THE
ROSE AND
THE THORN

ALSO BY NANCY LENZ HARVEY:

Elizabeth of York

THE ROSE AND THE THORN

THE LIVES OF MARY AND MARGARET TUDOR

BY NANCY LENZ HARVEY

MACMILLAN PUBLISHING CO., INC.
New York
COLLIER MACMILLAN PUBLISHERS
London

Macmillan Publishing Co., Inc.
866 Third Avenue, New York, N.Y. 10022
Collier Macmillan Canada, Ltd.

Library of Congress Cataloging in Publication Data
Harvey, Nancy Lenz.
    The rose and the thorn.
    Bibliography: p.
    Includes index.
    1. Margaret Tudor, consort of James IV, King of Scotland, 1489–1541.
2. Mary, consort of Louis XII, King of France, 1496–1533. 3. Henry VIII,
King of England, 1491–1547. I. Mary, consort of Louis XII, King of France,
1496–1533. II. Margaret Tudor, consort of James IV, King of Scotland,
1489–1541.
III. Title.
DA784.3.M3H37   941.1′04′0924 [B]   75–22442
ISBN 0–02–548550–4

First Printing 1975

Printed in the United States of America

For Jane and Claude
and
In Memory of Sadie

CONTENTS

LIST OF ILLUSTRATIONS

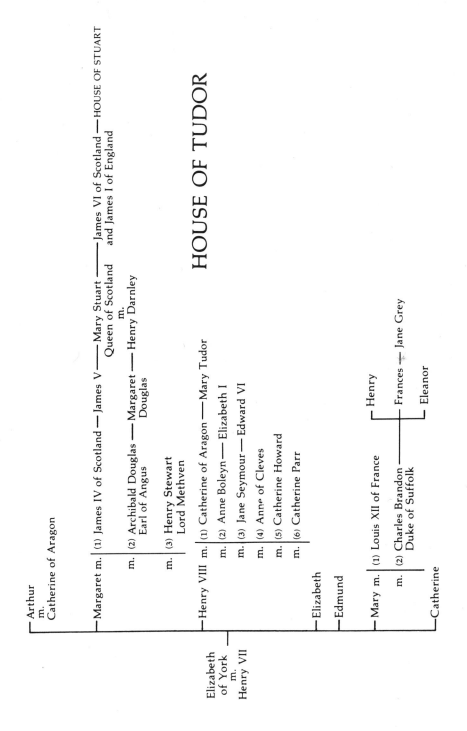

HOUSE OF TUDOR

PREFACE

THE LIVES OF TWO PRINCESSES WHO HAPPENED TO BE SISTERS ARE presented here as a single story. Although the two were not closely knit in either a sororal or political sense, they offer an interesting study in comparison and contrast. The externals of their lives were much alike. Margaret and Mary Tudor, like their more famous brother Henry VIII, shared a heritage which thrust them into international prominence. In addition to the advantage of royal birth, the two princesses exercised the drive of the Tudor will, delighted in the foot-stomping rhythms of the sixteenth century, and revelled in the magnificence of extravagant waste of the Renaissance court. Both girls were married young to men much older. When those husbands died, both Margaret and Mary—as did their brother—allowed passion to overrule policy and sought "their hearts' desire." Behind the glittering patina of outward similarities—and there were many—lies another story of contrast which led each princess toward the solitary darkness of despair. The ironies are heavy throughout.

For these reasons, I have intertwined the stories of the lives of Margaret Tudor Queen of Scotland and Mary Tudor Queen of France and Duchess of Suffolk. Both women have left through their own correspondence a rich legacy, illuminating not only the complex events of which their lives were a part, but more importantly, revealing much of their personalities and the workings of their minds. Where possible I have allowed the weight of the narrative to be carried in the words of Margaret and Mary. To simplify matters for the reader, I have regularized spelling and imposed paragraphing where there was none. I have left untouched, however, the capricious use of capitalization and the somewhat gnarled syntax because both underscore the emphases of their authors and provide a key to the perceptions of Margaret and Mary Tudor. The result is a certain distancing by this writer who found in Margaret and Mary—even through the dimness of four hundred years—personalities so strong that they would not yield to being more or less than what they were. Once again the will of the Tudors defies subordination.

The labor of this book was eased by many: the unnamed and sometimes unknown keepers of the manuscripts of the British Museum and the Library of Congress; the patient and persistent unknown at the National Portrait Gallery who sent three times a batch of illustrations to the illiterate in my university postal office who consistently confused the "return-to-sender" slot with that for my office. Although I will in all probability never be able to thank those helpful and responsible persons privately, I wish to thank them publicly. There are also others I would like to thank here: Carole Bowman for the genealogical chart; H. C. Waugh for his anecdotal tour of the chapel and grounds of Linlithgow Palace; Mary-Berenice McCall and Elizabeth Armstrong for their careful reading and criticism of the manuscript; Julie Dietrich and Dick Hinners for their research assistance; Alvena Stanfield for typing the manuscript; Ray Roberts for his constant encouragement; the Penrose Fund of the American Philosophical Society and the University of Cincinnati Research Council for financial support for travel, research, and the rarest commodity—time to write; and my family and friends who listened to distracted mutterings of a writer preoccupied with other persons and distant places.

N. L. H.
Cincinnati
1974

THE
EARLY YEARS

CHAPTER ONE

*My most dear lord and father, in the most humble wise that I
can think, I recommend me unto your Grace, beseeching you of
your daily blessing, and that it will please you to give hardy thanks
to all your servants the which by your commandment have given
right good attendance on me at this time. And especially to all
these ladies and gentlewomen which hath accompanied me hither,
and to give credence to this good lady the bearer hereof, for I have
showed her more of my mind than I will write at this time.*

*Sir, I beseech your Grace to be good and gracious lord to
Thomas, which was footman to the Queen my mother, whose
soul God have pardon; for he hath been one of my footmen hither
with as great diligence and labor to his great charge of his own
good and true mind. I am not able to recompense him, except the
favor of your Grace.*

*Sir, as for news I have none to send, but that my lord of Surrey
is in great favor with the King here that he cannot forbear the
company of him no time of the day. He and the Bishop of Murray
ordereth everything as nigh as they can to the King's pleasure. I
pray God it may be for my poor heart's ease in time to come. They
call not my Chamberlain to them, which I am sure will speak
better for my part than any of them that be of that counsel. And
if he speak anything for my cause, my lord of Surrey hath such
words unto him that he dare speak no further.*

*God send me comfort to his pleasure, and that I and mine that
be left here with me be well entreated such ways as they have
taken. For God's sake, Sir, hold me excused that I write not myself
to your Grace, for I have no leisure this time, but with a wish I
would I were with your Grace now, and many times more, when
I would answer.*

As for this that I have written to your Grace, it is very true, but

*I pray God I may find it well for my welfare hereafter. No more
to your Grace at this time, but our Lord have you in his keeping.
Written with the hand of your humble daughter*

Margaret.[1]

With this letter the prolific correspondence of Margaret Tudor,
newly created Queen of Scotland, began as she turned to her family in the distance of southern England for solace and comfort.
The loneliness, the sense of alienation in a foreign land, the petu-
lance, the anger, the frustration, the jealousy, and the sheer agony
of homesickness of a girl not yet fourteen remained to mark and
mar the rest of her life.

Born at Westminster Palace, November 29, 1489, this first
daughter of Henry VII and Elizabeth of York combined within
her person the warring passions, the rival blood, the ancient strife
of the houses of Lancaster and York. From her Lancastrian grandmother, Margaret inherited her name and ambition but none of
the sagacity, none of the intellectual curiosity, and little of the
religious fervor of Margaret Beaufort Countess of Richmond.
From her father she inherited position and preeminence, his
Tudor will and determination, but nothing of his caution,
nothing of his stoical reserve, nothing of his passive countenance
which hid an alert and politically sensitive mind. From her Yorkist grandfather, Edward IV, Margaret inherited a vivacity and lust
for life, a delight in the magnificence of pageantry and the bejewelled costumes of velvet and gold, the thrill in a touch of ermine about the wrist, the passion for pleasures physical. But she
lacked his easy familiarity which drew love and political support
from all levels of society. From her mother, Margaret inherited a
joy and talent for music, a fondness for children and all things
small, but nothing of her beauty, her quiet charm, or her compassion for the poor.

Margaret Tudor was both the victim and product of her heritage. She had innate intelligence which she never disciplined. She
had power which she never controlled. And she had ability that
she rarely exercised. She was from birth the pampered princess of
the English court. From the moment she was placed in her golden
cradle lined with ermine and covered with cloth of gold, every cry
was answered by Alice Bywymble the nurse or Anne Maylande
and Margaret Troughton the rockers of the royal crib.[2]

No expense was to be spared, no luxury ignored by a loving mother and a doting father. Although often accused of avarice, Henry Tudor delighted in his growing family. Theirs would be the fruit of patient years in exile, theirs would be the true victory of Bosworth Field, theirs would be the kingdoms of the earth and the responsibility of nurturing an infant dynasty wherein the name of Tudor would dominate throughout time.[3]

With the hope of succession firmly established in the three-year-old Prince Arthur, this birth of a daughter was a welcomed one. Even her birthdate seemed propitious. It was St. Andrew's Eve. With a sense of the future and a taste for symbolic gesture, Henry urged his daughter's christening the following day—the day designated to honor the patron saint of Scotland. Moreover, his daughter was christened in the little church near Westminster Abbey dedicated to the canonized Queen of Scotland, St. Margaret.

Within hours of her birth, Margaret Tudor was wrapped in twelve yards of fabric red and gold furred with ermine, accompanied by her royal aunts and uncles, the lords and ladies of court, her godmothers the Countess of Richmond and the Duchess of Norfolk, her godfather John Morton Chancellor of England and Archbishop of Canterbury, and carried to the silver font. Upon her immersion and the blessing of the Bishop of Ely, the congregation lighted candles, and suddenly the darkness of the church was pushed back by the brilliance of torches, shimmering garments, flaming banners, and the singing exultation of the choir. The child was welcomed into the bonds of Christianity, her spiritual future secured and her political future—on this St. Andrew's Day—tentatively outlined.[4]

Marriage alliances were the hope, however, of the future; for the moment the infant was carried with processional pomp to receive the blessings of her mother and father. Her gifts of golden bowls and goblets set with jewels were put aside, and the child returned to her nurses and rockers. Then the courtiers moved with easy procession into the pageantry of the Christmas season. When, however, measles struck at the heart of gaiety, the court took quick retreat by water to Greenwich, a favorite home of all the Tudors. There the festival continued with plays and hunting, dancing and banqueting until the house itself was exhausted. The family gathered its baggage, boarded its barges, and moved up river to Sheen and establishment of the royal nursery.[5]

During the next years, the population of the nursery grew. Within fourteen years, eight children were brought to life by Elizabeth of York and Henry Tudor. But the high rate of infant mortality ignored the fact of royalty, and a son George and a daughter Catherine died within days of birth. The others, however, seemed healthy and were expected to assume quickly the political assignments of the king. By the time Arthur was three years old, he had discarded his baby clothes for the robes of royal estate. He was dressed with the spurs and sword of knighthood and given the sceptre and crown as Prince and Viceroy of Wales. Margaret, as soon as she could walk, was swathed in gowns of velvet and caps of lace to become the squat, somewhat dumpy, miniature of her future self. But wherever she toddled, she was the focus of attention—especially for the ambassadors of Spain, France, Scotland, and the Netherlands. She was after all the princess royal, she was a political commodity, and she might well become the queen of any of these strange men with their unintelligible sounds and their searching, peering eyes. With future alliances always in mind, they documented her demeanor, her round face, her brown eyes, her golden hair, and crammed their notes into bulging portfolios.

But the nursery stage was not hers alone once Arthur was given his own household. Before Margaret was two years old, a fair-haired brother named for his father was born June 28, 1491. The following year, a sister named for her mother was born and within four years brought something of the knowledge of death to the nursery. That gloom dispersed, however, with the appearance of another sister—this one named Mary was born March 18, 1495.[6] Three years later another brother Edmund, destined to live only into his third year, came to Sheen. For wherever the royal infants chose to be born, their residence through the 1490s was most often at the king's beloved manor on the banks of the Thames. And so at Sheen, amidst its green richness, its abundant gardens and parks, its swans and ducks and deer, its quiet country splendor, the children grew; and the court on occasion came to them or called them to London.

The first public call was not long in coming. The date was All Hallow's Eve, 1494, and the occasion was the creation of the three-year-old Prince Henry as Duke of York and Lord Lieutenant of Ireland. Although the ceremonies centered on Henry, his midnight vigil before the cross of St. Stephen's Chapel and his reception into the Order of the Knights of the Bath in the Great Hall of Westminster, Margaret wedged her way into the festivities.

Seated with her parents and brother under the canopy of estate, Margaret watched the breaking of spears and the charge of horses. She heard the clang of sword against armor, the groans of combatants as they gasped and choked in dusty sweat beneath their helmets. And under the eternally pious eye of her grandmother, Margaret resisted the temptation to cheer too loudly or sway to the rhythms of the minstrels. She must maintain the dignity of royalty. As the trumpets signalled the day's end and the heralds pronounced John Peach victor, Margaret drew herself to the full height of five years' growth and presented to the kneeling Sir John the ruby ring of victory.[7]

Tourneys and jousts, dancing and masquing would remain the favored pastime of the Tudor children so that when they came to power, it was often murmured that they indulged themselves to excess. Life, however, was not always spent in war games. There was that dreadful night, for instance, when amidst the Christmas gaiety at Sheen with all the family assembled, fire flamed out in the king's chambers. Within hours, much of the palace was burned while the frightened family huddled in the chill of dawn and watched the enormous torch, once a home, light the night. Although the royal nursery would move to Eltham Palace near Greenwich, the older children watched the remnants of their childhood smolder in the ashes of Sheen.[8]

Often the problems of court pushed into the nursery conversations, and there were whispers and conjecture over contenders and imposters to the throne. There were stories from the north of Perkin Warbeck who claimed to be their mother's brother, the prince who had really died in the Tower with his brother the boy-king Edward V. There were tales of Perkin's persuasion of the King of Scotland's support—how he had not only recognized Perkin as Duke of York and rightful possessor of the throne of England but had welcomed him into the Scottish nobility, married Perkin to a cousin, Lady Katherine Gordon. There were days of tension when James IV invaded the north and rode stirrup to stirrup with the imposter. There were stories of the destruction of villages when the inhabitants rushed into the countryside rather than support insurrection. And there was certain alarm and confusion the day that Henry VII led his army to meet Perkin's second invasion, this time in the south. In that battle there was success, and the royal children awaited with amazement and curiosity as they learned that the Lady Katherine Gordon was being sent to stay with their mother. There was disappointment, too, that nothing about her looked like a traitor—she was rather like everyone else except that she spoke the language in such a strange way.

Perkin Warbeck was himself now a captive and an object of humiliation, his feet bound to his horse, his head covered with mud and slime hurled by the vulgar. But rather than live out his life in prison, he escaped the Tower to the priory near Sheen itself. There he was caught, locked in the stocks of the royal palace, and made the "object of every kind of mirth." Later he was led through the streets of London through greater humiliation, as the citizenry tossed their slops from windows and the filth slid from his face onto his body. The twenty-three-year-old imposter was beheaded at Tyburn.[9]

In the meantime the Scottish king repented his hasty support, realized the stability of Henry VII's government, recognized that the internecine War of the Roses was finally over, and perhaps grew weary of the frequent border wars so costly in men and money and so futile in lasting achievement. He sent an embassy to the English court to treat for peace and to ask for the hand of its oldest daughter, Margaret Tudor. Henry considered the offer as confirmation of his earlier belief that Margaret was destined for the throne of Scotland. It would be good for both countries to have this blood tie, to enter into a peace which held the potential for permanence. But the father would not hurry the negotiations. Royal dowries were not quickly decided, and Margaret was not yet ten years old.[10]

Henry was content to leave his daughter to the pastimes of childhood: the lute which she played well, as did all the Tudor children; the card games, in which she delighted, especially when she won; the wild hunts, on which she rode with great enthusiasm and ability. It was enough that she learn a little Latin to strengthen her soul, that she speak enough French to engage in the repartée of court. No one forced upon her the tasks of more rigid study. It was simply not worth the tantrums, the tears, and the ragged nerves of the tutors.

Unlike her brothers, Margaret did not like to study. She did not follow the intellectual interests of Arthur who was already conversant in Latin, Italian, French, and Spanish, and was a potential classical scholar. And although she rivalled her brother Henry for dominance of the nursery, it was Henry, when only nine years old, who challenged a poem from the great Erasmus.[11] Margaret was not interested. She was not the avid reader that Arthur was or that Henry was to become. She had no interest in the past or in politics or in the future for that matter. It was enough that she know how to read if she wanted to; it was enough that she be able to write. What matter if her spelling was guided only by the sounds she spoke—what were scribes and secretaries for if not to handle such matters? Instead let her shoot at the butts; she had a good eye for the bow. Let her ride her horses; let her delight in her gowns and growing jewel collection. Let her enjoy the festival of court. She learned, mainly through the dominating discipline of Margaret Beaufort, to handle herself well in public, to perform her duties with charm and dignity. What need she more than that? Let her frivol away her days if she wanted—it was in marriage that her real role lay and that would come when it would come.[12]

There was, however, marriage in the air. It was the center of the courtiers' conversation as they smirked and smiled with knowing eyes, of the ambassadors' whisperings in crowded corridors, of the seamstresses who stitched away on the royal velvets, damasks, and the omnipresent cloth of gold. Marriage was the talk of the cooks, the bakers, the farmers who wheeled into the courtyards the cumbersome carts loaded with vegetables, fruits, fish and fowl of every variety. Marriage was the topic of the priests and friars as they fingered their beads and mumbled in their incense, of the artists and artisans as they painted their banners and draped them from the houses of London, of the carpenters and lumbermen as they hammered the lists and platforms into place. It was the food of the gossips and the point of the bawdy gesticulations of the marketplace, the pubs and taverns, the highways bulging with the traffic of tourists rushing to London and the halls of the royal residences. The Prince of Wales was to marry the Spanish Infanta, and the festival was to include all England.

He was their darling, this heir to the throne. Handsome, intelligent, this quiet and sombre boy of fifteen was the symbol of the end of the long and fitful fight for the throne. He was the red rose and the white, as the ballad went, and he would one day be king. He was Arthur, the fabled hero come again. Now he was to marry, and his bride was the dark-eyed Catherine of Aragón. The wedding had been the matter of diplomatic discussion since the prince was a year old; and now that the bride was sixteen, her parents Ferdinand and Isabella allowed her to sail for England.

Catherine arrived with her entourage at Plymouth, October 2, 1501. As she moved toward London, more and more courtiers joined her train in welcome until finally Prince Henry and later the king himself went out to meet her. Upon her entry into London, each Spanish lady mounted her mule from the right and was escorted by an English lady mounted on her palfrey from the left. So that throughout the entire procession, the ladies sat back to back as though they had argued. But the laughter of the crowds changed to cheers, and the cheers began to swell through the streets of London. These were happy days of festival and game punctuated only briefly by the solemnity of the services at St. Paul's Cathedral on November 14. The brilliant alliance with Spain—one of the most prestigious powers of all Europe—was now secured by marriage, and it brought pride to the hearts of the English and hope to the Tudor family. Now the possibility of dynasty would push into another generation, and the king and his queen toasted as the trumpets sounded and the drums spoke. In the streets, the royal toasts were matched by those of the dancing, singing folk, for there were fountains which spewed wine while bonfires lit the night.[13]

Throughout these events Margaret watched and practiced in her mind's eye her own wedding, the day when she would be the center of all men's eyes and the object of every man's toast. Even now she and Henry could outdance the bridal couple. Arthur tired quickly, and his bride danced with her ladies to stately Spanish measures. But Margaret and Henry leapt and bounded to their own music; their vigor surpassed all others, and Henry ripped off his doublet and danced in his soaking shirt. He and his sister became the center of attention. For them the courtiers cleared the floor and applauded, and their parents laughed into tears. Still Henry and Margaret danced on revelling in the attention, the adoration. It was this to be a prince and princess—the admired of all admirers. And Margaret danced fiercely and flirtatiously knowing that the ambassadors of Scotland would write well of her to their king.

No sooner had Arthur and Catherine been waved off to Ludlow to take up the government of Wales than the ambassadors of Scotland pressed hard for a date and time of the marriage of Margaret to James IV. Their king was a hopeless profligate, and royal bastards meant political problems. Each journey, each pilgrimage that he took left the mark of the Stewart features upon a newborn face. Hopefully his insatiable appetites would contain themselves in the holy bonds of matrimony. What matter if he were a thirty-year-old man of the world and the English bride only twelve; their political alliance meant practical peace. The raids by the border bandits and the attacks by pirates would end. Scotland and England being of one island should and would be at one peace.

There were, however, some amongst the councillors of Henry VII who questioned the Scottish marriage. What if the Tudor princes should die, or die without begetting sons? What if the succession should pass to Margaret or her heirs, what then of England? Would it not then pass to foreigners? The king answered: "What, as God forbid, all my barnes be dead; if Margaret justly succeedeth . . . for seeing the use now is, that the less come to increase the more, Scotland will come to England, and not England to Scotland." His words became prophetic—the future would prove him true.[14]

On July 12, 1499, the peace agreement—the first in almost two hundred years—between the two nations was signed.[15] To prevent reprisals for border raids, nearly impossible to eliminate completely, both kings agreed to refrain from attack and to leave the responsibility for suppression and punishment to native control. Each king became responsible for the acts of his own subjects. Furthermore, the treaty—signed under papal sanction—made the violator of the pact subject to immediate excommunication.[16]

Since the prospective bride and bridegroom were within the forbidden degrees of kinship, Henry VII petitioned the pope for a dispensation. It was, for a price, forthcoming.[17] On January 24, 1502, the marriage treaty was concluded. It maintained that the King of England would pay as dowry ten thousand pounds; the King of Scotland, one thousand pounds yearly together with the gift of all the lands, castles, manors, and rents usually apper-

taining to the queens dowager. Furthermore the treaty stipulated
that James' betrothed be allowed to keep at least twenty-four English servants in addition to the usual Scottish domestics and that
"her household shall be maintained in due splendor, at the expense of her husband." In the event of his death, Margaret was to
have two thousand pounds yearly and the possession of her dower
lands.[18]

Once this treaty was signed, there was no more cause for delay.
On January 25, 1502, the court assembled at the newly restored
palace of Sheen, renamed Richmond in tribute to the king's
hereditary title. Among those assembled in the queen's chamber
was Prince Henry Duke of York strongly conscious in this his
eleventh year of his importance as the king's second son. With
him stood his sister, the Princess Mary, whose six years of life
seemed one continuous pageant. Then in marvellous procession
and accompanied by their royal aunts and uncles, the chief peers
of the realm, the archbishops of Canterbury and York, the lords
temporal and spiritual, the ladies of the court, and the representatives of the great foreign powers, the prince and princess joined
the king and queen, the bride, and the Scottish delegation. James
IV had sent as his proxy Patrick Hepburn Earl of Bothwell together with the Archbishop of Glasgow and numerous priests and
peers of Scotland.

Every man and woman, elaborately arrayed in their finest
robes, each marked with the insignia of his house, moved to the
music of the minstrels into the chapel for mass. There the Bishop
of Chichester, Richard Fitzjames, delivered the sermon and the
Host was shared by Margaret and Bothwell.

The procession returned to the queen's chamber, newly decorated with the banners of the Tudors and Stewarts. Everywhere
there was entwined the new heraldic device of the English rose
and the Scottish thistle. With the king and queen settled under
the canopy of estate, with Henry and Mary seated on stools at
their feet, with the court arranged around her, Margaret stood
in the place of honor. The ceremonies began with readings of
the papal dispensation and the treaty between the two nations. The
Archbishop of Glasgow then turned to the king, the queen,
the Princess Margaret and asked if there were any impediment to
the marriage. There were none. King Henry then asked the Archbishop of Glasgow, the Earl of Bothwell, and the Elect of Murray,

"whether it was the will and mind of the King of Scots, and full intent, that the said Earl of Bothwell should in his name, assure the said princess?" The Scots gave assurance. The Archbishop of Glasgow then demanded of Margaret if she were entering into this marriage of her own free will. And although it was probably the first time that her wish had been consulted, she rose and knelt before her parents and said, "If it please my Lord and Father the King, and my Lady my Mother the Queen." Henry Tudor and Elizabeth of York kissed and blessed their daughter. The moment had come for the exchange of vows.

The Archbishop of Glasgow intoned the words first to the Earl of Bothwell:

> I Patrick Earl of Bothwell, Procurator of the right Excellent, right High and mighty Prince James by the Grace of God King of Scotland, my Sovereign Lord, having sufficient Authority, Power, and Commandment to contract Matrimony *per verba de presenti*, in the Name of and for my said Sovereign Lord, with thee Margaret, the First begotten Daughter of the right Excellent, right High and mighty Prince and Princess, Henry by the Grace of God King of England, and Elizabeth Queen of the same, as by the Procuratory of my said Sovereign Lord, at this present Time openly read and published, more plainly appears, by virtue of the same Procuratory, and as Procurator of my said Sovereign Lord James King of Scotland, and in his Name and Behalf, and by his special Commandment, contract Matrimony with thee Margaret, and take thee into and for the Wife and Spouse of my said Sovereign Lord James King of Scotland, and all other, for thee, as Procurator foresaid, forsaketh, in during his and thine Lives natural, and thereto as Procurator foresaid, I plight, and give thee his Faith and Truth, by Power and Authority foresaid committed and given to me.

And Margaret answered:

> I Margaret, the First begotten Daughter of the right Excellent, right High and mighty Prince and Princess, Henry by the Grace of God King of England, and Elizabeth Queen of the same, wittingly and of deliberate Mind, having twelve Years completed in Age in the Month of November last be past, contract Matrimony with the right Excellent, right High and mighty Prince James King of Scotland, the Person of whom Patrick Earl of Bothwell is Procurator; and take the said James King of Scotland unto and for

my Husband and Spouse, and all other for him forsake, during
his and mine Lives natural; and thereto I plight and give to him,
in your Person as Procurator aforesaid, my Faith and Truth.[19]

With these words, Margaret Tudor became the twelve-year-old
Queen of Scotland. The trumpeters in the balcony joyfully and
triumphantly saluted the young queen, and the minstrels joined
in happy melody. With much kneeling and bowing, kissing of
hand and cheek, the Scots emissaries saluted their monarch. It
was a moment for Margaret of supremacy and grandeur—even her
brother Henry must kneel before her. Although the boy had
raged, thrown a royal tantrum when told that etiquette demanded
that he salute his sister, he bowed to his father's demands and
knelt.[20] Elizabeth took her daughter by the hand and led her to a
banquet for the ladies as the king led the gentlemen to a separate
banquet in his chambers.

In London, proclamation of Margaret's proxy marriage was
read at Paul's Cross, and the clerics and priests solemnly sang a Te
Deum. Then the city itself went hysterical with joy. It was a
holiday and the streets were lit with bonfires; once again the fountains spouted wine, and the bells of the city took up the song and
answered one another.[21] London, so far away from the effects of
border wars, saw the marriage as a symbol of peace; but the further north one looked, the fires burned less brightly and the singing was less spontaneous. In the north, there was both suspicion
and hope.

The next three days were spent in tournaments, jousts, and
festival—and all was for Margaret's honor. It was she whom the
combatants saluted as they went to the tilts. Among them was her
old friend Sir John Peach who broke spear after spear for her
pleasure and the applause and cheers of the crowd. The noise, the
tumult, quieted when Peach and Sir Rouland de Veilleville called
for their "great" spears, spears twelve inches in diameter. There
was silence so still that all heard the slamming shut of the visors,
the pawing hooves of the horses, the mad thunder of the gallop as
the two men hurled themselves—spears pointed—at each other.
Great was the clamor as wood smacked against metal, and Peach's
spear shattered into three pieces. Despite the impact, both horses
kept their feet and both knights kept their seat. It was the best
spear-breaking that ever was seen. And the silence of suspense

split before the applause of approval. Then Margaret awarded all the prizes of the day.

So this was what it meant to be a queen—to be worshipped, to be adored, to have men fight for and in one's honor, to stand regally apart and give prizes to the victors. It was to have new dresses, badges, crowns. It was to have all bow before her presence. It was, she decided, splendid to be a queen.[22]

But what did it mean to be a wife? The evening of her proxy wedding, slightly heady from the events of the day and the wine of the night, she was led by her ladies to her chamber. There amidst the new hangings of velvet and gold, the entwined thistles and roses, she was undressed and put to bed under the embroidered sheets and coverlets. Within moments the laughing men of court brought Bothwell, in his dressing gown, into the room. He stood there fully clothed except that his left leg was naked. Slowly, shyly, Margaret did as she had been told; she extended her right foot and ankle from beneath the cover. Bothwell with all decorum moved to her side and touched her leg with his naked thigh. The room erupted with applause—the marriage was consummated.

Margaret was left with her dreams and her questions. She would not, as the treaty stated, go to Scotland until she had reached her fourteenth birthday. Her father had been quite emphatic about that. For the moment it was enough that she now was addressed as the Queen of Scotland. It was enough that she have the homage of her brother and sister. Thus with her wardrobe filled with new gowns and shoes, caps and stomachers, she returned to the routine of her days, the cards, the lute, dancing and hunting.

For her father these were the celebrated results of his careful and calculated policy of prudent alliances to the honor of his family and the security of his country. Although Henry VII had wrested the crown from Richard III, the Tudor king was essentially a man of peace. Wars, he felt, were expensive gambles; and like his daughter with her cards, he hated to lose. Consequently, he preferred talk, diplomacy, and negotiation. With Arthur married to the Princess of Spain, England gained prestige and one of Europe's strongest powers as an ally. With Margaret now married to the King of Scotland, there would be peace in the north.

By securing these two alliances, Henry VII felt no need to hasten the marriage of his second son. Perhaps it would be better not to have him marry at all; perhaps he would be able to serve his brother better as a priest, as the archbishop of Canterbury for instance. To keep the prince free of marital pledges would give flexibility to future planning. With the young Mary, however, it was different—it was wise to be scanning constantly the marriage market. Princesses were harder to place. But there was potential in the two-year-old Charles Archduke of Austria, grandson of Ferdinand of Spain and Maximilian the Roman emperor. The English king sent his ambassadors to view the child and make vague inquiry. No need, however, to hurry; the future seemed secure.

On April 2, 1502, all of the planning of Henry VII collapsed. Arthur Prince of Wales was dead and his bride of five months was violently ill from the plague. The king was desolate. His firstborn, so much like him in looks and habit, so much the pride of his tutors and subjects, so much the hope of the early years of the reign, was gone. Henry wept and called his queen to him. She held him with words of comfort and promise. They were, she said, "both young enough. . . . God was still where He was. . . ." They would have other sons.

Throughout the court there was great sorrow. The wedding banners, the hangings of the royal household, the glittering gowns of court were all exchanged for those of mourning. As Arthur's body was carried from Ludlow to the cathedral of Worcester, the April skies darkened, and the rains filled the carriageway. Villages tolled their bells, and the English stood along the roadside to watch the passing of their prince. Outside Westminster Palace, where the royal family gathered, all London seemed to stand at the gates and weep in the April rain.[23]

Inside the palace, the king and queen moved sorrowfully, mournfully, through their routines of daily living. Most often they knelt in the chapel, and weeping priests intoned the funeral mass. Their prayers and offices, their chants of petition and adulation lasted throughout the days and continued throughout the nights. For the royal children there was a certain sorrow for their brother's death, but this sorrow was tempered by youth and circumstance. Margaret, of all the children, had known her brother best. And he felt closest to her; for when he died, he left to his sister—not his bride or his brother but his sister—all of his personal property, his jewels and plate and his best robes and gowns.[24] Margaret, although she demonstrated her grief, was still locked in her own affairs; she was after all a twelve-year-old queen, and Arthur had been out of her life for years. It was not until much later that she would come to realize the meaning for her of his death.

For Mary, Arthur's death meant more of a reflection of the feelings of those around her. She was seven years old and knew her brother only from a distance—the handsome young prince whom all adored but who was rarely at court. For Henry, however, life was immediately and irrevocably changed. Although his investiture as Prince of Wales was delayed ten months until it was certain there was no possibility of Catherine's being pregnant, Henry became instantly the hope of the future.

After Arthur's death the family as a whole became more closely knit. The children stayed less frequently at their apartments at Eltham and followed more often the peregrinations of the court to Greenwich, Richmond, Woodstock, or Westminster. Into their midst came the Princess of Wales, Catherine of Aragon. Still pale and white from the sickness she had shared with her husband, she took up residence with the Tudor daughters. She really wished to return to Spain, but that would mean a return too of her enormous dowry and an end of the splendid alliance. Her father-in-law demurred. She was too ill, he said, for such a voyage. So she too travelled with the court and took as her closest friend the young Princess Mary.

Mary was, even as a child, the prettiest of the Tudor daughters —preface to becoming one of the most beautiful women of the age. Already she was developing the tall, slender stature of her mother and with it her gentle disposition and delicate constitution. Both were prone to frequent illness in sharp contrast to the vigor and vitality of Margaret and Henry. Like them Mary had the Yorkist golden hair and the strong Tudor will, but by choice she and Elizabeth of York sought the quiet solace of music rather than the foot-stomping rhythms that excited Margaret and Henry. With so much attention showered on Margaret and her wedding, and Henry and his new importance, Mary was drawn to the quiet, lonely Catherine. But the three girls were often together, and the differences in personality were only heightened by the contrast in appearance: Margaret, moon-faced and plump; Mary, fragile and lovely; and Catherine, dark, handsome, and strangely melancholy.

In the evenings the princesses sat with the queen, listened to their minstrels and the queen's fool Patch, gossiped over their cards and chess, and read loud the stories of that famous Arthur of long ago. In the days they walked and rode, enjoyed the richness of the English spring, moved through the profusion of vibrant flowers, and took to their barges and boats for rides along the Thames. But this year of 1502 was a long year. Too much had happened, too many lives had been touched and changed for life to be as it was. Awareness of the sudden mutability of human events had shattered the seeming security of the royal household.

When Arthur died, his mother's health began to fail. In spite of that she was again pregnant. Elizabeth of York had never been a strong, vital woman, although she was a fertile one. Each of her numerous pregnancies had meant long terms of confinement and longer days of illness. Still she was only thirty-seven and the knowledge that she was to have another child somehow made the loss of Arthur easier to bear. Nothing could, she knew, replace him—the past could never come again—but a new child always meant hope. It stood for life itself.

The months of 1502 dragged themselves to a close. Christmas at Greenwich was quieter. There were, of course, the usual masquings and festival, the great Feast of Lights, the antics of the local folk who brought their dogs and bears to play and tear at one another for the pennies of the rich. But the joy of these days was mitigated for everyone except Prince Henry, confident now that his brother left no posthumous heir to mar the way to the throne.

The family, however, was restless. They left Greenwich for their apartments in the White Tower of the ancient citadel. Somehow its very walls seemed to threaten time. The Tower of London. Dark, massive, it defied the sea and held up the sky. It seemed to have been forever, and behind its quiet strength the family took refuge. There Henry VII planned his own monument to the glory of God and the name of Tudor—a new chapel at Westminster Abbey. If he and his sons must die, theirs should be the greatest monument. And so in the darkened rooms of the White Tower, Henry gave much of his days and most of his nights to planning the reaching spires, the stretched vaulting, the bosses of roses and portcullises, the glorious windows. This chapel of Henry Tudor became his expression of faith and belief, of hope and immortality. It was his personal challenge to time.

Scarcely had the building defined itself in stone when its vaults were readied for its first occupant. Elizabeth of York, Elizabeth the Beloved as her people called her, was dead. She had taken her chamber on the uppermost floor of the White Tower and given birth to a daughter. She named her Catherine for her favorite sister and the lonely Princess of Wales. Three days later, on what should have been her thirty-eighth birthday, Queen Elizabeth died. Her body was embalmed, dressed in its robes of estate, placed in its coffin of black velvet, and brought to the sombre Norman Chapel of St. John, one floor below the room in which she had died. There her sisters and daughters became the chief mourners while her husband retreated in grief to secret chambers. He ordered a magnificent funeral, but etiquette prevented him from participating in the embellished gesture of farewell.

Every citizen of London lighted a candle as though to light the way of this last progress of their queen. Through the streets of the city her body was borne, and the funeral effigy dressed in her robes only heightened the sense of loss. She seemed to move amongst her ladies, she seemed to be there with them, and yet she was not. At every corner children stood and sang her praise and prayers for her soul. The city was wet with the tears of its citizenry. It was enough that the old must die, but why the young too? The royal family and a nation wondered and grieved.[25]

With the queen's death, Henry became increasingly introspective and spent less time in public audience. After the period of mourning ceased, he allowed the banquets and the feastings of hundreds of courtiers and hangers-on to begin again, but of them he wanted no part. He stayed alone much of the time. He preferred to work over his accounts and his notes and plans for his chapel at Westminster. He sought conversation with only a few: Peter Torrigiano the architect of Richmond Palace and decorator of the chapel; Bernard André and Polydore Vergil his historians in residence. Of his son Prince Henry, the king saw little. The week after Elizabeth's death, the king allowed his son's investiture as Prince of Wales, gave him a household of his own, and turned him over to his teachers.[26] He and the boy would never understand each other, and what did that matter? In the long run, every man must live his life himself. All the king could do was to give his son the best of tutors, secure the throne through careful policy, and leave a treasury large enough to answer political and domestic needs. To these purposes he framed the last years of his life. With so much death about him, the king began to feel the weight of his

own mortality. Life was a struggle he was not sure he wanted any-
more. He would finish the tasks before him and leave the problems of the distant future to the vigorous son who seemed so
anxious to succeed him.

First among the unfinished affairs was the delivery of Margaret
to Scotland. King Henry in the spring of 1503 sent his ambassadors north with word that the Queen of Scots would arrive in
August. Although the marriage treaty allowed that Margaret not
come until she obtained her fourteenth birthday, the weather of
December and January would make a difficult journey even more
uncomfortable. The preparations for departure moved forward at
Richmond and those for the royal reception began in Edinburgh.
In all the towns and villages, the abbeys and castles along the
route, seamstresses were gathered to stitch new livery for the parties of welcome while the artists and carpenters set about new
banners and pageants.

Margaret bid farewell to her brother, sister, and sister-in-law at
Richmond, but the full impact of the leave-taking was lightened by
the excitement of adventure. Her father and many familiar faces
of court were members of the escort for some of the journey.
Through the first days of riding and the two-week stay at Collyweston, home of her grandmother the Countess of Richmond, the
entire outing seemed as one colorful, glorious picnic in the country. It was a relief to them all to be away from the duties and
strictures of court formality and the chambers still rich with the
memory of Queen Elizabeth.[27]

The significance of the coming departure touched Margaret's
consciousness as she said good-bye to her father. Before the gathered court, he gave her his blessing and a prayer book in which he
had written: "Remember your kind and loving father in your
good prayers." On a blank page opposite the prayers for December he wrote again: "Pray for your loving father, that gave you
this book, and I give you at all times God's blessing and mine.
Henry R."[28] She knew she would in all probability never see him
again, never see her family or country again. That was the nature
of royal marriages; she was leaving to join a husband she had
never met and become queen of a land she did not know.

The young queen, with her carts filled with handsome gowns
and jewels, her litter richly arrayed with the arms and badges of
her heritage, her ladies and gentlemen horsed in handsome trap-

pings, her minstrels with their new livery and shining instruments, her trumpeters with their heraldic banners and glittering trumpets, mounted her palfrey and was given by her father to the Earl of Surrey. He would take the queen and her companions through the rich and rolling fields of England northward into Scotland. On July 8 she left Collyweston, on the banks of the Welland, and started toward the city of York. Through the days of travel, villagers and farmers gathered at the roadside to watch the royal progress, to cheer their princess, and to offer gifts of fruits and cakes, wine and beer.

Slowly the procession moved from Grantham to Newark and Tuxford, to Doncaster and Pontefract, to Tadcaster and York. Wherever they went, the local nobility in their finest tunics, local clergy in their best habits, mayors and aldermen in their handsome scarlet gowns rode out in greeting from each village, town, and city. As Margaret entered one village or left another, the patterns of reception became familiar. One group of escort left as a new one rode out. In every village the bells sang out in welcome, and the Bishop of Murray, the chief Scottish emissary and escort, offered the cross for the queen to kiss. Often there were pageants symbolizing the visit and the purpose of the journey, always there were priests and children who sang greetings and praise.

Before entering the larger towns, the queen retired to her litter and her company retired to barns or bushes to change their travel dress for the more elegant velvets, damasks, and cloths of gold. Sometimes the queen rode one of her richly bedecked palfreys; at other times she sat in her litter which was slung between two handsome coursers. At all times she was surrounded by three handsomely appointed footmen in their tunics embroidered with the Tudor portcullis.

Of all the entries into English towns in that long travel northward, the entry into York—the capital of the north—was by far the most dramatic. Her already lengthy and impressive train grew steadily as the queen neared the city. At Tadcaster, the sheriffs and officers of York, twenty-four in all, rode out to greet her—each man with his horse well trapped, his servants newly costumed, and the gentlemen themselves in richly embroidered velvets. Two miles from Tadcaster, Lord Scroop and his son and servants added another twenty horses and men to the glittering procession. Four miles from Tadcaster the chief ladies of York and their gentlewomen rode out in greeting. And two miles from York the chief nobleman of the area came with his footmen and henchmen, his Master of the Horse, his officers of arms, his knights and gentlemen, numbering three hundred in all. He was Lord Northumberland, in a crimson gown embroidered at collar and cuffs with rich stones, boots of black velvet, and spurs of gilt. From his horse a crimson velvet cloth, embroidered with the Northumberland arms and badges, stretched to the ground. With much saluting and salutation, Margaret greeted this latest escort who would stay with her until Edinburgh. Now, however, she must ready herself for York—a gown of cloth of gold, a collar of precious stones, a sash of gold which swept the earth.

For the entry itself, the queen sat in her litter amidst a profusion of cushions, each embroidered with her arms and badges. Her palfrey, richly dressed, was led behind the litter. As the procession ordered itself for this impressive march, four orders of mendicant friars came out to lead the way with lighted torches. The child-queen entered the city to the music of the minstrels and sackbuts, the trumpets and drums, the tolling of the great bells of York Minster. Along the streets the burgesses cheered and bowed in their robes of scarlet and black, from the windows the ladies, nobles, and commons waved and cheered in salute, and along the rooftops boys scampered and whooped.

The procession wound through the city gate toward the cathedral where the queen heard mass. She then retired to the palace. The next day, again with great procession and rejoicing, she returned, more richly dressed than before, to the cathedral for high mass. After mass she received at the palace the Duchess of Northumberland with much kissing and familiarity, festival, masquing, and dancing. The York reception was the most brilliant of the entire journey and a welcome respite from days of riding the palfrey or swaying in the litter.

On July 17, with the streets crowded to suffocation, the windows jammed to overflowing, Margaret mounted her palfrey for the final procession through Northallerton, Darlington, Durham, and Newcastle. There she paused to hear the children singing her praise, to celebrate with lavish banquets, frantic dancing, and games. At Newcastle, her company was joined by Lord Thomas Dacre Warden of the Marches who would become a long-term confidant. Now he became another escort through the lonely and moody hills of the north. By July 29, the company reached Berwick, the border castle which had changed so often from English to Scottish control and back again. Here Margaret was allowed the luxury of hunting and the clotted gore of bear-baiting when dogs and bears gnawed and clawed each other for sport.

On August 1, Northumberland dressed his horse, his men, and himself in their most gorgeous apparel yet—some in cloth of gold, some in cloth of silver, some in cloth of gold and silver. He was determined to make the entry into Scotland the most impressive that any Scot had ever seen; for Northumberland saw Scotland merely as a country to be patronized, a paltry country existing mainly through the pillage of border raids, a country goaded by the French to be a constant itch in the side of the English.[29] Northumberland wanted the Scots to realize that their king's marriage to an English princess was a more than generous gesture; it was more than they deserved. And Margaret, richly arrayed in her jewels and golden collars, her hair and dress threaded with pearls and gold, lay amongst the glittering pillows of her plumed litter and shared Northumberland's attitude.

Surely Margaret felt every bit the queen with her magnificent array and retinue of eighteen hundred ladies and gentlemen richly horsed and richly dressed. Such a retinue, such splendor and display, such obvious wealth proved—in her mind—that she was indeed a person of note from a rich and powerful nation. She saw herself as the grand English princess making a triumphant entry into a weakened land.

As the English procession neared Lamberton Kirk, there were many who were surprised by the magnificent array of the official Scots party of welcome. The Archbishop of Glasgow and the Earl of Glasgow were also surrounded by hundreds of handsomely dressed knights and lords, ladies and gentlemen, henchmen and servingmen. They too bore their badges of honor and wore their silks and damasks, their cloths of gold and silver. They, in addition, were surrounded by multitudes of common folk all handsomely dressed in their best tartans and kilts and gowns. At the sight of the queen's approach, the Scots trumpets were raised glistening in the sunlight, and their rich melody belted against the heavens. In the distance the bells of every steeple called and answered and echoed in greeting. It was, noted a herald, a goodly sight to see and hear.

As Margaret was helped from her litter, the well-wishers knelt to welcome her. Then the chief members of both parties retired to a newly built pavilion for music and refreshment. From the pantries about the pavilion came bread and wine, fruits and meats, and everyone enjoyed this seemingly impromptu picnic. When it was over, Northumberland leapt to his horse and spurred it into much rearing and leaping to the great pride of his friends and the scattered applause of the spectators.

When the procession reassembled, the progress of Queen Margaret was increased by a thousand Scots—half on horseback and half on foot. This enormous entourage wound its way through the undulating hills of southern Scotland. Through Coddingham and Haddington and Dunbar and the villages in between. The slow procession beat the roadways into dust while villagers gathered upon the hillsides and shepherds stood among their flocks to watch this splendid entry of their new queen. Some brought food; some, drink; some, gifts of heather; some, golden cups. It was as though wherever the procession moved, the nation became one grand party of welcome. Always the church bells tolled, often the cannon charged the air with salutes which echoed and reechoed against the countryside. Everywhere people cheered and children tried to run the length of the procession. Through it all Margaret rode her handsome pony or waved from her litter. All this festival and rejoicing she knew was hers, and the pleasures and splendors of the hard and steady travel were softened by the adulation of these her subjects. There was no time for her to think or to assimilate the happenings about her. Every action, every event, was arranged for her pleasure and her entertainment. The world itself seemed to stand in welcome and praise.

On August 3 she was greeted as queen and mistress by Lord and Lady Morton and offered the keys to the castle at Dalkeith. It was here she would stay until her entry into Edinburgh, her wedding and coronation. As most of the company sought lesser lodgings, the queen settled into her chambers with her English ladies. She was not settled for long, however, when she learned that the king was coming. With little preparation and less formality, James IV King of Scotland dashed into her chambers. For this chance meeting—though planned to the smallest detail—the king, dressed in his hunting habit of embroidered crimson velvet and his hawking lure over his shoulder, hastened to his bride. He bared his head and Margaret curtseyed. Then the two bowed, saluted each other and kissed, and talked a long space together.

Although the courtiers and the ladies and gentlemen of both English and Scottish parties extended themselves in elaborate courtesies and pretended to be occupied in the pleasantries of the evening, all eyes surreptitiously watched the royal but solitary pair held together in close conversation. For political reasons, both parties had much to gain. Both countries had long been torn by faction and needless wars, and this marriage held the happy potential for peace. It was possibly a marriage of nations as much as it was the marriage of persons. It was, for the moment, and would remain for years, a basis of concord between two otherwise fractious neighbors.[30]

But political circumstances aside, each courtier must have mused at the seemingly ill-matched pair upon whom the destiny of nations rested. There stood the new queen, not yet fourteen years old, resplendent in her gowns of gold and glittering jewels. Although raised amongst princes, she was unknowing in the ways of men and policy. She was very much a wayward, willful girl, imperious in her bearing and dignified in her demeanor. But she was still very much a child dressed in the gowns of womanhood. James IV, on the other hand, was thirty years old and a king for nearly half his life. He was handsome, debonair, worldly, had marked his journeys and progresses with numerous amorous interludes. He had through the years taken a number of royal mistresses, the latest of whom had been mysteriously poisoned at breakfast.[31] There were many who knew he was still grieved by the loss of Margaret Drummond, and there were many who knew of his great love and care for his royal bastards. How would Margaret react once she knew of the amorous intrigues and the living proof of their intensity? How would James adjust to this child-bride of so limited experience? Whether the royal couple would be happy was of little consequence to those who stood and watched. As long as their nations remained at peace, as long as there was festival at court, as long as royal scandal did not interfere with national policy, as long as this union secured the throne through direct heirs and marital alliance, both English and Scots needs would be fulfilled. The marriage would be a brilliant political success, and that was its true value.[32]

CHAPTER TWO

JAMES IV KING OF SCOTLAND WAS A MAN OF MANY VIRTUES. From his birth on March 17, 1473, until his accession to the throne sixteen years and eighty-five days later, he had been carefully tutored and skillfully educated in the liberal arts, in politics, in diplomacy, in horsemanship and the joust. His mind and body had been equal to the challenge. He spoke fluent French, German, Italian, Spanish, and a multitude of Scots dialects. He was deeply read in theology and history, and was sincerely committed to serving his people.[1] Within only a few years of his kingship, he had subdued most of the unruly subjects of the south; and by travelling yearly to the far northern reaches of the kingdom, he had won the loyalty and respect of the Highlands. To insure justice to all men, he established well-regulated courts, often surprised the justices with his own presence, and made equality under the law swiftly and fully available to men of all estates. To improve and to continue his system of jurisprudence, he insisted that the sons of all the nobility and landed gentry be educated—for therein lay the future of his courts.[2]

To expand and develop the economy of the nation, James IV encouraged fishing and busied himself with shipbuilding; and—like his brother-in-law, the future Henry VIII—the King of Scotland often inspected the shipyards and was not unknown to take the helm of a new ship to test its seaworthiness.[3] Furthermore, he was a busy monarch who loved to travel his land. Sometimes his visits were announced, at other times he travelled incognito. In so doing, he developed a spirit of respect and camaraderie among subjects of differing levels and walks of life. And often when dressed merely as a travelling pilgrim, alone, on foot or horse, he would spend the night in some low cottage to learn from his subjects their attitude toward their sovereign and what he did. In consequence, he was a man much beloved.[4]

In his court James sought to emulate the famous courts of Burgundy and France and to surpass the growing fame of the court of England. Since luxury and magnificence and ostentatious display were the measuring rod of success, he sought to make his court as opulent as any. He encouraged his nobility to spend lavishly for their clothes and those of their servants, and many a gentleman was forced into indebtedness to the king in order to save face with his peers. Excessive expenditure weakened the wealth and consequently the power of rival chieftains—and that strengthened their reliance on and allegiance to the crown. Court itself, whether at Edinburgh or Falkland, Stirling or Linlithgow, was a continuous scene of revelry, pageantry, amusement, gaming, masquing, tournament, and jousts. The king entered into every facet and fancied his court the rival of any in the world and not unlike that of the fabled King Arthur. He was, in short, an incurable romantic.[5]

In stature and person, James was a handsome man, athletic and able, intelligent and inquisitive. Of him, Erasmus noted: "He had a wonderful face of intellect, an incredible knowledge of all things, an invincible magnanimity, the sublimity of a truly royal heart, the largest charity, and the most profuse liberality. There was no virtue which became a great prince in which he did not so excel as to gain the praise even of his enemies."[6]

However, despite his dedication to his people, his love of law and order, his strengthening of a central government, his dash and bravado, his ability to do, his love of being king, and his romantic flair for the role, James IV was a haunted man. When yet a boy, he had been the unknowing accomplice of ambitious men who had hacked his father to death after the desperate battle of Bannockbourn. How great a role James played in the revolt against his father, no one—not even James himself—knew. But that he had in some way usurped a throne and been smeared by the blood of patricide, he felt to be his private guilt. As an outward punishment for his inner shame, he had fashioned a belt of iron to which he added more links each year. This heavy and constant weight, however, was not enough. In the midst of happier moments, gloom would burst forth in his soul and darken his countenance.

In such moods, he would rush from whatever frivolity or game he was engaged in, and whip his horse into a lather to reach the distant shrine of St. Duthlac at Tain or St. Ninian at Whithorn. Other times he would flagellate himself before the cross, weep away the nights in prayer and fasting, or disappear for days in a darkened cell of some religious house.[7]

James' religion, no doubt begotten in guilt and nurtured through his quest for absolution, bordered on fanaticism. He never cut his hair or beard, he observed all offices and precepts of the Church, he ate no meat on Wednesday or Friday, and never rode his horse on Sunday. Whenever there was important business to contract, he always heard two masses beforehand.[8] His greatest desire was to harness the powers of Europe into one mighty crusade to the Holy Land—a project to which all heads of state paid lip service but one to which James alone was truly dedicated. He hoped to be the admiral of the crusade fleet.[9]

Excessive piety—indeed this piety which bordered on madness—was typical of James' life. He knew nothing of restraint, and that lack of moderation penetrated every facet of his life, every desire, every action. He ordered a dumb woman and her two young children into solitary confinement to discover what language the children would speak.[10] He capriciously supported the idle claims of Perkin Warbeck against all reasonable arguments and listened instead to the romantic mystery of the "lost" prince of the Tower. And it was the same lack of temperance which catapulted him into the arms of every willing, winsome woman.

Now that the King of Scotland had to marry, he might have convinced himself that his amorous affairs were a part of the past. His insatiable pleasure in sexual delight, however, was only diverted by the romantic delusions of his forthcoming marriage. Throughout the first meeting with Margaret at Dalkeith, James was the personification of the ideal knight. When in the presence of his lady, he kept his head bare, his bonnet in his hand, as a mark of humility. When they shared a basin to wash their hands before eating, he insisted the queen rinse her hands first. Throughout the dancing and masquing of the evening, he sat at her feet. When it was time to leave, he reverently kissed all the ladies, called for his horse, and flung himself into the saddle without touching the stirrup.

Margaret's emotions throughout her first days in Scotland were more than mixed. The dialect of the Scots was difficult to follow, and she found herself relying heavily on her own ladies for conversation and company. She was delighted with the parties and celebrations, but they were becoming repetitious. She was exhausted from the long journey from London, and during her first night at Dalkeith the fire bells ripped the quiet of the night. Fire devoured the stables; and her favorite palfreys, who had so faithfully carried her from home, died in the flames. The little queen's grief was inconsolable. She had lost her mother and brother and left her father and home forever, and now the horses that she best loved were also gone. Was there nothing that would last? Was there nothing of her past that could remain? She was thirteen years old, and life as she had known it seemed, was, gone forever.

When the king heard of the fire, he, "flying as a bird that seeks his prey," raced from Edinburgh to comfort his bride. He ordered her residence changed to the castle of Newbottle a half-mile away. He ordered parties and dancing, encouraged Margaret to dance with her friend the Countess of Surrey. When it was time for wine, he served her himself. He asked her to play for him the clavichord and then the lute; he ordered his gentlemen to sing. He worked away at softening her grief. If her chair did not suit her, he gave her his own. He shared with her his cup and plate. And although Margaret adored his attentions and his little courtesies, they too grew familiar and served only as momentary distractions from the loneliness she felt. If only her horses had not died it would have been better. Now their loss only intensified the loss of mother, father, home, and all things familiar.

Margaret had been in Scotland nearly a week. On August 7 amidst the almost continuous dancing and banqueting, the noise of the trumpets, minstrels, and sackbuts, a present from the king arrived—new palfreys, white like those she had lost, handsomely appointed with golden harness, velvet saddles, and embroidered cloths. Perhaps these would lessen her sorrow. It was the least a knight could do for his lady. Moreover James busied himself in providing the constant entertainment of more singing and more dancing. No young girl, he romanticized, could continue to grieve or be homesick when surrounded by constant merrymaking.

On August 8 the queen lavishly dressed herself in a new gown of cloth of gold and black velvet furred with ermine, increased the splendor with jewels and pearls, necklaces and collars, and prepared for Edinburgh. Once more she entered her litter, newly fitted for this latest and grandest procession, and watched the ordering of the procession—her horses, her ladies, her gentlemen of England, each one paired with a lady or gentleman of Scotland. Hundreds formed before and after the queen while thousands lined her way. Halfway to the capital the king sent out a tame doe for the queen to hunt, for her skill with the bow was well known. But the queen refused; she would wait until she and James might run the course together.

Within moments James galloped up—the horse in gold, the king in purple. He leapt to his feet, gathered the queen in his arms, kissed her with a resounding smack, and leapt again into the saddle. Before him rode the bishops and earls of Scotland, but the king reined his prancing stallion so that he might ride by the side of his bride. Overcome with romantic ardor, he then decided that he and Margaret must ride the same horse together. Another horse was brought; James and a page rode double to test the horse's going. The horse reared, pawed, and stomped the ground; and James, with an excessive display of concern, dismissed both horses and mounted one of the gentle palfreys of the queen. Then Margaret mounted behind him, and they rode toward Edinburgh.

No sooner had the procession begun again when shouts and screams came from the wooded hillside. From a newly built pavilion rode a knight in armor, behind him sat his ladylove. Another armed knight rode out of the thicket, galloped toward the pavilion, seized the lady from her horse and carried her away. The first knight blew a challenge, the second knight returned, both grabbed their spears in a mock trial by combat. James and Margaret galloped forward calling "Peace! Peace!" The combatants dropped from their horses onto their knees, declared their case, and James appointed a joust to settle the quarrel. Once the vizors were raised, the two knights were discovered to be Sir Patrick Hamilton of an ancient and powerful family and Patrick Sinclair, Esquire, who became a great friend of Margaret's.

The procession reordered and moved again toward Edinburgh, but within half a mile James ordered the tame doe to be released and followed by the swiftest greyhound. To the good fortune of the doe and the disappointment of the crowd, the doe eluded the hound by racing through the streets of the city and reaching its home park at Holyrood House, the newly built palace of the king.

At the gates of Edinburgh, friars and clerics presented relics—including the arm of St. Giles—to be kissed, and James insisted that Margaret precede him in the ritual. Along the streets were platforms of pageants and "angels" of welcome; one "angel" flew down to give Margaret the keys to the city. On other platforms stood figures from mythology, and "Paris" presented Margaret with the golden apple. At another station the "Virgin Mary" married "Joseph" while "Gabriel" whispered at her ear. Throughout the city fountains ran with wine, the church bells rang, and spectators rich and poor alike mashed themselves into the windows or shoved through the walkways to stretch and strain to glimpse this fair sight of their new queen and their handsome king. It was a day to memorize and describe to one's grandchildren. It was the day in which the poet William Dunbar declared:

> . . . the flowers did rejoice,
> Crying, at once, Hail, be thou richest ROSE!
> Hail herbs' Empress, hail freshest Queen of Flowers,
> To thee be glory and honor at all hours.
>
> The common voice up rose of birds small,
> Upon this wise, Oh, blessed be the hour
> That thou was chosen to be our principal;
> Welcome to be our Princess of honor,
> Our pearl, our play, our plain felicity;
> Christ thee comfort from all adversity.[11]

The next day was the wedding. By eight-thirty in the morning, the procession became a shimmering stream of cloth of gold, golden chains, jewelled collars, horses as richly dressed as their riders, and minstrels and trumpeters shattering the morning mist. James in white damask and black velvet, with sleeves and hose of scarlet satin, stood with his black bonnet in his hand. The costume of Margaret, as etiquette demanded, was a matching gown. Now for the first time, she wore the crown of queen. The marriage itself was performed by the Archbishop of Glasgow and the Archbishop of York, and the king and queen shared the Host at mass. The trumpets signalled their union. And as the service ended, James gave Margaret the sceptre; she was then anointed with holy oil and became in fact the Queen of Scotland.

When they walked from the church or through the banqueting

halls of Holyrood, James was ever tender of his bride, his arm
about her waist. At the banquet James insisted that Margaret be
served first as the fifty dishes were held before them. And when
the feast was over, he commanded the Marchmont herald to pro-
claim in the queen's name alone gifts of celebration: "Largess, To
the high and Mighty Princess Margaret, by the Grace of God,
Queen of Scotland, and first Daughter engendered of the very
high and very mighty Prince Henry the seventh, by that same self
Grace, King of England."

The gifts and the banquet were only part of the grandness of
magnificent splendor—splendor evocative of the glories of so
noble a couple. As neither was modest in looking to the future
with hope, neither king nor queen was modest in looking to the
past for comparable glory. Thus in the wedding chambers, the
tapestries represented the history of Troy, and those in the royal
apartments illustrated the lives of Hercules, Coriolanus, and Solomon. In the newly glazed windows were the arms of England and
Scotland, and on the bosses there were thistles and roses interlaced
with crowns.[12]

The visiting English were astonished at the brilliance of the
moment and its setting. The old feelings of superiority and con-
descension wavered. There was much to praise.[13] But the holiday
was soon over; and while the English friends and attendants prepared for home, Margaret wept. For her Scotland must now be
home—Scotland with its lonely hills, its gusty heights, its sombre
fog that made reality itself less than a memory. To this land she
had been destined since birth, to this land she had been brought,
and it was in this land that she would be left to fulfill her role as
brood mare for a nation. The young queen wept while England
and Scotland rejoiced. The marriage was good policy.

The Earl of Surrey, who had taken great pains to cultivate
James' friendship—much to Margaret's frustration and jealousy—
told King Henry that James was foolish in many ways. He was too
hopelessly caught in dreams of glory and romanticized reality; but
because of his commitment to some grandiose ideal of knighthood, he was a man of his word and could be trusted.[14]

The marriage treaty so long nurtured to fruition by Henry VII
proved to be for these last six years of his reign what he hoped it
to be. James controlled border raids with increasing fervor and
punished violators with such swiftness of justice that the crimes

soon ceased altogether. With that frontier secured and Henry's encouragement to his son-in-law to stay disengaged from other foreign alliances, the kingdom of Scotland achieved a period of peace and reached a level of prosperity it had never known before.[15] The marriage *per se* would have mighty and far-reaching consequences of which many might dream and some fear. But a hundred years later the great-grandson of James Stewart and Margaret Tudor rode south to London as James VI of Scotland to become James I of England and to unite forever the two thrones under a single rule.

That particular reality was, in all probability, never part of the dreams of James IV. There were too many variables. Margaret, it was true, was second in line only to her brother for the English throne, but Henry VII still lived and was searching for another bride. Prince Henry, the heir apparent, was lusty and virile. He would marry. He would, no doubt, have sons.

Reality for James IV rested in the moment. He had his young bride, and he was attentive to her needs and generous in his affection. He was certain theirs would be a fruitful union. He knew that in time there would be heirs aplenty to his own throne. In the meantime he sought to fill the queen's days with pleasure. There was, however, little the royal pair had in common except their love for music. Both played well the lute and clavichord, but James had special fondness for the organ which he had carried from court to court wherever he travelled. Many an evening passed while Margaret's minstrels, in their Tudor livery of green and white, sought to rival the music of James' whistlers, bagpipers, and harpers in their Stewart livery of red and yellow. But in the early years of Margaret's residence, James' fool "English John" was forced to temper his ribald humor against the southern neighbor.[16]

The court, composed of innumerable entertainers, courtiers, and hangers-on, exhausted the food supplies of a neighborhood, turned freshened rooms with their rush and herb-scented floors into rank and smelling sinkholes, and caused their slops and garbage to overflow limited facilities. Consequently the court—like all courts of the day—was forced to move frequently to allow the buildings to rest and air themselves. This was true even of the newly constructed but still incomplete palace of Holyrood near the Abbey. A mile away was Edinburgh Castle perched high upon its hill, where gale-like winds would blow. To Margaret, this castle was "a sad and solitary place, without verdure and by reason of its vicinity to the sea, unwholesome."[17] A few miles away was the palace of Linlithgow with its purer air and sloping hills and broad waters, its boats and birds, which brought reminiscences of the childhood homes on the Thames. The favorite residence, however, was Falkland Palace, resting well in the countryside, its pointed towers barely visible through the great trees of extensive parks. Here the deer roamed freely, and the king and queen found another basis of understanding—the hunt. Both loved the mad and frantic ride through bush and over log, loved the singing of the hounds and the desperate chase, loved the frenzied, screaming bloody moment of the kill. In such manner the months moved into years, and the royal progresses became familiar sights as, amidst the courtiers and servants, Margaret and James rode—she with her twenty-three carts of luggage and he with his single baggage horse.[18]

Religion, however, was not one of their shared passions. For James it offered temporary respite from whatever anguish haunted his dreams. For Margaret it was a ritual through which she must occasionally go in order to secure the safety of eternity. But neither the pleasures of heaven nor the fires of hell held for her much meaning. James might disappear in sudden gloom to one of his hermitages to humiliate his body and flagellate his soul, but Margaret let it be known from the beginning of their marriage that the occasional mass was enough for her. Instead she held court at her dower castle of Stirling. There the days and nights would pass in unbridled revelry and were recorded by the mocking pen of her friend Dunbar. He wrote "Of a Dance in the Queen's Chamber":

> Sir John Sinclair begouth to dance,
> For he was new come out of France;
> For if any thing that he do might
> That one foot gaed aye[a] unright,
>   And to the other would not agree.
>   Quoth one, Take up the Queen's knight;
>   A merrier dance might no man see.

[a] ever went

Then came in Maister Robert Shaw:
He looked as he could learn them all;
But aye his own foot did waver,
He staggered like a strummel-aver,[b]
   That hap-shakellit above the knee:
   To seek from Stirling to Stranaver,
   A merrier dance might no man see.

Then came in the Master Almoner[c]
A homelty-jomelty juffeller[d]
Like a stork staggering in the rye;
His hips gave many a hideous cry.
   John Bute, the fool, said, Woe is me!
   He is bedirten—Fy! fy!
   A merrier dance might no man see.

Then came in Dunbar the maker;
On all the floor there was no one frakar[e]
And there he danced the dirrye dantoun;
He hopped like a filly wanton,
   For love of Musgrave, men tell me;
   He tripped, while he tint his pantoun:[f]
   A merrier dance might no man see.

Then came in Mistress Musgrave;
She might have learned all the laiffe;[g]
When I saw her so trimly dance,
Her good carriage and countenance,
   Then, for her sake, I wished to be,
   The greatest earl, or duke in France:
   A merrier dance might no man see.

Then came in Dame Dontibour;
   God knows if that she looked sour!
She made such grumblings with her hips,
For laughter no one might hold their lips;
   When she was dancing busily,
   A blast of wind soon from her slips;
   A merrier dance might no man see.

---

[b] stumbling horse   [c] Dr. Babbington   [d] a clumsy, awkward fellow
[e] more active   [f] his shoe   [g] the rest

When there was come in five or six,
The Queen's Dog[h] began to rax
And of his bond he made a bred [i]
And to the dancing soon he him made;
    How mastif like about went he!
    He stinketh like a tyke, some said;
    A merrier dance might no man see.[19]

Thus the years passed with the royal pair caught up in their separate interests and coming together for the affairs of court. Peace seemed secure with England, and the last of Margaret's dowry installment, ten thousand gold nobles, was delivered by Henry VII's commissioners on the couples' second anniversary.[20] James continued his correspondence with France, but ignored its urgings to reactivate the border forays. He was content to work toward national prosperity, encourage the growing industry, visit his shipyards, and dally in science. When for ten nights in August, 1506, a comet lighted the summer skies, all Scotland stood in awe and wondered what it meant.[21] James felt he knew. His wife was pregnant with their first child. The comet meant a glorious life for the boy—the king knew this first child would be a boy. And the comet, like the eastern star of old, heralded the new prince. No matter that the comet came in August and the birth of the prince was still many months away; it was a marvelous sign, it was a harbinger of the great event. As the birth of the prince neared, James ordered each man in Edinburgh to ready a new torch, to have a new suit of clothes, and to come to the Abbey when the bells announced the birth.[22]

On February 21, 1507, the Abbey bells pealed the long-awaited news, and the citizenry dropped their tasks, closed their shops, grabbed their torches, and moved as one to Holyrood House. It was true, the seventeen-year-old queen "was delivered of a bonny barne." On the morrow with great procession and joy, accompanied by lords and ladies of the land, he was brought by his godparents Robert Bishop of Glasgow, Patrick Earl of Bothwell, and the Countess of Huntley to the Abbey and named James Prince of Scotland and Lord of the Isles. None knew on that happy, long-wished-for day, that a year hence they would bring

---

[h] James Doig, the queen's wardrobe keper   [i] sprung away

him to his grave. The queen, however, participated in none of these celebrations; instead she lay weak and near to death. The king, with the knowledge of his past upon him and fear for the future of his wife and child, became a pilgrim on foot to the shrine of St. Ninian near Stirling. There he wept and refused all comfort. But the court physicians later assured him that the moment he reached the shrine, the queen recovered.[23]

The sad pattern of birth, death, and great sickness became the curse of James Stewart and Margaret Tudor. On July 1508, a daughter was born, but she was no sooner christened and named for her mother when the child died. Margaret "was again in great peril of death."[24] Once more James became a tearful pilgrim, and Margaret recovered. When another child was expected in the autumn of 1509, James spent much of the summer at the shrine of St. Duthlac at Tain while Margaret remained at Holyrood. There in October she was delivered of a prince of Scotland and named him Arthur—for her dead brother and the king from whose house the queen was said to descend. But this child too was doomed to die the following July at Edinburgh Castle.[25]

These unhappy events only strengthened James' belief that he, his soul, and his house were damned by patricide. He became a man fevered with apostolic fervor. He lengthened his days of fasting, increased his time at prayers, whipped and flayed his body, and added heavier chunks of iron to the already massive belt at his waist. He was a man more conscience-ridden, more driven than ever, and he sought relief through public humility and service. The idea of a holy crusade to defeat the infidels and to free the Holy Land became through these years his personal challenge. He urged Ferdinand of Spain, Louis of France, Henry of England, and Maximilian the Holy Roman Emperor to the endeavor. They were more realistic than he and continued to agree *pro forma* to the cause, but refused overt commitment. Since the King of Scots alone could not hack away at the pagans abroad, he hounded the heretics at home. And many were the smoking fires of human flesh of those who dared to challenge the ways of the Church of Rome. For these efforts of diligent piety, Pope Julius II declared James "Protector of the Christian Faith" and sent in token the symbolic purple diadem and the sword with a golden sheath set in precious stones.[26]

James' piety was, of course, heightened by this notice of Rome, but it by no means meant great changes in his court or in his behavior. Even more he fancied himself the model prince—devout and pious and a man of arms who "ever brought away the palm, ever bore the bell, and ever won the victory."[27] To complete the image he continued his interest in science. Alchemy, the art of changing base metals into gold, particularly fascinated him. He financed much experimentation, lighted the fires himself, watched the miracle of changing metal. Flying also teased his imagination, and he encouraged the Abbot of Tungland in his efforts. One day at Stirling the nobility gathered to see the abbot strap to his shoulders gigantic wings. He planned to fly from the highest point of the castle into France. However, no sooner had he leapt into the air than he plunged to the ground—writhing with a broken thigh amidst the twisted wings. He blamed the failure not on the idea but on the fact that the wings had been made of feathers of divers fowls rather than those of the eagle. He never flew again.[28]

Throughout these early years of marriage, there were for Margaret many good days and many bad. But there were never any that were easy. There was too much that was and continued to be foreign. Her husband was nothing like her father. While Henry's court was rich, James'—in spite of his love of display—was bankrupt. While James vowed eternal devotion, his wife learned quickly of his lascivious past and his present affairs.

He might weep and lament the children she bore and lost, he might seek his shrines to renew her health, but he always turned those trips to personal pleasure. While she lay, possibly dying, in childbed, James managed visits to his mistress Jane Kennedy, the mother of his bastard Alexander Stewart. Such infidelities Margaret never forgave, and she resented James' idea that Alexander leave his studies in Germany to become the eleven-year-old Archbishop of St. Andrews.[29] Her father had never been unfaithful to her mother—that the world knew. But James, she felt, made her the laughingstock of the court; she was always, it seemed, the last to understand what others had long known.

Margaret kept up public appearances. She endured the pain of childbirth and the anguish of infant death. But she feared each pregnancy, feared each birth, feared the long days and nights of pain and suffering, feared the thought and reality of death. Yet yearly this was the life she must expect; for her there were no choices. It was to this kingdom she had been sent; she had been born to be a queen. She was the fertile showpiece. That was her inheritance. And if she wanted the devotion of a husband and the love of his people, she must provide an heir for the throne. Then her existence and the expense of her keeping would be justified.

With these thoughts in mind, Margaret occasionally accompanied James on his various pilgrimages. She would show herself before the saints and the people and hopefully gain the support of both. When, however, ambassadors from England brought gifts from her father—horses with rich harness and saddles—she wanted to go home. These ponies were so like those lost in the awful fire five years ago that the old, urgent homesickness returned. She wanted to go home.[30] That, however, was impossible. Instead she prodded and probed the ambassadors for news of her father and family.

King Henry, they said, was beginning to show the effects of the anxiety and tension that had marked the years of his youth in exile and his tenacious hold on the crown in manhood. Although he spoke of marriage, he seemed to be thinking of death. The cough of consumption more often wracked his body, and it was believed his days on earth were not long. Prince Henry, however, grew stronger and more handsome. Now he jousted with the most valiant of the tourney, and he usually won. When he wrestled with his boyhood friend, Charles Brandon, or challenged him to tennis or the butts, the prince invariably won. Furthermore he composed songs, accompanied himself on the lute, translated the classics, wrote poems in English and Latin. He was the scholar, the athlete, the personification of vital youth. He was the joy of his people.

Princess Mary, on the other hand, was fast becoming the most beautiful young girl at court. At thirteen, she was already tall and lovely, and her face resembled the delicate features of her mother. When her mother had died and her sister had left for Scotland, the young princess found in the lovely Catherine of Aragon a friend and confidante. The two became great friends and often sat together stitching at the same embroidery or sharing the same keyboard. They walked and talked and sang together. When in 1506, news came that Philip the Handsome and Joanna of Castile had been forced by storm and wind to land on the English coast, the girls were delighted. For Mary, the arrival meant a renewal of parties and pageantry much neglected since the death of Queen

Elizabeth. For Catherine, the arrival meant an unexpected re-union with her sister.

The court roused itself to the event. With minstrels filling the air with music, seamstresses stitching new gowns, artists brightening faded banners, the old days seemed to come again. But the guests were singularly diasppointing. Joanna showed little interest in Catherine, or in anyone else for that matter. She merely sat and stared at Philip, and occasionally a wild and frightened look entered her eyes. She loved him desperately, some said insanely. Under her gaze, Philip was especially dour. Time and time again Catherine and Mary tried to coax him to dance, and each time he replied that he was a mariner not a dancer. Mary played upon her lute and then upon the clavichord, and "she was of all folks there greatly praised that in her youth in everything she behaved herself so very well."[31] Philip, despite his taciturnity, was impressed, and long he talked with the king about policy and about the future. By the end of the visit, the two agreed that Mary should marry Philip's son—Charles Prince of Castile and Burgundy.

The marital treaty itself, its details of dowry and diplomatic give-and-take were completed in December, 1508, mainly through the efforts of King Henry's ambassador Richard Fox Bishop of Durham—the same ambassador who had been instrumental in the Anglo-Scots alliance. Content with the extraordinary success of the agreement, Henry directed the City of London to offer all possible demonstrations of celebration. He had, after all, engaged his daughter to a boy-prince of brilliant political attachment. Charles stood to inherit through his mother the kingdoms of Castile and Spain, and through his grandfather Maximilian the vast holdings of the Holy Roman Empire. Henry's sombre facade cracked in delight; he had, he maintained, "a wall of brass about his kingdom, when he had for his sons-in-law a King of Scotland and a Prince of Castile and Burgundy."[32]

The Prince of Castile was in 1508 only eight years old; his bride, thirteen. To bind both parties to agreement, the proxy marriage was performed December 16, 1508, at Richmond Palace. Once again foreign legates and ambassadors joined the leading English nobility assembled in pageantry and ceremony to witness this marriage of the last of the Tudor daughters. Mary, draped in handsome, bejewelled gowns, gathered her ladies in the chambers which were formerly those of her mother. Together the ladies came into the Queen's Presence Chamber where her father waited with Charles' proxy Lord de Bergues and the Archbishop of Canterbury. After the salutations, presentations, and the archbishop's sermon, de Bergues took Mary by the hand and spoke for Charles. And Mary responded in French: "I Mary, by you John, Lord of Berg[ues], commissary and procurator of the most high and puissant Prince Charles, by the grace of God Prince of Spain, Archduke of Austria, and Duke of Burgundy, hereto by his commission and special procuration constituted and ordained, by your means and signifying this to me—take the said Lord Charles to my husband and spouse, and consent to him as to my husband, and spouse. And to him and to you for him, I promise that henceforward, during my natural life, I will have, and repute him as my husband and spouse; and for this I plight my troth to him and to you for him."[33]

Throughout this recital Mary stood with "most sad and princely countenance, having no manner of person to rehearse the words of matrimony to her uttered, [and] spoke perfectly and distinctly in the French tongue." To the amazement of the ambassadors, Mary fulfilled her part with such dignity and ready, uninterrupted speech that "for extreme content and gladness the tears passed out of their eyes." The king, however, was nothing amazed. He had disciplined and schooled all of his children for such public performances; he expected perfection. It was not so much sternness on his part as a recognition of the power of public display. It was a political tool which could win or lose the respect, the admiration, and the love of subjects. And Henry was never one to slight small details; he had built a crown and established a dynasty out of care and caution. He had taught his children the same policy from which Mary and Henry were to profit in their youth.

Thus it was with paternal pride that the king watched the exchange of vows and his daughter's peerless performance. De Bergues in reverent manner kissed the princess and placed upon her finger the ring of gold. It was her first gift from Charles. In addition he sent a K for Karolus embellished with diamonds and pearls and engraved *"Maria optimam partem elegit quae non auferetur ab ea."* His grandfather sent an orient ruby and a large diamond set with pearls.[34] After the wedding banquets and dancing, Mary was led to her chamber to await the consummation of her marriage. Like her sister before her, she lay naked beneath the coverlets and touched with her leg De Bergues' thigh.

For three days the celebrations continued. Foremost in the lists of the tourney was the handsome Charles Brandon who ran many courses, broke many spears, and took many prizes. While the days were rounded out with bullfights, bear-baiting, hawking, and hunting, Charles of Castile wrote to Mary from his court in Flanders: "My good Mate, With good and as cordially as I can, I recommend myself to you. I have charged the Lord of Bergues, and my other ambassadors ordered to your country, to inform you of the same good condition of my person and affairs, begging you to believe the same and to let me know by them of your health and good tidings, which is the thing I most desire, as knows the blessed Son of God, whom I pray, my good mate, to give you by his grace your heart's desire. Your good husband, Charles."[35]

It was not what one would call a love letter, but it was typical of the staid decorum and restraint of an overly serious, melancholy boy. Throughout Flanders and the Netherlands, the marriage was a popular one, and these sentiments found more joyful expression in contemporary ballads. In the shadows of the bonfires and amidst the fountains of wine, the populace sang:

> Arouse yourselves, ye sleepy spirits.
> Whoever are friends of the English,
> Let us sing Ave Maria!
>
> Dame Mary shall join the fleece of gold,
> And the enclosure of the castles, eagles, and lilies.
> Arouse yourselves, ye sleepy spirits.
> Whoever are friends of the English,
> Let us sing Ave Maria!
>
> . . . .
>
> For during ten thousand years from this
> There will not be nor has been in the country,
> Such a peace, such an alliance
> Arouse yourselves, ye sleepy spirits.
> Whoever are friends of the English,
> Let us sing Ave Maria!

We all pray, great and small,
That the kings may be all good friends,
And peace throughout the world.
Arouse yourselves, ye sleepy spirits.
Whoever are friends of the English,
Let us sing Ave Maria!

And that at last in Paradise
All may sing
With voice and heart purified:
Arouse yourselves, ye sleepy spirits.
Whoever are friends of the English,
Let us sing Ave Maria![36]

Mary played the role of the love-sick bride. Wherever she went she fondled a small, unflattering portrait of Charles. She declared that she wished for his presence at least nine times a day.[37] Legally she was not to see her bridegroom for six more years—not until Charles had reached his fourteenth birthday. In reality she would not see him until many years later and under different, unexpected conditions. For the moment, plans and preparations continued in both countries. Charles' aunt and guardian the Archduchess of Savoy, who had been instrumental in the arrangement of the marriage, sent her new niece handsome gowns in the Flemish fashion and notes on European etiquette. At Calais, where Mary should first enter the Continent, elaborate plans developed concerning the hangings of her chamber, carpets for the floors and tables, mattresses and bolsters for her bed. These too would be utilized under later and differing circumstances.[38]

The winter of 1508–1509 was working, however, in subtle and insidious fashion, undercutting the dreams and work of years of labor. Amidst the stone chambers of Richmond Palace, where the wind blew and chilled even this newest of royal homes, the king was being consumed by the ravages of consumption. Although he had quieted many of his days and nights with solitary and lonely study, he coughed away his remaining strength. There were days when he seemed well, but there were also days when his servants had seen him gasping, white-faced, for air. Now, however, there were few hours when his body ceased to quiver and strain. Now his eyes hollowed out, his flesh sagged from his bones, and the sinews of his neck were taut with pain. Although he survived this last winter, his strength and will were gone. The greening meadows, the quickening flowers, the fresh and soothing breezes delighted him no more. His work, he felt, was finished. He had taken a weakened, war-stained throne and bolstered it to a position of strength, power, wealth, and respect. That must be his legacy to his kingdom and his son; for his daughters, he had done the best he could. Margaret as Queen of Scotland had her kingdom, her husband, and her treaties. There was nothing more to be done than to leave to her some personal gifts of jewels and robes, some of which had been Arthur's.[39] The king had hoped to do as much for Mary. The marriage with Charles of Castile would prove, no doubt, a sound alliance. Already the boy was heir to the estates of his grandfathers, Maximilian and Ferdinand, now that his father was dead and his mother hopelessly insane.

Henry VII knew that he could not live to see Mary leave for Flanders. He simply could not wait out another six years. So with a certain frustration born of exhaustion, yet with a determination to provide well for the future of this third of his remaining children, Henry VII added with customary caution the codicil to his will which would cover any unforeseen contingency:

> And whereas we for the dot and marriage of our said daughter, over and above the cost of her traduction into the parties of Flanders, and furnishing of plate, and other her arrayments for her person, jewels and garnishings for her chamber, which will extend to no little sum nor charge, must pay and content to the said prince of Spain the sum of fifty thousand pounds in ready money at certain dates expressed in the said treaty. . . . And in case it so fortune, as God defend, that the said marriage by the death of the said Prince of Castile, or by any other chance or fortune whatsoever it be, take not effect, but utterly dissolve and break, or that our said daughter be not married by us in our life, nor after the same have sufficient provision for her dot and marriage by the said these Estates, we then will that our said daughter may have for her marriage fifty thousand pounds payable of our goods. . . . So and in none otherwise that in her said marriage she be ruled and ordered by the advice and consent of our said son the Prince, his council and our said Executors; and so that she be married to some noble Prince out of this our Realm. . . .[40]

This final gesture completed his earthly responsibilities, and Henry VII, with his handkerchief ever at his mouth, turned his face to the wall to consider responsibilities spiritual. On April 21, 1509, in the twenty-fourth year of his reign, Henry VII died at Richmond.

Henry's body was embalmed, dressed in its robes of estate, placed in its black velvet coffin, and honored at Richmond for many days. It was brought by a chariot, surmounted by an effigy of the king—a crown on its head, the orb and sceptre in its hands—to London on May 9. There his cortege was met by the clergy with their prayers and dirges, children with their lighted candles and songs, and the citizenry in their black garments of mourning, with their rosaries and their solemn countenances. The first obsequies were held at St. Paul's Cathedral; but for his final rest Henry VII was taken to his beloved chapel at the Abbey. There his horse, in its magnificent trappings, along with the king's coat of arms, his personal banner, his sword, shield, and helmet were offered at the altar. As the choir sang *Libera me*, his body was lowered into the vault, and the Lord Treasurer, the Lord Steward, the Lord Chamberlain, the Treasurer, and the Comptroller of the king's household broke their staves of office, their symbols of authority, and cast them into the grave. The heralds, in turn, removed their coats embroidered with the badge of Henry VII, hung them upon the hearse and with great lamentation cried: "The noble King Henry the Seventh is dead." As they turned again to the altar, they donned new coats and cried with joyful voice: "Long live the noble King Henry the Eighth, King of England and of France, Sire of Ireland."[41]

It was in truth a time of mixed emotion. For a nation, there was a sense of the old order passing—an order symbolic of the tumultuous years of the fifteenth century. The century that saw the end of the fratricide, the carnal waste, the fields of blood and festering flesh which had so often punctuated the years of the Wars of the Roses. Henry VII had put an end to that. Through politic and diplomatic marriage he had united the claims of rival factions in spite of other claimants to the throne with less questionable lineage. Through policy and diplomacy he had built a government disentangled from costly foreign intrigue. By creating out of the survivors of the wars a new nobility which owed many of its titles and nearly all of its wealth to Tudor supremacy, he brought new stability and loyalty to the throne. Through careful and cautious economy he amassed a treasury more than equal to domestic demand. These were the legacies he left his only son, and as Henry VIII assumed the government, there were few who questioned his right and none who could seriously challenge his claim.

Henry VIII took the crown in the full splendor of his youth. As one chronicler noted: "The features of his body, his goodly personage, his amiable visage, princely countenance, with the noble qualities of his royal estate, to every man known, needeth no rehearsal, considering that (for lack of cunning) I cannot express the gifts of grace and of nature that God indued him with all."[42] Within weeks of his father's death, Henry VIII married his brother's widow Catherine of Aragon. On June 24, amidst the golden splendor of pageantry the two were anointed as King and Queen of England. In the days and weeks which followed, each moment sumptuously filled with banquets, tournaments, dancing, gaming, and surprise entertainments, the fourteen-year-old Princess Mary had little time to mourn her father or to consider the meaning of his death. She had ever been her brother's favorite sister, and for these his first grand weeks of monarchy, he ordered for her new, more handsome gowns. He insisted on her presence at all ceremonies and tournaments. He desired her participation in the masquing and dancing that followed. Sometimes the king himself was her partner, often it was his best friend and longtime companion Charles Brandon—second only to Henry in tournament success and ballroom charm. Thus through the weeks of June and throughout the months to come, Mary danced her way along the confusing road of conflicting emotions. Her father was dead, but she was fourteen and would live forever.

The news of the death of Henry VII brought greater sadness to the twenty-year-old Queen of Scotland. Although she had not seen her father since he gave her the book of prayer, the gift of farewell, she had always loved him and felt his presence. She still did—in spite of the congratulatory letters which she and James sent to the new king. It was when she heard, amidst the descriptions of coronation festival, that her grandmother the Countess of Richmond had died June 29 that the awareness of loss began to widen. She knew that the two great forces of her early life were gone, and she could only wonder about their ramifications. When she thought of her old home and the places she had loved, she had seen her father and grandmother. Now that they were no more, even the solace of memory was utterly changed. She had through the years come to accept Scotland as the inevitable, but it would never be home. She felt more an alien than before.

CHAPTER THREE

IMMEDIATELY UPON THE DEATH OF THE OLD KING, HENRY VIII and James IV renewed the treaties which restrained them from border skirmishes and retaliation. Furthermore, the two renewed the treaty, under the sanction of the pope, which subjected the violator to war and immediate excommunication.[1] All became brotherly love and concord as the two exchanged frequent notes. In answer to Henry's continued verification of concord, James wrote:

> After our most hardy recommendation, dearest brother and cousin, We have received your loving Letters written with your own hand, where through we understand good and kind heart ye bare to us, of the which we are right glad considering our tenderness of blood. God willing we shall bare the same to you, the which ye shall perceive in deed, if it pleasure you to charge us, as knoweth our Lord who have you in his keeping. At our Abbey of the Holy Cross the xi. day of June with the ill hand of your Cousin.
>
> James R.[2]

Politically the two nations seemed little affected by the change in command. In Scotland, James felt secure that his brother-in-law would yield to the experience of the older king. Margaret assured him that she and Henry were the most devoted of siblings, that he would follow her advice. He was, after all, her younger brother. But she forgot, for the time, how much they were alike—imperious and strong-willed. She forgot the youthful Henry's rage when he was forced to pay homage the day she first became Queen of Scots.

Henry, on the other hand, was delighting in being king. He revelled in the attention and adoration, the splendor of costly clothes, the devotion of his new bride, the power of his word, the throngs which lined his halls and corridors, the cheers of the multitude, the parties and tourneys he could now have at whim. He found pleasure in surprising his queen with gay masquings and would burst into her chamber in disguise, sometimes as Robin Hood, sometimes as a knight errant ready to defend her honor. He was thrilled by magnificent pageants—mountains glistening with golden trees which opened to reveal the children's choir.[3] When his son Prince Henry was born January 1, 1511, Henry's joy was boundless. In honor of his wife, he ordered a pageant which contained a forest, complete with hills and dales, trees and flowers of gold and green velvet. In their midst was a castle of gold guarded by foresters and archers. The entire pageant was drawn into the hall by two enormous beasts, a lion and an antelope. "When the pageant rested before the Queen, the . . . foresters blew their horns . . ." and the forest opened and disclosed plumed knights engaged in mock jousting.[4]

On another occasion the king, queen, and his entire court were dressed in gowns and robes covered with the gold initials of Henry and Catherine. As usual the commoners were invited to watch the royal couple eat and dance. In exuberance and joy, Henry invited them to join the fun and snatch for their own the golden letters. Although some gentlemen swung from the chandeliers or climbed the rafters to protect their garments, the mob claimed its due. Within moments the fine gowns of the nobility were shredded, and the king himself was stripped to his hose and doublet. Then the crowd was thrust from the hall by armed guards. The nobility laughingly gathered its rags and sat down to banquet, but it was Henry who most enjoyed the fracas.[5] He loved to indulge his people and move, either in his own person or in disguise, amongst them.

Into all these festivities Henry swept the young Princess Mary. She was not only a favorite of his, she was an exquisite ornament to his court. Her wit sparkled, and her open frankness was disarmingly winning. Like her brother and their Yorkist ancestors, she had an easy grace, a charming simplicity, and majestic dignity which won people of all estates to her. She loved people. She loved the gay days and brighter nights of Henry's court, and she was devoted to Catherine of Aragon. The shock of her father's death was absorbed in the pleasures of being a princess, and Henry catered to her whims.[6] He would keep her near him until she must go to Flanders to fulfill the marriage contract. But that was years away.

Mary, however, continued to carry the portrait of Prince Charles with her. When there was a quiet moment or a need to turn the conversation, she would bring out his picture, gaze wistfully at it, and wish for his presence. This so-called affair with the boy she had "married" but had never seen, had developed almost into a ritual where the form was kept but the meaning lost. It was only when Charles' aunt, Margaret of Savoy, sent patterns of the latest Flemish fashion or news of the foreign court, that the union with Charles took on any real meaning.[7] She was, however, the Princess of Castile and held a position at the English court second only to the king and queen. And her days and nights were kept so busy with delightful splendors of court that she no longer had time for the rigors of the schoolroom. When her brother became king, Mary thought of herself—and was treated—as an adult. She was the golden princess who followed closely wherever the queen went.

When Henry's infant son died two months after his birth,[8] Mary wept with her brother and his queen. But there would be other sons; deaths of infants were expected occasions. And as Henry was confident in the future, he soon swung his court into heightened festival. The torches of Westminster Palace blazed more brightly, the logs in the hearth burned more brilliantly, and the dancing, masquing, and pageantry became more frantic. When the old palace burned in 1512, the king took no pains to rebuild it. It represented too much of the past seriousness of his father's reign. Instead he redecorated and expanded the other palaces and built new ones. And the royal circle moved from palace to palace as though on extended massive holiday.[9]

In Scotland, Margaret and James had reached through the years a workable relationship. Although she could neither appreciate nor understand his numerous infidelities, she ceased to rage against them. When his natural son Alexander Stewart came home from Germany to become the eleven-year-old archbishop of

St. Andrews, Margaret gradually accepted the child.[10] She saw
James' concern and treatment of the boy as recompense for sins
committed. She had spent enough nights by her husband's side to
know something of the dreams which scorched his soul and
burned his conscience. Moreover, he remained tender towards
her.

Both James and Margaret saw her numerous confinements as
political responsibility, and James came to regard them with fear
for her pain. She thanked him for that. And when one by one the
children died, they shared their grief. When their Prince Arthur
died while yet an infant, this "prince of so singular expectation . . .
was buried with many a salt tear." The grief of the royal parents
was so great that they were unable to remain in Edinburgh Castle
where the child had died. In haste and pain they moved to Stirling.[11] But the change brought no real respite from sorrow, the
death of the son only heightened the sense of guilt of the father.
He grew more desperate in his encouragement to the crusade to
the Holy Land. He sent dispatches to all Christian monarchs, he
wept and prayed for the plans he constantly discussed, and he set
again to the task of enlarging his navy.

James called all the carpenters and shipwrights of the land to
build the grandest ship of all time. It would be his flagship. It
would take him to the Holy Land. Only this great act would bring
the absolution he needed, would lift the stain of patricide from
his blood and give him sons who would live. With his usual frenzy
and proclivity for excess, the king denuded the forests of Scotland
—save that of his private hunting preserve at Falkland—to build
his grand ship. By 1511 it was completed and named the *Great
Michael*. Margaret and her ladies watched as James, in his golden
suit fashioned like that of a mariner, took the helm for the ship's
maiden voyage. Even the ambassadors who stood upon the shore
agreed that no navy on earth could rival the fleet which contained
the *Margaret*, the *James*, and now the *Great Michael*—with its
impenetrable walls ten feet thick.[12]

James wrote of these activities to the pope, Julius II. He noted
how the King of France, though suffering from the gout and incapable of an active part in the crusade, had encouraged him to be
ready when the pope should call. James was ready with his new
fleet, he would follow wherever the pope might summon, and he
would "gladly shed his last drop of blood in the cause of Christen-

dom."[13] James was desperate for the great cause which might alleviate his greater guilt.

Margaret thought him foolhardy, but what was the point of protest? He was ready to leave her with an heirless throne, and she knew she could not reason with his fanaticism. Instead she willed strength into the new babe which now kicked in her womb. She would make him strong through sheer force of will. She would guard his days and nights. This child, she determined, would live. He would live to be a king. She would make it so. James might put all his faith in God, but she put her faith in herself.

So with greater pomp and confidence Margaret received ambassadors, flattered them, condescended to them, took a greater interest in intrigues of government. She travelled more and showed herself more often to the people. She knew the power of public appearance—every Tudor did. And she was no less capable in charming a crowd than any member of the family. She visited many towns and many places, but the most famous visit was to Aberdeen, long known for its flair for pageantry and display. With word of the queen's coming, the town council had ordered all the burgesses to be "ready with their arrayment made in green and yellow, [with] bows, arrows, brass, and all other convenient things according thereto" in order to impersonate the foresters of Robin Hood.[14] The respectable band greeted the queen, but the visit itself was best recorded by William Dunbar, friend, priest, and courtier of Margaret Tudor.

> Blithe Aberdeen, thou beriall[a] of all towns,
>   The lamp of beauty, bounty, and blitheness;
> Unto the heaven ascended thy reknown is,
>   Of virtue, wisdom, and of worthiness;
> High noted is thy name of nobleness,
> Into the coming of our lusty Queen,
>   The well of wealth, good cheer, and merriness:
> Be blythe and blissful, burgh of Aberdeen.
>
> And first her met the burgess of the town,
>   Richly arrayed as becomes them to be,
> Of whom they chose four men of reknown,
>   In gowns of velvet, young, able, and lusty,
>   To bear the pall of velvet crimson

[a] brightest

Above her head, as the custom has been;
  Great was the sound of the artillery:
Be blythe and blissful, burgh of Aberdeen.

A fair procession met her at the Port,
  In a cap of gold and silk, full pleasantly,
Syne[b] at her entry, with many fair disport,
  Received her on streets lustily;
  Where first the salutation honorably
Of the sweet Virgin, goodly might be seen;
  The sound of minstrels blowing to the skies:
Be blythe and blissful, burgh of Aberdeen.

And syne thou gart the Orient Kings three,
  Offer to Christ, with benign reverence,
Gold, sence, myrrh, with all humility,
  Showing him King, with most magnificence;
Syne how the angel, with sword of violence,
Forth of the joy of Paradise put clean
  Adam and Eve for disobedience:
Be blythe and blissful, burgh of Aberdeen.

And syne the Bruce, that ever was bold in stour,
  Thou gart as Roy come riding under crown,
Right awful, strong, and large of *portrature[c]*
  As noble, dreadful, mighty champion:
  The noble Stewarts syne, of great reknown,
Thou gart upspring, with branches new and green,
  So gloriously, while gladded[d] all the town
Be blythe and blissful, burgh of Aberdeen.

Syne came there four-and-twenty maidens young,
  All clad in green, of marvellous beauty,
With hair detressit[e], as threads of gold did hang,
  With white hats all embroidered right bravely,
  Playing on timbrels, and singing right sweetly;
That seemly sort, in order well beseen,
  Did meet the Queen, her saluting reverently:
Be blythe and blissful, burgh of Aberdeen.

The streets were all hung with tapestry,
  Great was the press of people dwelt about,
And pleasant padyheanes[f] played prettily;

---

[b] afterwards   [c] visage   [d] delighted   [e] hanging in tresses   [f] pageants

The lieges all did to their lady lout,[g]
  Who was convoyed with a royal rout
Of great baronesses and lusty ladies sheen;
    Welcome, our Queen! the commons gave one shout:
Be blythe and blissful, burgh of Aberdeen.

At her coming great was the mirth and joy,
  For at their Cross abundantly ran wine;
Until her lodging the town did her convoy;
    Her for to treat they set their whole ingenuity,
    A rich present they did to her propine;
  A costly cup that large thing would contain
    Covered and full of coined gold right fine:
Be blythe and blissful, burgh of Aberdeen.

O potent Princess! pleasant, and supereminent,
  Great cause thou has to thank this noble town,
That for to do thee honor, did not spare
    Their gear, riches, substance, and person,
    Thee to receive on most fair fashion:
Thee for to please they sought all way and mean;
    Therefore, so long as queen thou bear the crown,
Be thankful to this burgh of Aberdeen.[15]

When the king and queen were in residence together, she sought to play upon his fondness for game and pageantry. She encouraged his participation in disguises. There was the day, for instance, when he pretended to be a foreign knight and defeated in the lists all who challenged him. She encouraged games and plays both religious and secular and invited to court the biblical presentations of Corpus Christi Day and the merry gaming of the Morris dancers.

Despite, however, the semblance of harmony in both English and Scots capitals, tensions slowly—almost imperceptibly—began to grow. Margaret waited in Scotland for the legacy which her father had left her in England. But the months passed into years, and Henry VIII neglected to send the jewels. James saw the refusal as a personal affront.[16]

Whenever the English ambassadors came to the Scottish court, Margaret would in private ask about her legacy. On one such

---

[g] bow

occasion Dr. Nicholas West, the English ambassador, answered that he was ready to deliver the jewels "so that the king would promise to keep the treaty of peace." To which Margaret asked, "And not else?" Dr. West responded, "No, for if he [James IV] would make war [Henry VIII] . . . would not only withhold that, but also take from them the best Towns they had."[17]

Margaret, in consternation, immediately wrote her brother:

> Right excellent, right high and mighty Prince, our dearest and best beloved Brother. We commend us unto you in our most hardy wise. Your ambassador Doctor West delivered us your loving letters in which ye show us that where ye heard of our sickness ye took great heaviness. Dearest Brother We are greatly rejoiced that we see ye have respect to our disease, and therefore We give you our hardy thanks, and your writing is to us good comfort.
>
> We can not believe that of your mind or by your command we are so unfriendly delt with in our father's Legacy, whereof we would not have spoken nor written had not the Doctor now spoken to us of the same in his credence. Our husband knows it is withheld for his sake, and will recompense us so far as the Doctor shows him. We are ashamed therewith; and would God never word had been thereof. It is not worth such estimation as is in your divers letters of the same; and we lacking nothing; our husband is ever the longer better to us, as knows God, who right high and mighty Prince, our dearest and best beloved brother, have you in governance. Given under our Signet at our Palace of Linlithgow the xi. day of April.
>
> Your loving sister, Margaret.[18]

The crack in the truce had appeared. Neither king, however, seemed ready or anxious to war over a handful of jewels. Margaret encouraged restraint on both sides. The crack, however, widened in spite of her protestations. Henry, eager to prove himself a leader of men and commander of the army, and anxious to display the military dexterity of his ancestors, sought to make valid the title which he bore—Henry the Eighth King of England and France. Like the famous Henry V, the new Henry would bring the French to their knees. The eighth Henry would show the world his mettle—and in this enterprise he was encouraged by his father-in-law Ferdinand of Spain as well as the Emperor of the Romans Maximilian and Pope Julius II.

All three men were anxious to pluck the feathers of the French, although none wished to spend his own resources to do so. If, however, the passionate Henry could be prevailed upon to engage France, to draw her attention away from the southern borders, then the objectives of the southern monarchs would be served. Maximilian even offered to serve as a soldier in Henry's army if that prince would lead the way. Henry could not resist this chance to test and prove himself in the world arena. He had, in short, outgrown the lists of the tourney; he would enter the lists of the world.

France, however, was an ancient ally of Scotland. The treaty known as the "auld alliance" had been part of French-Scots policy for centuries. James considered an attack on France a challenge to his own honor. He too had been itching for battle. He had hoped it would be against the Infidel sitting in Jerusalem. If that were not possible, then the English would have to do. He began to think seriously of war.

In the meantime, the King of Scots' adored navy had been touched to the quick by the seizure of some vessels and the murder of his captains by the English. James had commissioned Andrew Barton in 1509 to man the seas and protect Scots enterprise against Dutch pirates. Barton had been so successful that he not only engaged the pirates in battle but filled a hogshead with their severed heads and sent the trophy home to James.[19] For two years Barton had sailed the channel in search of pirates. Any vessel he captured, he labelled a pirate ship—regardless of its country of origin. In the course of this to-and-froing, he intercepted English ships, pillaged them, and brought vessels, men, and cargo into Scottish harbors. In retaliation, Henry sent out his own men-of-war under the leadership of the Lord Admiral of England, Sir Edmund Howard. A sea battle followed. Amidst the shivering, writhing boats, with the cannon smoking and rebounding, Andrew Barton was killed by the admiral's brother Lord Thomas. With the Scots under guard and the decks glued with their captain's blood, the Howards brought Barton's *Lion* and her sister ship *Jenny Perwin* into the Thames.[20]

James was incensed. His kingdom had been challenged directly. His honor was at stake, and his dream of pilgrimage had received a devastating blow. With time and effort he could replace the ships, but Barton had been a brilliant seaman and no one could replace him. In rage and sorrow, James demanded restitution from his brother-in-law. Henry retorted that the affairs of pirates were not the affairs of princes. He wanted no more talk of the matter.[21]

Despite the protestations of his wife and against her better judgment, James prepared for war against England as Henry prepared for war against France. Now James knew what the great earthquakes of 1508 had foreshadowed. They had shaken both realms, and he saw them as a portent of the mighty cataclysm to come.[22] Now he knew too what the great comet had spoken as it lighted the August skies of 1511 for twenty-one nights. While all others who saw or heard of it feared, James knew it to be the sign of flaming victory.[23]

The king heightened his religious fervor, he prayed and scathed his flesh until it bled in painful humiliation. He grew to love the sting of the whip and the weight of his iron belt. They showed how sorry he was. They showed the great penitence he felt. Now if God would only show him favor, he would avenge his honor. It seemed he got his sign. On Easter Eve, April 11, 1512, the queen while at her dower castle of Linlithgow gave birth to a new prince and named him James.[24]

Once again Margaret was sick unto death; once again James undertook his barefoot pilgrimage in prayer and supplication. But this time when he sent news of the prince's birth to the courts of France and Denmark, he also asked for military supplies to use against the English. He received congratulations and gifts for his wife and son, and armaments to use against their kinsman.[25]

While Henry prepared for war against France, the emissaries sent frantic dispatches between England and Scotland. James talked increasingly of his wife's inheritance which her brother failed to send. He spoke of an attack against France as a challenge to Scotland and an affront to his honor. Margaret urged peace to James. She urged restraint to Henry. And to his ambassadors, she spoke of James' increasing support from France. While in fact Margaret was not an active agent of England, she was an active advocate. She wanted peace with England and saw with increasing anguish the rupture between her "dearest brother" and her "dearest husband." To obey the one was to dishonor, if not to betray, the other.

In the meantime Louis XII of France promised James "grant of a whole *disme* 'throughout all his realm, on this side and beyond the Mountains, to be levied by the King of Scots within a year after the peace was made'; also a number of men of arms and shipping."[26] What could England do to match this obvious love of France? James asked of the English ambassador Nicholas West. West hesitated; he wanted James to express his terms for peace in writing. This the king refused, saying he feared any written statements might be used against him in France. West, however, learned of a French convoy under the command of the Frenchman de la Motte. His passage was long overdue. The ambassador urged Henry that "the biscuit and beer that de la Motte bringeth is to victual the great Ship and other[s]. I pray God he be, or may be taken by the way; for his taking were worth to your Grace ten thousand marks; for by him ye should know all the secrets of the King here."[27]

The arguments and intrigue continued with utmost courtesy, and before Dr. West left for England he met with Margaret. The two lamented the widening drift of interests, and West described the interview: "Howbeit she said she had done the best that was in her power, and so would continue, and without further communication of her Legacy or any other matter she delivered me tokens to your Grace, to the Queen, and the Princess [Mary], and prayed me to recommend her to your Grace; and so I took my leave. And she commanded me to be brought to see the Prince, and so I was; verily he is a right fair child, and a large of his age."[28]

In his final meeting with the king, the ambassador was told by James: "Yea my brother shall do right wisely since he hath enterprised so great a matter, as to make war upon France, which he cannot well perform and bring about to turn his army upon us and thereby excuse him of going into France." Whereupon West flung out the final taunt by answering that James "should right well understand that if he would break with your Grace [Henry VIII], your Grace was able to perform your Voyage into France, and also to withstand him and his power, and in case he made you war it might somewhat trouble your Voyage, but not let [prevent] it."[29]

In spite of the differing claims of interest neither Henry nor James seemed ready to war with the other. They were, after all, still bound by the marital treaty which both had willingly renewed in 1509. They were not only bound physically by Margaret, they were bound spiritually by the threat of excommunication by the Church. Both kings fancied themselves princes of the Church. Henry, however, had given himself to the cause of Rome in its war with France. James was tied politically to France, but he wanted more desperately to serve the Church. He lamented the fact that Henry's admiral Sir Edmund Howard was killed April 25, 1513, in an attempt to capture French ships. James noted that the "valiant knight's service and other noble men that must on both the sides apparently be perished, If War continue, were better applied upon the Enemies of Christ. . . ."[30]

Henry responded: "if he [James] will promise faithfully to keep his bond foresaid to me I shall incontinent with all the consent of my nobles make him Duke of York and governor of England to [until] my homecoming. For the affairs of England may either come of me or him, and I have none as yet that is lawful of my body, but I heresay Margaret my eldest sister has a pretty boy, apparently to be a man of estimation. I pray God to bless him and keep him from his enemies and give me grace that I may see him in honor and estimation when he comes of age, that I may entertain him according to my honor and duty."[31]

The plea was to no avail. Henry, accompanied by Catherine and Mary, left with his handsomely appointed army for Dover in June, 1513. There he made Catherine the Regent of England, and he commissioned the Earl of Surrey—the same who ten years earlier had conducted Margaret to Scotland—to take an army northward and guard against Scottish invasion. Henry said to Surrey: "My lord, I trust not the Scots, therefore I pray you be not negligent." Surrey answered: "I shall do my duty, that your grace shall find me diligent, and to fulfill your will shall be my gladness." Surrey spoke the words with difficulty as he wanted desperately to be among the party going to France. Later with a more settled mind he spoke bitterly of James: "Sorry may I see him or I die, that is the cause of my abiding behind, and if ever he and I meet, I shall do that in me lieth to make him [James IV] as sorry if I can. . . ."[32]

With great lamenting on the part of the ladies and to the great huzzas of his men, Henry VIII blew his gold whistle. The ships lifted anchor as the gilded sails unfurled. He was ready to prove his right by conquest for England and St. George:

The Rose will into France spring,
Almighty God him thither bring,
And save this flower which is our King.
This Rose, this Rose, this royal Rose
Which is called a noble thing,
The flower of England, and soldier King.
These April showers which are full sweet*
Hath bound this Rose not yet full blown
In France he will his *levies* shoot.
His right to conquer, his enemies to know.
This Rose, that is of color red,
Will seek his enemies both far and wide,
And with his beams he will France light.
Saint George Protector be his good guide.
God send this flower where he would be,
To spred his flowers to his rejoicing,
In France to have the victory;
All England for him shall pray and sing.
Jesus and Mary, full of might,
God be his guide in all his right;
Sweet Saint George our Lady's Knight
Save King Harry both by day and night.[33]

Henry gathered his forces in Calais and joined the advanced troops led by Charles Brandon, the newly created Viscount Lisle. Together they marched in glittering array toward the town of Thérouanne. Once there they plotted the coming battle. Into their midst rode the Scots herald with James' list of grievances. The borders, he maintained, stood under challenge and were readying for battle, the treaty into which Henry had entered violated the honor of the Scots, the death of Andrew Barton remained unrequited, and Margaret's legacy was yet to be released. "Herefore we write to you this time at length [the] plainness of our mind, that we require and desire you to desist from further invasion and utter destruction of our brother and Cousin the most Christian king [Louis XII]. . . . Certifying you we will take part in defense of our brother and Cousin. . . ."

To this challenge Henry thundered: "We cannot marvel, con-

---

* Weather probably prevented the earlier departure.

sidering the ancient accustomable manners of your progeniteurs, which never kept longer faith and promise than pleased them. Howbeit, if the love and dread of God, nighness of blood, honor of the world, law and reason, had bound you, we suppose ye would never have so far proceeded, specially in our absence. . . ." The gauntlet had been thrown down and snatched up. Henry immediately sent word to Catherine to prepare in all haste for war. He ordered Surrey to prepare against the Scots, to move northward, and to ready for defensive action against invasion.[34]

Henry's confidence in affairs at home gained quick reenforcement by his affairs in France. On August 22, the city of Thérouanne fell. Basking in the glow of military victory, the English army swept the French before them in the battle at Guinegate, which was quickly named the Battle of the Spurs—the only implement used by the French that day. Then the King of England, in the midst of fallen French banners, sat down before the gates of Tournai.[35]

News of these victories spread quickly to Scotland and burned like salt in the wounded pride of James IV. He sent messengers to all parts of his land, to every chieftain, to prepare himself and his men for war. Although bound by oath to obey the directive, there were many amongst them who spoke against battle. The long peace with England had been a prosperous interlude many hated to interrupt. The clergy, however, were anxious for war. They saw the absence of the English king as an open invitation to easy victory. And it was to the clergy that James listened.

The turning point in James' decision came, however, from France. All the world knew of James' proclivity for romance and idealized knighthood, and upon these most unpolitic and undiplomatic characteristics, the French began to play. The ailing Queen of France, Anne of Brittany, sent to James a special message carefully worded and padded with the phrases of chivalric appeal. She asked that he advance but three feet onto English ground and strike a blow for her honor. To seal the request, she sent him a ring from her *own* finger.[36] Such an appeal was irresistible to James. The question was decided. He had been asked as a Christian knight to do a noble deed for the Queen of France. What knight could say nay?

Margaret pleaded in vain. Her arguments, her tears, her pleas were answered with accusations: Did she not love England more than Scotland? Did she not serve her brother rather than her husband? Did she not see her words as treason? Was she nothing better than spokeswoman for the enemy?

Undaunted when appeals to reason failed, Margaret worked upon her husband's emotions, his fears, his superstitions. She began to weep in her sleep and whisper in her dreams. She spoke of pearls melting into chains; she tore at her eye in pain—screaming that it was ripping from its socket. With the other eye, she saw her husband falling from high places—towers, precipices, heaven itself. But these mighty demonstrations were dismissed by James as "mere dreams." And Margaret's retort was ready:

"It is no Dream that ye have but one Son; and him a weakling. If otherways than well happen unto you, what a lamentable day will that be, when ye will leave behind you, to so tender and weak a Successor, under the government of a Woman, for inheritance, a miserable and bloody war?

"It is no dream that ye are to fight a mighty people; now turned insolent by their riches at home and power abroad. That your Nobility are indigent ye know, and may be bribed to leave you in your greatest danger. What a folly, what a blindness is it to make this war yours; and to quench the fire in your Neighbor's house of France, to kindle and burn up your own in Scotland? Ye have no reason to assist the French, as ye have to keep your promises to England, and enjoy Peace at home. Though the English should make a conquest of France, will they take your Crown, or disinherit their own race? This is even as the left would cut off the right. Should the Letters of the Queen of France (a woman twice married—the first half in Adultery, the last almost Incest—whom ye did never nor shall never see) prove more powerful with you than the cries of your little Son, and mine, than the tears, complaints, curses of the Orphans and Widows which ye are to make?

"If ye will go, suffer me to accompany you; it may be my Countrymen prove more kind towards me than they will to you; and for my sake yield unto Peace. I hear the Queen my sister will be with the Army in her husband's absence; if we shall meet who knows what God by our means may bring to pass."[37]

From these entreaties James turned brusquely away. No, he maintained, Margaret sounded like a jealous wife; and his honor, his very knighthood, were at stake. There would be no turning back, no hesitation. To tighten the allegiance of his men, parlia-

ment at his request ordained "that if any man is slain by Englishmen or dies in the army his heirs shall have ward, relief, and
marriage" under the guardianship of the crown.[38]

While at her palace of Linlithgow, Margaret made another
plea. Kneeling before James in open court she called again for
restraint, wept bitterly at the events which tore from both sides
her allegiance and loyalty. Her final word was that "if he must
enter war with her brother, at least not to conduct his forces in
person; but to look upon his infant son, and reflect that upon him
alone rested all the hopes of his parents, and of all affectionate
people."[39] That too was impossible, the king responded. If her
brother could lead his men in war, so would the King of Scots—for
his was the better fight. With that, James returned to his prayers
and masses at St. Michael's Church at Linlithgow.

But Margaret's resources were not yet exhausted. While the
king sat, sad and dolorous at prayer and meditation, an ancient
long-haired man clad in a blue gown and carrying a huge pikestaff
in his hand, appeared in the chapel. With apparent desperation,
he pushed the noblemen aside and moved quickly and forcefully
toward the king. James, sitting beneath the ancient banners of his
fathers and staring fixedly at the bleeding cross, paid no heed to
the confusion. The old man came steadily forward, however, and
with little reverence leaned down on the king's desk and said: "Sir
King, my mother sent me to thee desiring thee not to pass at this
time where thou art purposed, for if thou does thou will not fair
well in thy journey nor none that pass with thee; further she bade
thee not *mell* with no women nor use their counsel, nor let them
not touch thy body nor thou theirs, for if thou do it thou will be
confounded and brought to shame."

The king turned away, thinking of these words. When he turned
again to speak, the ancient one had vanished—some said in a puff
of smoke "as he had been a blink of the sun or a whip of the
whirlwind." None could say where he went, and he was never
seen again.[40]

The old man's emphasis on adultery made James suspicious—
the words echoed of Margaret's sermonizing. The entire charade
he saw as a ruse on her part, and he paid no heed. But later when
so much was lost, there were many who believed the ancient man
in blue to have been a messenger of heaven.[41]

The king prepared for invasion and moved to Holyrood House.

The highland chiefs arrived in Edinburgh with their men and equipment—enough to last a battle forty days. As men jostled each other and talked of war, James daily pushed through the throngs to supervise the preparations of the arms at Edinburgh Castle. Foremost amongst the artillery were the famous cannons of Edinburgh—the Seven Sisters. With the desperate groans of the horses and the shouts of sweating men, the great cannons began to slip down the courtyard of the castle, down the long rough road of High Street, and on toward war. While the days of preparation were charged by the challenge of victory, the nights were broken by shrill and threatening portents of evil. No one knew whether the warnings were of "vain persons, night walkers, drunken men, or if it was but a spirit," but there were many who took the warnings in fear and tossed prayers and pennies into the waiting dark.[42]

Margaret came to Edinburgh and again begged James to listen to the dire portents of the warning voices. Again she reminded him of the single, fragile heir who played alone in his cradle at Linlithgow. Again she urged the king to wait until the little prince was older, until he had reached maturity and had the security of brothers yet unborn. These entreaties "for the weal of her husband and the common weal of the country and also for the love that she bore to her brother the King of England" came to naught.[43]

In late August James bid a noisy farewell to Edinburgh, and in a gesture of trust and reconciliation he created Margaret regent of the realm in his absence. By the twenty-second of the month he was engaged in border raids and minor skirmishes—attacking a village here and burning fields and homes there.[44] He had taken at last those three steps and more for the French queen.

The English, however, were not unknowing of the sporadic but definite preparations in the north. Queen Catherine sent Thomas Howard Earl of Surrey again to the north. From London, Catherine directed much of the operation and wrote to Wolsey in France: "You are not so busy with war in Thérouanne as I am encumbered with it in England. . . . They are all here very glad to be busy with the Scots, for they take it as a pastime. My heart is very good at it, and I am horribly busy with making standards, banners, and badges."[45]

Surrey continued his march northward, and James stormed the tower of the castle at Furd. It fell quickly to him and Lady Heron an English prisoner of the castle, fell into his arms. The lady was won and she was willing. James forgot in an instant the earlier warning of Dunbar's "Thistle and the Rose":

> And since thou art a King, thou be discreet;
> Herb without virtue thou hold not of such price
> As herb of virtue, and of odor sweet;
> And let no nettle vile, and full of vice,
> ... Nor let no wild weed, full of churlishness,
> Compare her to the like's nobleness:
> ... Nor hold no other flow'r in such duty
> As the fresh ROSE, of color red and white.

While the Lady Heron tempted, toyed, and teased the King of Scots, her daughter similarly entertained his son Alexander Archbishop of St. Andrews. The games continued and Lady Heron drained the king of his energies and information. The news of his men, their armaments, and their position, she relayed to Surrey. And while the English forces gathered their men, increased their strength, and moved closer to confrontation, James dallied with his mistress for nearly three weeks. It was all the time Surrey needed.

In the meantime the Scots, many hesitant about the battle from the beginning, grew restive. The army of fifty thousand which had answered the call and marched from Edinburgh began to drift away. The weather was wet and raw, the food supplies dwindled, and many a soldier who sat around an evening's fire gathered his goods and disappeared by dawn. No one seemed to know the English forces were so near at hand.[46]

From Newcastle, Surrey challenged James to battle on Friday, September 9. To envenom the challenge his son Thomas Howard, the newly created Lord Admiral who was responsible for Barton's death at sea, added that he was ready to answer for the death of the "pirate." James' hand was forced. Against the advice of his lords he led his encampment across the river Till through the Cheviot Hills and took a strong position on the hill of Flodden from whence he could watch the advancing English army. In order to clear his name and answer the challenge of Surrey, James sent a herald with the message: "The great damage wrought by your king to me and mine provokes me now to arms, and not proud arrogance, false in my promise, as ye falsely allege. Neither pretend we any other cause of battle, which, by God's grace, we shall defend, the day appointed."[47]

James and his army sat at their strongly defended and strategic posts and with silent cannon watched the English maneuver for position. Surrey sought to lure James from his excellent encampment by appealing to his famed "honor"; Surrey wrote to James: ". . . it hath pleased you to change your said promise and put yourself into a ground more like a fortress or Camp then upon any indifferent ground for battle to be tried, wherefore considering the day appointed is so nigh approaching I desire now of your Grace for the accomplishment of your honorable promise you will dispose yourself for your part, like as I shall do for mine, to be tomorrow with your host on your side of the plain of Milfield, in likewise as I shall do for mine, and shall be with the subjects of my sovereign Lord on my side of the plain and of the said field to give you battle betwixt xii. of the clock and iii. in the afternoon, upon sufficient warning by you to be given by vii.[th] or ix of the Clock in the morning by the said Pursuivant. . . ."[48]

James refused on the grounds that an earl must never dictate to a king. Surrey, ever flexible of mind and confident in the personality of his adversary, moved his army in plain view without protection over the bridge of the river Till. The master gunner of the Scots raced to the king, fell on his knees and begged permission to shoot. He knew he could destroy the enemy. But James felt himself constrained by honor and refused to seize the advantage. Like a man gone mad, he raged at his gunner: "I shall hang thee, quarter thee, and draw thee if you shoot any shot this day, for I am determined I will have them all before me on one plain field and try them what they can do all before me."[49] The English crossed the river, and the Scots guns remained silent.

Throughout the morning of September 9, the English forces pulled into formation. The day of battle was at hand. Back and forth across his front, James was fancying himself a leader of men although this was his first real military campaign. In vain his councillors urged him to another position to watch the action, not fight himself, to heed the warnings of the night before. Mice had gnawed through the leather of his helmet, making it impossible to fasten; the cloth of his tent had appeared at dawn red and wet as though soaked with blood. And in the early morning's light a "hare started amongst them, which having a thousand arrows, daggers, and other kind of things bestowed at him, with great noise and shouting, yet she escaped from them all and without hurt."[50] These signs and portents and the petitions of his men seemed rather to flay James into unreasoned rage. He grew furious and retorted: "My lords, I shall fight this day with England [even though] ye have all sworn the contrary; though you would all fly from me and shame yourselves, ye shall not shame me as ye devise. . . ."[51]

On seeing the English move toward Branxton Hill, a mile north of Flodden, James ordered his camp to be burned, and under its smoke he gave up his strong position and moved to the lesser hill. By the time the smoke had cleared, the two armies were nearly face to face. It was after four o'clock in the afternoon, but the challenge had been made and must be met. The ordnance from both sides began to explode. Yet while the Scots gunners were slain by English shot, the Scots cannon—too highly mounted —overshot and little harmed their enemies. With horror at what was happening and the sudden impatience which drew them to folly, the Scots left the advantage of the heights and raced down the hill. Their spears were too long and their daggers too short to offer much defense, for the English with their shorter halberts sliced away at the spears and gored the flesh before the rushing Scots could recover. Gradually the English moved up the hill, slipping and stumbling over fallen, writhing limbs. Behind them stood their archers who continued their constant piercing rain of arrows which arched so high and dropped with such force that many a Scot was drilled to the ground. Right and left the best of the Scots were slain. And as the English gained ground, the Scots leaders Hume and Huntley withdrew from battle.

In the center of the action, the men of the Scots army drew into a tighter circle about their king. While Surrey surveyed the action and directed the battle from a distance, King James IV fought like a foot soldier. Around him the muddy ground turned red, and the Scots ripped away their shoes to grip better the earth. It was all to no avail. When darkness forced an end to battle, the English withdrew, not knowing who had won the field. They sat in the silence of the night and waited while the fields and streams ran red. This

time there were no fires to light the night, no food, no rest—only
night sounds and the heavy breathing of exhaustion and the cries
of the dying.

At dawn, Surrey found his army resting alone. The Scots had
disappeared; their dead and dying were left behind. Already some
bodies had been stripped naked. Here and there an arm twitched,
a leg moved—some eleven or twelve thousand Scots lay dead. As
the victors moved up the hill, the bodies of the Scots already
picked clean by the scavengers of the night lay three and four
deep. At the center of the action, a circle of the dead lay tightly
ringed about their king. James IV was dead. With him lay his son
Alexander, thirteen earls, fourteen lords, a bishop, two abbots,
and knights and gentlemen of nearly every noble house of Scotland.

> O Flodden Field the ruin to revolve
>   Or that most dolent day for to deplore
> I nill[a] for dread that dolour to [you] dissolve
>   Or show how that prince in his triumphant glory
> Destroyed was what needed process more
>   Not by the virtue of English ordinance
> But by his own wilfull misgovernance.
>
> Alas that day had he been counselable
>   He had obtained laud, glory, and victory
> Whose piteous process being so lamentable
>   I nill at length to put in memory
> I never read in tragedy nor story
>   At one journey so many nobles slain
> For the defense and love of their sovereign.[52]

The ones who stood and looked marvelled at the "lack of discretion in the king which would needs run upon his own death,
[which] amazed the minds of all men, and brought them unto
such perplexity, that they knew not what to do. . . ."[53]

The English foot soldiers seized the supplies of the enemy; and
having had nothing but water to drink for three days, found the
Scottish beer much refreshing.[54] Orders were given for the Scots

---

[a] will not

harness and artillery to be gathered and sent to Berwick where much of it was sold.[55] Orders were given for the wounded to be gathered and the dead to be buried, and then an intensive search began for the body of the king. Since he had ten men dressed in his coat of armor—a usual precaution when any king took the field—identification of his body remained for years a matter of doubt. The English maintained that he was found and recognized by Lord Dacre "who knew him well by his privy tokens."[56] The Scots maintained otherwise. Some said that in the midst of the smoke of battle, four knights known only to each other rode onto the field, horsed the king, and brought him to Kelso.[57] Others alleged that he had escaped the battle whole and sound and disappeared in sorrow and humiliation from the land. He had, it was said, become a pilgrim and taken himself on solitary crusade to his beloved Jerusalem. There he was said to weep away his days before the Holy Sepulchre and to remain the rest of his life in devout and saddened pilgrimage.[58]

Surrey placed the body, pierced by arrow and spear, in a cart and brought it to Berwick. There he showed it to Sir William Scott Chancellor and Sir John Forman the Sergeant Porter "which knew him at the first sight and made great lamentation." Satisfied that the right body was in his possession, Surrey ordered it embalmed and wrapped in lead. It was stuffed amongst other articles and secretly brought to Newcastle and finally south to Richmond Palace to await the pleasure of Henry VIII.[59]

While these proceedings passed, Surrey sent to Catherine news of his victory and the bloody coat of the king. It was with a note of triumph that she wrote to Henry: "My husband, for hastiness with [the Herald] Rougecross I could not send your Grace the piece of the King of Scots' coat which John Glenn now bringeth. In this your grace shall see how I can keep my promise, sending you for your banners a King's coat. I thought to send himself unto you, but our Englishmen's hearts would not suffer it. . . ."[60]

As the bloody trophies went southward, the dolorous news swept northward. Scarcely a home was left without a weeping widow, a crying sister, a sobbing child. The flower of Scots manhood festered on the fields of Flodden; their armaments were in the carts of the English and trundled slowly away. And the impact of the overwhelming loss to a nation as a whole and the citizenry in particular brought shock, dismay, and near paralysis. The country, barren and broken, stood vulnerable to inroads and on-slaughts from the south. There seemed few men left to fight, supplies and munitions were lost, and the bleeding remnants of the army scattered into the hillside. No one seemed to know anything of the whereabouts or condition of the English. Were they even now moving through the silent fog toward the capital? Were they waiting at Berwick and Newcastle for reenforcements from the south? Or was the English army wearied and worn; was it in truth dispersed? Rumor carried fear, and its contagion swept into the villages and surrounded the capital itself.

Margaret had waited through the long days of James' absence at Linlithgow with her son, the infant Prince James. To them had come word of the border skirmishes, of the foolish castle raids, of James' affair with the Lady Heron. More news followed as the battle of Flodden drew near, as it happened, as it ended only hours later in bloody catastrophe. All reports were scattered, confused, and conflicting. Whether James lived or died was in doubt. Had he really been seen at Kelso? Was he dead? There were many at court and throughout the country who either could not admit of his death or fervently believed he lived. His famous iron belt, for instance, had not been found at Flodden. Had he laid it aside for the day of battle? Had scavengers stolen it away? Did the king now wear it with increased sorrow; did he now move only in darkness, too filled with shame to face the living?

Amidst the lamentation and the gossip, the hand-wringers and the hangers-on, Margaret's realistic, practical nature pierced the prevailing paralysis of confusion. She summoned the few remaining councillors and statesmen and arranged at least temporary government. Not knowing the predilections of her brother or those of his officer the Earl of Surrey, she sent word to the remaining men of Edinburgh. The city was ordered to look to its weapons, to ready the defense of the capital, to answer the sound of the common bell if the English should draw near. The order ended with the stern mandate: ". . . let no woman be seen clamoring and crying in the streets, but let them pass to church for prayer or busy themselves at home with their domestic tasks."[61]

Within days of the Flodden tragedy, Margaret sent "loving letters" to her brother urging peace for her kingdom, protection for her son, and renewed truce between the two realms.[62] Henry

answered that "if the Scots want peace, they can have it. . . ."[63]
Then she summoned a parliament general to meet at Stirling
Castle. On September 21, 1513, she caused her son now a year, five
months, and ten days old, to be crowned King James V. It was not
an occasion for joy, but one of great sadness; and while the priests
intoned the ritual of coronation, there were many who wept aloud
at the necessity. The event would be ever known as the "Mourning Coronation." But Margaret feared betrayal, and so she placed
a heavy guard about the infant king.

James IV, before leaving for his disastrous duel with death, had
named Margaret regent of the realm and tutrix of their son. His
will verified his wish and when it was "publically seen and approved" Margaret was given by parliament the authority of regent
and the care of her son with the understanding that she remain a
widow and follow the advice of a council of four: the Earl of
Angus, the Earl of Arran, the Earl of Huntley, and the Archbishop of Glasgow James Beaton. It was a diplomatic measure on
many sides.[64] Margaret was still the sister of the King of England,
and Scotland was in no position to face any reprisal or any demands Henry VIII might make in her name. Secondly, she had
the sentimental support of the commons. And thirdly, the late
king himself had named her to the position of power. For the
moment her position was strong while not impregnable. Although
there were some nobility who fretted at a woman's reign—and an
Englishwoman at that—they were for the moment silent and did
nothing.

The queen mother was not yet twenty-four years old. Physically
she had developed into a large woman, though none would ever
call her handsome or beautiful. She did, however, have a will of
iron and certain intelligence. She was generally popular with her
subjects and could exhibit a charming grace and warm dignity
when the occasion demanded. She had, it is true, been indulged
by her father and her husband, and like them she was used to
having her way. But those who supported her in the first frantic
days following the disaster of Flodden Field hoped and perhaps
believed that she could develop a talent for diplomacy and leadership. At least they were willing to give her the chance. She was the
king's mother, after all, and she carried within her another child
of James IV. Whatever else might be said for the queen, she had

the protection of her brother's interest and army, and for the moment she was the only one who could safely protect the interests of the young king and his unborn brother.

Margaret was thus accepted by the parliament as regent, and none could quarrel with her policy and that of her council during the early days of regency. The defenses of Edinburgh had been strengthened, plans for defense of the borders were underway, what arms and munitions could be recovered were put into commission, and arrangements for the ransom of Scots prisoners were made. Edinburgh Castle was reenforced. The king had been crowned without interference and returned to his cradle.[65]

When Henry VIII heard the news of the victory of Flodden, he caused celebrations to be made in his camp as it lay in siege about the city of Tournai. Amidst the rejoicing, the King of England wrote of James that "he has paid a heavier penalty for his perfidy than we would have wished." Part of the price of that perfidy was excommunication. James had technically broken the peace with England, and his body was denied Christian burial.[66]

With the fervor of a forgiving champion, Henry petitioned the pope in James' behalf and planned an elaborate funeral at St. Paul's Cathedral. Henry himself would be chief mourner. But before that could happen, Henry had more battles to win and more parties to give, and by the time he returned to England, his enthusiasm for the burial of his brother-in-law had disappeared.[67] The pious Catherine, in the meantime, was undecided about what should be done with the body. She had it transferred from Richmond Palace to the monastery at Sheen. The body remained uncoffined and unburied in its lead wrappings in the basement of the monastery. It stayed there for decades.[68]

THE
MIDDLE YEARS

CHAPTER FOUR

THE VICTORY IN SCOTLAND FIRED THE IMAGINATION OF HENRY IN France. After the masses and bonfires of celebration, Henry VIII luxuriated in his watered-blue-silk tents while the siege heightened about the city of Tournai.[1] The town was surrounded and daily the English cannon beat at the walls, gates, and towers. With no hope of relief, there seemed no reason to resist. The city fathers were forced to give the lie to the motto engraved upon the walls: "Thou hast never lost thy maidenhood." The flags of truce went up, messengers from both sides met, discussed, and agreed to terms. Henry, with his usual garments of gold and his penchant for the flamboyant, called out with magnanimity: "Sirs, he that asketh mercy of us shall not be denied. . . ."

Charles Brandon Viscount Lisle was created governor of Tournai and with six thousand men entered the city, seized its towers and walls, searched out its homes and churches. Then Thomas Wolsey Master Almoner called the four-score thousand citizens to fall upon their knees in homage to their new king. On October 2, Henry in great triumph, imagining himself the ancient Caesar, surrounded by henchmen, spearmen, axmen, and footmen, entered the city. With so much grand work behind him, he decided it was time to have a party.

He ordered the tournament lists to be built, his banners to be dusted, his tents reordered, and invitations to be sent to Charles of Castile and his aunt Margaret of Savoy, who held court only twelve miles from Tournai. The royal couple came with torch-light procession and were joined by Margaret's father and Charles' grandfather, the Holy Roman Emperor Maximilian. In Charles' honor, Henry and Lord Lisle challenged all comers, and the king excelled everyone in his equestrianship, his agility, and his breaking of spears. It was a great festive occasion and Henry talked much of the approaching union of his sister Mary with the young prince. Maximilian was delighted with everything and called the King of England variously his son, his brother, his king.

Lord Lisle, all this time, was trying desperately to catch the notice of Margaret of Savoy. She had already lost two husbands and seemed unwilling to involve herself with a third, but she was adept at the game of courtly love. Gracefully and with dignity she ignored Charles Brandon's advances. When Brandon succeeded in playfully stealing her ring and bracelet, he claimed the tokens as a pledge of betrothal. This for Margaret went beyond chivalric conduct, and she offered to buy the jewels again. She was far too cautious a diplomat to allow betrothal rumors to spread, and she had nothing to gain from such a match.[2] She was of the most royal blood of Europe, of ancient lineage, and of comfortable estate. Brandon was of low estate and had inconsequential wealth. His father had brought fame to his line by falling before the Tudor standard at Bosworth Field. In gratitude Henry VII had brought the orphaned boy into the royal household. Brandon developed into an excellent athlete, but that was his major talent. His intellect was slight and his imagination lacking. He was merely an ambitious horseman, handsome and sturdy, who happened to be the closest companion of the King of England. For Margaret of Savoy that was not enough, and Brandon was too slow or too ambitious to realize it. Finally she appealed to Henry—more politically aware than his friend—to extricate her from the affair. That he did.[3] While Brandon persisted in his delusions of grandeur, Margaret and Henry spoke of the forthcoming marriage of Charles and Mary. They settled on the date of May 16, 1514, for Mary's departure from England.[4]

With the approach of early winter, Henry bid farewell to his royal guests, secured the government of his newly won territories, paid his soldiers, and sailed for England. He was Caesar returned, ever reining his horse, acknowledging the cheers, accepting the tokens of gratitude from his people. But he was also anxious to be home, and he hurried toward Richmond Palace and the waiting Catherine. There the two exchanged stories and congratulations for battles won and celebrated with accustomed pageantry. To

mark the victory, the Earl of Surrey for his triumph against Scotland became the Duke of Norfolk, and Charles Brandon for his
service against the French became the Duke of Suffolk.[5]

Amongst the well-wishers and spectators was the eighteen-year-
old Princess Mary. She had developed into a woman of unparal-
leled beauty, accomplished wit and intelligence, and fitted with
all the graces becoming her estate. More delicately framed than
either her brother or sister, she shared their strength of will and
purpose, their love of pleasure and magnificence, but not their
lust for power. Her future seemed as secure as her past as she
listened eagerly to the tales of Henry about her betrothed Charles
of Castile and his aunt Margaret of Savoy. He was, Henry maintained, a boy too solemn, too melancholy, too serious in demeanor,
but Mary with her winning ways would change all that. He assured his sister she would find an exciting, vital companion in the
Archduchess Margaret. She was a magnificent woman, politically
astute, sophisticated in the ways of the world, charming in her
deportment. Her court was one of the liveliest and lightest of
Europe. And it was one which awaited anxiously the arrival of the
English princess.

Henry ordered the preparations to begin for Mary's trousseau.
She must have the finest gowns, the handsomest banners, the
grandest procession to enter Flanders. Every manifestation of ostentatious display would grace her entry. She was his beloved sister and that the world must know. While Henry planned the
pageantry, Mary considered more carefully her exercises at the
lute and polished her performance at the clavichord. While standing for fittings, she even wrenched her attention from colorful
fabrics and delicious silks and furs to practice her French and
rehearse prepared speeches. Once again the well-worn portrait of
Charles was brought out for much caressing and many whispered
words, but the princess was now impatient with pictures and anxious to meet this husband of six years' standing. It was no longer
enough to be called the Princess of Castile—she wanted to be the
Princess of Castile. She wanted a court of her own. Henry had his
court and Margaret had long been Queen of Scotland; it was now
the turn of the last and the youngest. She looked forward to the
spring and her own departure.

The situation of Mary's sister was not, however, an enviable
one. From the moment of James IV's death at Flodden, there were

many who saw the absurdity of his death to be only slightly more absurd than his appointment of his wife as regent of the realm and tutrix of their child. Such designation was contrary to all Scots custom and tradition which allowed the regency to the man nearest in blood to the young king.

Margaret, however, had the sentimental backing of the commons, and many of the lords of Scotland were willing to support the directive of their late king. When the first challenge to her authority came from James Earl of Arran who, as the little king's uncle, claimed to be the nearest in blood and consequently legal guardian and regent, the lords of Scotland refused him. They were willing to support the regency of Margaret "so long as the queen kept her widowhood and her body clean from lechery."[6]

There were some, however, who felt that Margaret's devotion to English interest warped her judgment and twisted her government. She did rely heavily on Henry for advice and support, and it was known that Henry had made it clear to the pope in a letter written only a month after Flodden that he wished to control Scottish affairs. In order to do so, he demanded that the see of St. Andrews—left vacant by the death of the young Alexander—be suppressed and that bishoprics and prelacies made vacant at Flodden be filled at the will and interest of the King of England. Henry's attention to the ecclesiastical offices and appointments evidenced his awareness of the power and wealth of the Scottish church. His determination to control that power and wealth was underscored by threats of invasion.[7]

As a hint of broader action to come, he ordered Lord Dacre to renew border raids "to the most annoyance of the Scots that [he] possibly may. . . ." Dacre destroyed villages, burned crops, and carried away the sheep, cattle, and swine until the darkness of the moon forced him to wait another month for greater light. When Dacre renewed his destruction, he delighted in it. As he wrought calamity upon calamity, he joyfully wrote Henry: "There was never so much mischief, robbery, spoiling, and vengeance in Scotland than there is now, without hope of remedy, which I pray our Lord God to continue."[8]

Between Henry's policy toward domination of the Scots and Margaret's belief that the interest of Scotland and those of her son were inextricably bound with the interests of England, many of the Scots nobility saw the very independence of Scotland at stake.

Through the bitter winter of 1513–1514, matters grew more complex. There were a number of ecclesiastical benefices, vacated by the slaughter of Flodden Field, which needed replacement. Since the power had not been given to Henry, Margaret sought to fill the posts with her own supporters—an act which the disaffected nobility saw as merely another means of strengthening a regency they wished to remove.

The chief ecclesiastical seat of Scotland was that of the archbishopric of St. Andrews. James IV had long recognized its value and had consequently secured it for his bastard Alexander Stewart. With the boy's death, however, this rich and powerful position gained many claimants. Margaret put forward as her candidate Gavin Douglas Bishop of Dunkeld and uncle of the young and dashing chieftain the Earl of Angus. Andrew Forman Archbishop of Burges, Bishop of Murray, and Legate to Pope Julius was sponsored by the pope. John Hepburn Prior of St. Andrews was nominated to the post by the Chapter of Canons and gained the support of the estranged nobility.[9] A temporary compromise was reached through a neutral, but aged, priest, the highly devout and greatly respected Bishop of Elphinstone. He maintained he did not want the office; he preferred instead disengagement from worldly affairs. He wanted to think of spiritual matters and prepare his soul for death. But his wishes were disregarded, and he was nominated as successor to Alexander the late archbishop. With this uneasy compromise the ecclesiastical question rested.

If Elphinstone were to die, the critical arguments would begin again. To prepare for that day, the opposers of Margaret's authority sought to strengthen their position. They turned to France. It was France, after all, who had helped to bring Scotland to its low and tenuous state. Had the Queen of France not challenged James to take the famous three steps onto English soil, he would still be alive. Ironically now both were dead, and Anne's widower Louis XII considered marrying the widow of the King of Scots. Margaret, now heavy with James' posthumous son, could offer the proof of fertility but little more. Louis knew he could count on alliance with Scotland; it had no choice if it wanted to be free of England.[10]

The developing pro-French faction in Scotland began to pursue Louis. It was not marriage they wanted but one of the leading courtiers of France, John Duke of Albany. His father Alexander, brother of James III, had been banished from Scotland for attempted usurpation of the throne. There he had married into the French nobility, led a prosperous life, and died. His son Albany had never seen Scotland, he spoke only French and Latin, and his patriotism toward a land he had never known was questionable. He was, however, the closest in blood to the infant James V, and the pro-French faction negotiated with Louis XII for Albany's release. Once Henry VIII heard of the negotiations, he worked equally hard to keep Albany in France. Albany was loathe to leave his wife and family and the comfort of his vast wealth and estates to take on the confused and confusing state of Scotland. He was, however, willing to listen to the pleas of the foreigners who sought him out and offered the regency and control of the infant king.[11]

As the champions of Albany gained strength, Margaret on April 5, 1514, demanded and got the seals of government from the Secretary Patrick Panter, an outspoken supporter of Albany as regent.[12] Henry VIII, in the meantime, encouraged Dacre to continued border raids to remind the Scots of the danger of having England for an enemy. While these great political tensions fermented, Margaret's pregnancy forced her into confinement by the end of the month. Knowing full well that possession of the king meant possession of the government, she took her chambers near those of the little king at Stirling Castle. There on April 30, 1514, she gave birth to James' posthumous son and named him Alexander Duke of Ross. But through the days of confinement and the weeks of convalescence, her political strength waned. Her four councillors had assumed during her absence nearly all the power, and she became regent in name only.[13]

Henry VIII decided to take matters into his own plump hands. He would entrap the Scots by playing their own game. Louis, after all, had more to gain by winning a truce with England than by negotiating with the penniless Scots. Louis XII, wearied of wars on many fronts, recently widowed, prematurely old at fifty-two, gouty and pockmarked, was ready for peace. The two kings opened negotiations.

Henry, with his recent victories upon him, knew he had something of the upper hand and demanded one million five hundred thousand gold crowns and the territories of Thérouanne, Boulogne, and St. Quentin, or one hundred thousand crowns annually and a marriage between Margaret of Scotland and Louis of France.[14] Louis hesitated. He was anxious and willing to ransom French prisoners, he wanted the return of French territories, but he had heard of Margaret's growing stoutness, her rather coarse features, her arrogant ways. For his remaining years he wanted instead a younger bride, one that was malleable, inexperienced.

In the meantime, during the politically hectic spring of 1514, plans moved forward for the Princess Mary to consummate her marriage with Charles of Castile. According to their marriage treaty, she was to come to him when the prince achieved his fourteenth birthday. He would be fourteen in May. In England, her magnificent trousseau of splendid gowns and jewels, her mattresses, pillows, and coverlets, her wall hangings, banners, and tapestries, her gold and silver plate were readied. Her company was chosen, and Calais prepared for her reception. The Flemish court also filled with expectation, especially as the news of Mary's beauty spread. Of her, one correspondent wrote to Margaret of Savoy: "I saw the Princess Mary dressed in the Milanese fashion; and I think never man saw a more beautiful creature, or one possessed of so much grace and sweetness." Gerard de Pleine wrote of her: "I would not write to you about the princess until I had seen her several times. I assure you that she is one of the most beautiful young women in the world. I think I never saw a more charming creature. She is very graceful. Her deportment in dancing and in conversation is as pleasing as you could desire. There is nothing gloomy or melancholy about her. I am certain if you had seen her you would never rest until you had her over. I assure you she has been well educated. It is certain, from everything I hear, that she is much attracted to Monsieur [Prince Charles]; of whom she has a very bad picture. And never a day passes that she does not express a wish to see him 'plus de dix fois, comme l'on m'a affirmé.' I had imagined that she would have been very tall; but she is of middling height, and, as I think, a much better match in age and person for the prince, than I had heard or could have believed before I saw her."[15]

Ferdinand of Spain, however, was in no haste to complete this marriage of his grandson. Consequently he urged the counsel of Flanders to demur at Henry's inquiries about the specific day of marriage. To each query, vague replies were returned: Charles was still too young; he was too weak; he was too ill. Then the council, no doubt at Ferdinand's instigation, challenged the point of Mary's dower and concluded: ". . . the first agreement between the king her father and King Philip his father to be of none effect, since the Spaniards would not confirm the same, and the cause was, by reason that King Philip was not naturally born to be their king, but was king in the right of his wife [Joanna], and so they were not bound to his agreements made without their consent."[16]

Margaret of Savoy argued with the Flemish council and urged ready compliance with the earlier agreement. She believed and believed sincerely that the best alliance for her nephew was with England. After hearing of Mary, Margaret grew more confident in her choice. The girl would help balance the life of the overly serious boy. It would be a good marriage publicly and privately—a rare commodity amongst royal marriages. Unknown to Margaret, however, her own father Maximilian was also toying with the future of his grandson. Never a man to take his own word too seriously, he was negotiating another betrothal in spite of the proxy marriage between Charles of Castile and Mary of England in 1508. The emperor believed the stronger alliance to lie with a daughter of France. The English apparently discovered the emperor's duplicity before Margaret of Savoy either learned of the negotiations or could interrupt them. As a result the marriage which she had nurtured and developed for nearly a decade was no more.[17]

Henry would not allow his sister the ignominy of being jilted. He was, moreover, tired of the delays and indecisions of the Flemish council; so he seized the moment. On July 30, 1514, before the assembled nobility and ministers of state in a carefully rehearsed ceremony, Mary repudiated her marriage contract with Charles of Castile.[18] What she felt on this occasion is unrecorded, but she was too much of a Tudor to ignore the slights and constant delays of the Flemish council. She was, no doubt, weary of the charade of the declarations of devotion to a boy she had never seen. She was a blossoming young woman, exulting in the energy of youth and the power of her beauty. She was used to the adoration of the court and conscious of the flattery which had so much basis in fact. She was growing increasingly conscious of her effect upon men and was perhaps feeling herself drawn physically and emotionally to one so often in her presence—Charles Brandon Duke of Suffolk.

Brandon, confidant of the King, had long been part of the royal household; always prominent at court functions, he was virile, handsome, and a most available partner. Best known for his athletic accomplishments, his equestrian ability, his agility with spear, lance, and sword, he was also an accomplished courtier— schooled in the graces of the dance and idle chatter. While many of the established nobility saw Brandon as an upstart who gained preeminence through friendship with the king, Brandon saw himself as only slightly less than irresistible. He had annulled one marriage and fooled himself into believing that Margaret of Savoy would raise him to her own high estate. That failing, he had married again. Even then there were moments when he fancied a third marriage which would bring him into the royal family. But a princess of the blood royal seemed beyond his grasp; their birth, their stations in life were too far apart. Mary's future was beyond her control, and Brandon would not destroy his own career by incurring the rage of her royal brother. Reality, however, never prohibited dreaming, and Brandon surely had his dreams.

As soon as it was generally known that Mary was free from her commitment to Charles, formal negotiations for a similar contract were opened with France. Louis XII was interested. The more he heard of Mary's youth and beauty, her wit and charm, the more interested he became. He ordered serious negotiations. The Duke of Longueville, one of the French prisoners Henry had gained in the course of his foreign campaigns, was among the first to raise the question of Mary's marriage. And Henry answered: "Well, if he chooses to marry my sister, the widow of the King of Scots, the agreement shall be made."[19]

That, stated Longueville, was not the point. The point was Mary—Louis would have only the younger, prettier of the two. Henry, in contradiction of his father's will but banking on Louis' lust, offered Mary without dowry. Louis wanted the bride and he wanted peace with England, but not at any price. He counteroffered with a liberal, if not overly generous, settlement. If Henry gave four hundred crowns toward Mary's trousseau and those of her ladies, Louis would pay half of Mary's total expenses—two hundred thousand crowns. In addition, he offered the same jointure as that given to his late queen, Anne of Brittany. In the event of Louis' death, Mary was to have her dowry—all the goods which she had brought from England—together with her jointure of lands, and "all the jewels which Queens of France have used to enjoy after their husband's death."[20] The agreement was signed. On August 13, 1514, two weeks after repudiating Charles, Mary entered into another marriage, this time at Greenwich with the Duke of Longueville acting as Louis' proxy.

Again there was great feasting, dancing, and jousting on the open green stretches at Greenwich Palace. The whirl and wheeling of the gulls, the waters of the Thames crowded with barges mirrored the activities of the crowds of spectators who watched the celebration which marked at last a peace with France.

Mary must have wondered at the meaning of her pledge to the old and pocky Louis. At the least, she must learn to tolerate his fumbling advances; at the most—if he were as ill as many said—she would not be married very long. At any length it was better to be Queen of France than Princess of Castile. So it was surely with mixed emotions that she wrote to this second husband: "Sir, Very humbly I recommend myself to your good grace. I have received the letters which it has pleased you to write to me with your own hand, and heard what my cousin, the Duke de Longueville has told me from you, in which I have taken great joy, felicity, and pleasure; for which, and for the honor which it has pleased you to do to me, I hold myself ever indebted and obliged to you, and thank you as cordially as I can. And because, by my cousin, you will hear how all things have taken their end and conclusion, and the very singular desire that I have to see you and to be in your company, I forbear to write to you a longer letter, for the rest, sire, praying Our Creator to give you health and long life. By the hand of your humble companion. Mary."[21]

News of the marriage quickly came to Flanders where it was said the young Charles burst into his council chamber and demanded whether or not he was to have his promised wife. The councillors, excusing their own part in the domestic disaster, answered: "You are young, but the King of France is the first king in Christendom, and, having no wife, it rests with him to take for his queen any woman he pleases." Upon hearing these words, the white-faced, clenched-jawed Charles walked out of the chamber only to return with a young hawk upon his fist. He sat down and coolly, calmly, plucked the feathers of the hawk. Finally one councillor asked what the prince was doing, and Charles in quiet rage responded: "Thou askest me why I plucked the hawk! He is young you see, and has not yet been trained, and because he is

young he is held in small account, and because he is young he
squeaked not when I plucked him. Thus have you done by me: I
am young, you have plucked me at your good pleasure, and because I was young I knew not how to complain, but bear in mind
that for the future I shall pluck you." There were many who said
the story was apocryphal, but there were also many among the
English who believed and laughed at Charles' chagrin.[22]

This time, matters moved swiftly ahead. A second proxy marriage between Louis and Mary was performed in France on September 14 at the Church of the Célestines in Paris. Here Louis
not only bound himself to the marriage contract but swore before
the Bishop of Paris that if he failed in this bargain he was liable to
excommunication.[23] He hoped that within the week Mary would
sail from Dover.

As these plans went forward, rumors and confused reports came
from another quarter. In August, 1514, there had been another
marriage in the Tudor family. Less than a year after her husband's death, Margaret Tudor, without the consultation of her
brother or her council, had secretly married Archibald Douglas,
the nineteen-year-old sixth Earl of Angus. From a political view
the marriage was the single, most disastrous choice Margaret could
have made. It shattered her tenuous hold on the regency. It undermined the loyalty of those who had supported her out of sheer
devotion to the wishes of the late king. It alienated the love of the
commons who wished her to be a living memorial to James IV
and the pure, sanctified mother of James V. It broke the will and
testament of the late king which had allowed her the regency for
the duration of her widowhood. And finally the marriage destroyed the delicate balance of power—whoever held the person of
the king held also the power of government.

Angus, of ancient family, gained his title when his father died
three months after Flodden Field. Their faction, commonly
known as the Red Douglases, was a powerful clan rich in land and
fortresses and loyal supporters. It was this power which had made
the parliament declare him one of the four advisors to the queen.
But there was little else to recommend him to such a position. He
was young and without experience, he was powerful and wealthy
but without restraint. He was aggressive but no leader of men. He
was a blunt young man who demanded what he wanted. What he
did not get, he took.

He had haunted the court, played upon Margaret's vanity and her fears of losing her government and the control of her sons. For the moment Angus must have felt he had won all—the queen, the king and his brother, and the government itself.

Margaret, for her part, was captivated by the young husband who was nearly six years her junior. She was infatuated with his handsome face, his youthful physique, his demeanor, his little courtesies. She also saw him as a source of strength. He was wealthy; he headed a mighty clan. He was powerful and energetic, and with him she hoped to stand against the forces gathering about her, the forces that sought to overwhelm her, the forces that meant to take the reins of government from her hands and her sons from her arms. She had asked for guidance and support from Henry, but nothing of value had come. She had heard of the Anglo-French treaty which looked to peace between nations and overlooked the needs of Scotland and her own preservation.[24]

Margaret turned to Angus in passion and in need. He was the necessary masculine force to strengthen her tottering reign. She did not, could not, have anticipated the total meaning of her hasty marriage. It ripped away the remaining vestiges of government. Angus took everything into his own hands—her sons, her lands, her power. That was not what she had meant to happen. He took by force the Great Seal from Alexander Hume the chancellor and aroused the united wrath of opposing factions. Instead of gaining strength, Angus had hastened its loss.

The Earl of Arran, upon hearing of the queen's marriage, immediately gathered his kinsmen, friends, and retainers, armed them for possible battle and rode at the head of this imposing force across the country and into the streets of Edinburgh. There he declared the queen had violated her authority and the will of James IV. Arran, as near in blood to the infant king, demanded control of the government.[25] Parliament again rejected his claim. He was not the closest kinsman.

On August 26 Margaret and Angus were brought to heel by the Lords of the Council. They argued that Margaret had violated her right to the government by remarriage. Furthermore she must resign the regency in favor of Albany—the nearest kinsman of James V. Angus raged and fumed and swore he would not give way. Margaret with great tears and lamentation urged that giving the infant king and his brother into the hands of their uncle was tantamount to giving them over to their murderer. Must the Scots allow recent history to repeat itself? Did the council not know of the horrors visited upon her own family? Did they not know of the murder of her uncles—the youthful Edward V of England and his nine-year-old brother—by their uncle Richard III? Were the parallels not clear? Must she draw the equation? Must she name the Duke of Albany another Richard III? No, she would not suffer her James, her Alexander, to repeat the tragedy of Edward and his brother.

Her entreaties were ignored. Albany was the next of kin. Despite his allegiance to France and his hesitancy to take on the government of Scotland, parliament renewed its appeal to Louis XII to permit the duke freedom of passage. On September 18 parliament formally requested Albany to come "in all possible haist." Simultaneously letters and delegations sought the duke at the French court, hounded him in the green pastures of his own lush estates, and begged him to take the government of Scotland during James V's long minority.[26]

In October Bishop Elphinstone completed his long pilgrimage in life and left vacant the controversial see of St. Andrews. Immediately the factions of Scots politicians came close to civil war. Angus and his followers seized the castle of St. Andrews for his uncle Gavin Douglas. Within short order the chancellor, Lord Hume, gathered a stronger force and drove the Douglases out of St. Andrews. Then John Hepburn Prior of St. Andrews was placed in the archbishopric and maintained with armed troops. Not content with this victory, the Humes and their clan, their supporters and retainers, galloped into Edinburgh, blocked the streets and crossways, and stormed the castle itself. Margaret was forced to take her two small sons and flee toward Stirling. She was chased by the Humes and caught and brought—virtually a captive —back to Edinburgh.[27]

The kingdom erupted in confusing contests for power. As one chronicler noted: "The Realm now in such distress, all drew to factions and parties, some to defend the queen, some the nobility, all studied to their particular profit, either occupying his neighbors' lands, with force, or his neighbor's goods wrongfully, however he could. The Earls of Lennox and Glenkarne choosing a convenient night for their purpose mirk, windy, and stormy, when men might neither hear nor see, came to Dumbarton, and at the nether port of the castle, with engine of lead pipes subtly undermined, while at last through fraud, partly through arms, they shot out the captain Erskine and manned the house; between Angus and Arran now hot wars, all the land in trouble."[28]

Arran and Hume joined forces against those of Angus while Margaret paced the darkened corridors of that "sad and solitary place," Edinburgh Castle. She was more alone now than ever. She had pawned her jewels and lost her friends. She had no resources on which to call. Angus, having eluded Arran and Hume, circled the country with his army, burning and pillaging at will. Henry sent directives and promised support through his Warden of the Marches, Thomas Dacre. But nothing happened. The queen was locked in, and the world was locked out. Daily she expected that her sons would be permanently taken from her.

On November 21, with the belated help of Angus, the queen escaped from Edinburgh and made a headlong race to Stirling. There she dropped the portcullis and prepared to wait out her enemies. It was a calculated move on her part, for Stirling Castle was the strategic center of Scotland. Situated in the Midland Valley, with its strong fortress and its bridge over the Forth, it guarded all roads from the north and south, east and west.[29] With these fortifications, loyal retainers, and well-victualled larders, Margaret felt her position better than it had been. She was confident that Henry's armies would come, and at Stirling she would wait. She again wrote her brother:

> Right high and mighty prince and dearest brother, I commend me to you with all mine heart. I have received your loving and comfortable writings from a man of the lord Dacre's, the 22d day of November, wherein I perceive your fraternal love and kindness. I and my party were in great trouble of mind, till we knew what help you would do to us. I have shown the said writings to all my lords which were with me in my castle of Stirling the said day, whereof they were greatly comforted.
>
> My party-adversary continues in their malice and proceeds in their parliament, usurping the king's authority, as [if] I and my lords were of no reputation, reputing us as rebels; wherefore I beseech you that you would make haste with your army, both by sea and land, and in especial on the chamberlain which is post of this conspiration. . . . On that other side the prior of Saint

Andrews [John Hepburn], with the power of my contrary party,
has laid siege to the castle of Saint Andrews, which I would that
your navy would revenge; for it stands on the sea-side fore-against
Berwick by north.

I have sent my husband to break the siege, if he may, this 23d
day. I am at great expenses—every day a thousand in wages, and
my money is near hand wasted; if you send not the sooner other
succors of men or money, I shall be super-expended, which were
to my dishonor; for I can get no answer of my rents, as I showed
you before.

All the hope that my party adversary hath is in the duke of
Albany's coming, which I beseech you to let [prevent] in any wise;
for if he happen to come before your army, I doubt that some of
my party will incline to him for dread. I shall keep this castle with
my children till I hear from you. There is some of the lords that
dread that your army shall do them scathe, and that their lands
shall be destroyed with the fury of the army: wherefore I would
that you wrote to them that [neither] their lands nor goods shall
not be hurt, and, if so be, that they shall be recompensed double
and treble. The king, my son, and his brother, prospers well, and
are right lifelike children; thanked be Almightly God.

It is told me that the Lord's adversaries are purposed to siege
me in this castle. I would, therefore, that the chamberlain were
holden waking in the mean time with the borderers. I trow [trust]
that I shall defend me well enough from the others till the coming
of the army. I pray you to give credence to master Adam Williamson in other things as it is written to him, and thank him
for his good service, and the peril that he was in for my sake in
the ship that was broken, with other three ships that I have word
since that, departing of Scotland afore his ship, with a message
to the duke of Albany, wherein was Lion the herald, with other
messages direct from these lords adversaries, with letters sealed
with the great seal, which seal they keep masterfully from me and
my lords, and use it as they were kings. I trust that God is on my
party, which letted their message, and furthered mine.

I have given Saint Andrews to the apostolate of Arbroath, my
husband's uncle [Gavin Douglas], wherefore I would that you
letted all other competitors that labor the contrary in Rome,
and that you would direct to the pope's holiness upon the same
with the next that you send, and that you would direct writings
to me each month, at the least, how you will do, and what you
would that I did; and if my party-adversary counterfeit any letters
in my name, or if they compel me to write to you for concord,

the subscription shall be but thus—MARGARET R. and no
more, and trust that such writing is not my will.

Brother, all the welfare of me and my children lies in your
hands, which I pray Jesus to help and keep eternally to his
pleasure.

At Stirling, the 23d day of November. Your loving sister,

Margaret R.[30]

Henry urged Margaret to prevent Albany's coming; for his
part, he asked Louis to keep Albany in France. In the meantime,
he ordered Dacre to continue the border intrusions and simultaneously offered peace to Scotland under terms no one would
accept. With certain frustration, Margaret read her brother's ad-
monitions and felt the awful irony of the moment. She, who had
been only months ago the undisputed queen of the realm, was
now a captive in her own land. But she had her sons. Let the
others rage and war about her; as long as she had her children
nothing could legally be done in their name. She was a queen—
but no queen. She had no resources. She had nowhere to go. She
had few friends and no allies. And she must have wondered how it
all could have come to this point. She—Margaret Tudor—daughter, wife, sister, mother of kings, was surrounded and besieged.
How quickly her life had changed; how quickly her world had
overturned. It was not supposed to be this way, and she could not
help but curse the twists of fortune's wheel which had flung her so
low and raised her sister so high.

But for the trick of fortune, the whims of man, and the politics
of nations, Margaret might now be the Queen of France. Louis
had mentioned it, Henry had consented to it; but then suddenly
her sister Mary had taken her place. It was with envy that the
Queen of Scotland, sitting in the frozen chill of Stirling Castle,
read and heard of the Queen of France. Mary, the little sister
whom she still thought a child; Mary, the girl who had usually
been too weak or ill or indisposed to enjoy the hearty sports of
childhood, had developed into a strikingly handsome woman—all
the world seemed to speak of her beauty. Mary, who had always
seemed too puny by Margaret's standard, had suddenly achieved
the mighty throne of France. She had ever been, continued to be,
the adored of the adoring. The youngest, pampered child was
now the beautiful, pampered queen. It was all very hard to im-

agine. But the dispatches from England and France gave vivid and
visual proof, and the Queen of Scotland read and listened—behind
the cold, chilled walls of a besieged castle—with fascination tinged
with envy of the spectacle which framed Mary's every move.

The movements of the summer and fall were quick indeed.
Louis wanted none of the diplomatic delay which usually accompanied international agreements. He wanted this young wife, and
he wanted her immediately. He baited the English ambassadors,
sought their support, showed them the "goodliest and richest sight
of jewels," and laughed merrily as he said, "My wife shall not have
many but at divers times kisses and thanks for them."[31]

The earlier preparations for Mary's wedding journey to Charles
of Castile allowed her journey to Louis of France to go forward
with immodest haste. In addition to plate, tapestries, bedding, and
furnishings for her royal apartments, Mary's wardrobe was mag-
nificently sumptuous—even opulent by the extravagant standards
of the day. There were sixteen dresses of the finest fabrics, embroidered and bejewelled, designed in the French fashion; six
in the Italian fashion; eight in the English. She had jewels for her
hair, her head, her ears, her neck, her arms, her wrists, her fingers,
her waist. She had diamonds and rubies, sapphires and rich to-
pazes; she had ropes of pearls, chains of gold, garlands of flowers
delicately fashioned of silver and small gems. She had with her a
great silver seal bearing the arms of England and France, and her
privy seal of gold marked with a crown and four roses. In addition
to her personal wardrobe and possessions, she brought the hangings for her chapel and the images of silver-gilt of her favorite
saints—Edward the Confessor, Thomas of Canterbury, Catherine,
Margaret, Mary Magdalene, and George and his dragon. The banners for her troop bore the arms of her father, her mother, her
grandparents, and her own motto: "La volenté de Dieu me suffit."[32]

By mid-September the wagons and carts were packed, the thousand palfreys harnessed in crimson velvet, the hundred carriages
cushioned and pillowed, the musicians finely rehearsed, Mary's
company carefully selected and those of whose character Louis
opposed—dismissed.[33] Simultaneously the new queen was carefully rehearsed for the continuing roles she was about to play. To
equip her as Queen of France, Henry showered money, attention,
and affection on this his favorite sister. He had left no detail to
chance and went so far as to have John Palsgrave—one of Mary's

tutors—prepare for her the first French grammar text ever written. For her farewell gesture to London, Henry invited to court all the local merchants, both native and foreign. When Mary appeared in her costly woven gown of gold, the entire group was dazzled by her presence, her appearance, and her quick wit. But it was the jewel about her throat that caused the greatest whisper of amazement. It was the Mirror of Naples—a jewelled diamond "as large and as broad as a full-sized finger, with a pear-shaped pearl beneath it, the size of a pigeon's egg." It was Louis' wedding gift.[34] The merchants were so impressed that many raced home to dress themselves in new finery to accompany the queen to Dover.

All the court, the king and his Catherine, their lords and ladies, the merchants of London, representatives from all the guilds, and priests and clergy helped to form one of the longest and most extravagant processions ever to leave London. Everywhere villagers and townsmen, farmers and sailors, stopped to watch the moving spectacle as it travelled to the coast.

Once there, ships were pressed into service for Mary's crossing; then storms blew up, the wind was troublous, the weather foul, and travel impossible. One ship was driven ashore and wrecked, its cargo ruined and half its crew of six hundred men drowned. The royal progress, in spite of its magnificence, was halted, and the royal patience sorely tried. Henry disliked to wait for anyone or anything.

At the first sign of clearing, at four in the morning of October 2, Mary and her company shivered in the chill and windy mist of the port of Dover. There she took her leave of Catherine, a good friend and faithful. There she kissed her brother, impatient as always to be on to the next occasion. But as Mary clung to him, with her skirts whipping about them both, she wrung from him a promise—if she were to marry a second time, might she not choose a husband for herself? Anxious to have the moment gone, uneasy with the emotion of parting, nervous before her tears and fears, Henry gave his word. Yes, do this for him and England. Next time she might do as she pleased. Although neither expected Louis to live long, the promise was of little comfort. It had come to the moment of good-bye to the only family she knew, to the land that had been her home. As she boarded her ship for Boulogne and the sails billowed, the early morning fog shrouded the cliffs and wharf. Those she loved, quickly became dim, waving shadows and then they were gone. The sun would not shine that day.

Within hours the storm renewed itself. The men clung to ropes and hauled at the sails, and the women pitched and gagged in the tiny cabins of the hold. The little company of thirteen ships was quickly dispersed. Some were driven to Calais, some to Flanders, and Mary's own ship made its tottering, wave-lashed way to Boulogne. With the winds still at full gale, the captain lost control of his sails and rigging and the great vessel was blown ashore. Small boats swept out to the rescue, and Mary—sick of mind and body, her handsome sailing dress wet, heavy, and dripping—was gathered in the arms of one of her men Sir Christopher Garneys and carried through the slapping waves to shore. It was not the entry she had planned. Although there were many of the nobility and clergy standing in welcome, the soaked and seasick Queen of France wanted only rest and quiet. It took all her strength and the resilience of all her training to command her energies to the occasion. She was then taken to lodgings in Boulogne.[35]

From there, in continuous stages, the English escort moved southward to Abbeville where the wedding was to take place. On the day she was to enter Abbeville, Mary was met by more of the French nobility. Foremost among them was Francis Duke of Valois and Bretagne and Count of Angoulême—the dauphin and heir presumptive to the throne of France. He had married one of Louis' daughters and had sharply opposed this latest marriage of the king. He feared even the remote possibility that Louis might sire a male heir who would interrupt the way to the crown. But whatever his feelings, the marriage was going forward and Francis posed as a devoted courtier of the new queen. Never very fond of his own wife Claude, he seemed delighted with the beauty of Mary. He regretted that she was to be wasted on Louis.

Francis reined his horse to ride next to Mary in this glorious entry into Abbeville. By now the procession was fleshed out with Mary's entire English escort, horsemen, archers, pages, ladies in carriages and on horseback, musicians and minstrels, the queen's horses, her litter, her badges and banners, her canopy of estate, the seemingly endless carts which carried the royal gowns, plate, and furnishings. Peasants and townspeople looked and cheered as Francis and Mary rode by, sitting their horses, apparently lost in conversation. Suddenly a "hunting" party of fifteen hundred horses appeared. Leading them was King Louis himself, overcome with curiosity and impatience to see his bride. In spite of the fact that Mary and Louis were dressed in similar costumes—the meeting had been carefully planned—Mary pretended surprise, a little fear, and total ignorance. When the royal visitor was identified, she immediately started to alight. Louis would have none of that. Instead he spurred his horse to her, embraced her with a quivering arm, kissed her with wet lips, and whispered in her ear. Then as suddenly as he appeared, the king—with his curiosity satisfied and his imagination enflamed—took a secret way back to Abbeville. He wanted, he said, her entrance into the city to be the queen's alone. He would be there to welcome her.

The procession reformed, Mary's esquires in their silk and gold collars and chains, the ambassadors and noblemen of both parties rivalling each other in brocaded magnificence—their gold chains so heavy about their shoulders that they grew weary with sitting erect. Pride alone kept them—as they moved onward—in their saddles. Then came the banners, the trumpeters in scarlet damask, gentlemen carrying their gold maces with the arms of France and England, grooms in black velvet leading white ponies. In the midst rode Mary, whose animated conversation with Francis of Angoulême masked the thoughts and revulsion she had experienced at the moment of meeting Louis XII—fifty-two years of age, drooping with gout, his eyes red and wet, his lids hanging limply, his jaws slack. Although he tried gallantly to play the young lover he had once been, he could scarcely sit his horse. He had been reduced to an old and drooling man—a king still—but a man more dead than alive. And for whatever season, for as long as he lived, he would be her husband. Neither the flattery of Francis nor the splendor of her proud procession, the bright banners of red and white roses, the shining lilies of France, the music, the laughter of her ladies, or the march of the two hundred English archers could alleviate the coming dread. What had started as a triumphal entry had become, for the Queen of France, a march of death. Every step brought her closer to the living grave with the smiling corpse who wore a crown. Suddenly the heavens themselves seemed to share her sorrow, and the rains fell heavily as the procession reached the city.

In the city the procession paused for the party to refresh itself and for Mary to change into her wedding gown—a white gown with gold brocade. For this stately moment she exchanged her horse for the canopied litter, embroidered with its roses red and white of England and the lilies of France. About her was a circle of footmen and beyond them the Scots Guard. As the men of the city came out in welcome, the bells of the towers and churches answered the trumpeters in melody, and the cannon of the town walls rumbled forth persistent salute.

Mary, as queen, made her first formal entry into her new kingdom through the gate Marcade, travelled down the wet and muddied streets, passed the cheering throngs who whispered amongst themselves of her great beauty, looking "more like an angel than a human creature. . . ."[36] She was led past the pageants and songs of welcome to the Church of St. Wulfran to give thanksgiving for a safe crossing and journey; then she was taken to the Hôtel de la Gruthuse where King Louis XII waited with his court for his bride. Amongst the assembly stood Francis of Angoulême as the heir presumptive, the Duke of Longueville who had served as proxy in England, and the Duke of Albany who still toyed with the invitation of the Scots nobility to have the regency which Margaret still maintained at least in name.[37]

While Louis entertained his bride at a small dinner party, Francis and his wife Claude held a grand ball for the general welcome and pleasure of the English guests. As the French and English nobility danced and drank away the night, fire broke out in a shabbier quarter of the city. The squalid wooden houses fed the flames and consumed themselves while those who stood and watched were not allowed to sound the fire-bells. It was against the law to disturb the pleasures of the king. By the time the party was over, a vast section of the city lay in ruin, and there were many who walked among the ashes to salvage something left of what had once been home.[38]

The next day, Monday, October 9, was the feast of St. Denis, patron saint of France, and the auspicious occasion for the royal wedding. In order to allow the assembled nobility of England, France, and Europe to witness the ceremony, it was held in the saloon of the Hôtel, richly hung with cloth of arras, tapestries, and cloth of gold. Louis, in rich attire with his collars and orders about him, waited with the Archbishop of Rouen and the Bishop of Amiens for Mary to ride her palfrey from her chambers to the

Hôtel.[39] Her path was lined with her good English archers and the Scots Guard, and before and behind her came her gentlewomen in cloth of gold brocade. As the trumpeters heralded her approach, Louis raised himself from his chair of estate; as she approached, he doffed his bonnet, and the queen curtseyed to the ground—her rich golden hair falling about her shoulders. The king raised her, then kissed her, and seated her next to him under the canopy supported by the princes of the realm. The treasurer, Robertet, handed the king a necklace set with "a great pointed diamond with a ruby almost two inches long." This he placed about Mary's throat. The royal couple then heard mass and were married by the Cardinal of Bayeux. The contract was now sealed, and Mary left the chamber to dine with the ladies of France. At eight o'clock in the evening she was led by Madame Claude and her ladies to the chambers of the king. There she was undressed and left alone with Louis. The English rose and the French lily were now united, and the minstrels strutted their song:

> Princes, try to entertain to keep
> The Rose among the lilies of France,
> So that one may say and maintain—
> Shamed be he who thinks ill thereof.[40]

The next morning Louis was most jovial and gay, but by noon he was forced to his chamber by a severe attack of the gout.[41]

Perhaps it was anger at his own ill health or jealousy of the numerous English men and women to whom Mary so often spoke, perhaps it was that he wanted to share her attention with no one or feared too much Anglo influence in his French household that made him act precipitously on the day after his wedding. With apparently no cause, and less courtesy, he abruptly dismissed the entire English company—even a favorite sheepdog of the queen's household. The laughter of festival was immediately turned into great lamentation amongst the women and anger amongst the men. Many had left lucrative posts at home and tied their fortunes to those of the young queen. Others had come out of years of service and devotion. In spite of the fact that he had earlier approved the list of attendants, "there was no remedy"; the king had decided and spoken.[42]

Despite Mary's protestations and pleas, her attempts at tears and cajolery, Louis would not relent. Her fears after their first meeting had proved true—he was a gouty, drooling old man who sought to usurp her youth and poison her life. She could not bear the thought of losing her friends, especially Lady Joan Guildford fondly known by Mary as "Mother Guildford." She had long been something of a tutrix, advisor, and companion to the princess, and both had hoped she would long continue in the same capacity to the queen. That, Louis maintained, was impossible.

In anguish at the loss of her friends, in fear of being left absolutely alone in the French court with her doddering, decaying husband, Mary wrote to her brother: "My good Brother, as heartily as I can I recommend me unto your Grace, marvelling much that I never heard from you since our departing, so often as I have sent and written unto you. And now am I left almost alone in effect, for on the morn after marriage my chamberlain and all other men servants were discharged, and in like wise my mother Guildford with other my women and maidens, except such as never had experience nor knowledge how to advertise or give me counsel in any time of need, which is to be feared more shortly than your grace thought at the time of my departing, as my mother Guildford can more plainly show your Grace than I can write, to whom I beseech you to give credence. And if it may be by any mean possible I humbly require you to cause my said mother Guildford to repair hither once again.

"For else if any chance hap other than well I shall not know where nor by whom to ask any good counsel to your pleasure nor yet to mine own profit. I marvel much that my lord of Norfolk would at all times so lightly grant everything at their request here. I am well assured that when you know the truth of everything as my mother Guildford can show you, ye would full little have thought I should have been thus intreated; that would God my lord of York [Wolsey] had come with me in the room of Norfolk; for then I am sure I should have been left much more at my heart's ease than I am now. And thus I bid your Grace farewell. . . . By your loving sister, Mary, Queen of France."[43]

Apparently afraid that the one letter was not sufficient to stress the urgency of her necessity, Mary wrote on the same day to Henry's almoner, her "loving friend" the Archbishop of York Thomas Wolsey:

". . . the morn next after the marriage, all my servants, both men and women were discharged. Insomuch that my mother Guildford was also discharged, whom as ye know the king and you willed me in anywise to be counselled. But for anything I might do, in nowise might I have grant for her abode here, which I assure you, my lord, is much to my discomfort, beside many other discomforts that ye would full little have thought. I have not yet seen in France any lady or gentlewoman so necessary for me as she is nor yet so mete to do the king my brother service as she is. And for my part, my lord, as ye love the king my brother and me, find the means that she may in all haste come hither again, for I had as lief lose the winning I shall have in France as to lose her counsel when I shall lack it, which is not like long to be required, as I am sure the noblemen and gentlemen can show you more than becometh me to write in this matter. I pray you my Lord give credence further to my mother Guildford in everything concerning this matter. . . . Yours on while I live. Mary."[44]

The matter became immediately more complex than the simple dismissal of retainers and attendants of a homesick and lonely young woman when compounded by the fact that she was also a queen married to an aging king. Louis' health was more tenuous and fragile than the English had been led to expect. Certainly his condition was worse than he could or would admit. And the additional strains of the wedding celebrations, the excessive travelling, and the wooing of his bride were hastening his decline at a precipitous rate. Mary was too realistic and sensitive a woman not to recognize the fact that he might die at any moment. What then would be her situation? What unexpected political necessities might test this newest and latest foreign alliance? To whom then could the young queen turn for advice in order to assure the best solutions for herself, for Henry, for Margaret, and for England?

Although Henry seemed loathe to question the actions of this new brother-in-law and possibly disturb the equanimity of the alliance, Wolsey—certainly with Henry's knowledge—wrote a most diplomatic letter to Louis concerning the reinstatement of Lady Guildford and concluded:

"Since the king, my sovereign lord and master, your good brother, had ordered, on account of the true, perfect, and entire confidence which he had in Mrs. Guildford, that she should be with the queen, his sister, your wife, on account of the good manners and experience which he knew her to have, and also because she speaks the language well; in order also that the said queen, his sister, might be better advised, and taught by her, how she ought to conduct herself towards you, under all circumstances;—considering, moreover, that the queen, his said good sister, is a young lady, and that when she should be abroad, not understanding the language perfectly, and having no acquaintance with any of the ladies there, to whom she might disclose such feelings as women are given to, and that she had no one of her acquaintance to whom she could familiarly tell and disclose her mind; that she might find herself desolate, as it were, and might thereby entertain regret and displeasure;—which, peradventure, might cause her to have some sickness, and her bodily health to be impaired, which God forbid; and should such an accident happen, I believe, Sire, that you would be most grieved and displeased.

"And whereas, Sire, I have known and understood, that the said Mistress Guildford is at Boulogne, on her return here, and that she was entirely discharged; doubting lest the king, my master, should he know it, might think it somewhat strange, I have ventured to write to the said lady, to tarry awhile at the said town of Boulogne, until I had written you my poor and simple opinion on this subject, which, Sire I now do. And by your leave, Sire, it seems to me that you should retain her for some time in the service of the queen, your wife, and not discharge her so suddenly; seeing and considering that the king, your said good brother, has taken her from a solitary place, which she had never intended to quit, to place her in the service of the queen, his said good sister. And I have no doubt, Sire, that when you know her well, you will find her a wise, honorable, and confidential lady, very desirous and earnest to follow out in all things possible to her, your wish and pleasure, in all that you may order and command, whatever report has been, or may be made to the contrary."[45]

It was all that Wolsey could do. He asked and Louis refused. After a lengthy interview with the French king, Worcester the English ambassador detailed Louis' feelings toward Lady Guildford:

"My good lord, as touching the return of my Lady Guildford I have done to my power, and in the best way that I could, to the French king. And he hath answered me that his wife and he be in good and perfect love, as ever any two creatures can be, and both of age to rule themselves, and not to have servants that should look to rule him or her. If his wife need of counsel, or to be ruled, he is able to do it; but he was sure it was never the queen's mind nor desire to have her again; for as soon as she came to land, and also when he was married, she began to take upon her, not only to rule the queen, but also that she should not come to him, but *she* should be with her; nor that no lady nor lord should speak with her but *she* should hear it; and began to set a murmur and banding among ladies of the court; and then he swore that there was never man that better loved his wife than he did, but ere he would have such a woman about her, he had liever be without her; and he said that he knew well when the king, his good and loving brother, knew this his answer, he would be contented, for in no wise he would not have her about his wife.

"Also he said that he is a sickly body, and not [willing] at all times that he would be merry with his wife, to have any strange woman with her, but one that he is well acquainted withal, afore whom he durst be merry; and that he is sure the queen, his wife, is content withal; for he hath set about her neither lady nor gentlewoman to be with her for her mistress, but her servants, and to obey her commandments.

"Upon which answer, seeing he in no wise would have her, I answered him again so that he was content; and so I make no doubt but the king's grace would be, for the answer was well debated, ere I gave it. . . . My lord, the French queen told me that she loved my Lady Guildford well, but she is content that she come not, for she is in that case that she may well be without her, for she may do what she will. I pray God that so it may ever continue to his pleasure."[46]

Since Mary in this interview no longer outwardly opposed Lady Guildford's dismissal, the matter was dropped. Perhaps the older woman was being overly protective of her young ward; perhaps she was a busybody who vicariously delighted in the experiences of the king and queen; perhaps she thought she was doing her duty to Mary and England—hoping to gather any diplomatic insight which might be of later value. At any rate the lady, after her delay at Boulogne, returned to England and retirement.

In the meantime, Charles Brandon Duke of Suffolk brought a large English delegation to the coronation of Mary and the tournaments and games of celebration. Suffolk, in particular, and his

friends, in general, filled the void left by those friends already
dismissed. At the least they were a needed link with home; at the
most they were friends who could be trusted and in whom Mary
could confide. Of his first meeting with Louis and his new queen,
Suffolk wrote to Henry:

"Please it your grace, so it is that, on this Thursday, the 26th
day of October, my Lord Marquis Dorset and I came to Beauvais,
where the king and queen was both; and so we were brought unto
our lodging; and so as soon as we had made us ready, the king sent
Clermont for me, and showed me that the king's pleasure was that
I should come to his grace, myself, alone, and so I did.

"And when I came into the court, I was brought straight into
his chamber, where he lay in his bed, and the queen sitting by his
bedside; and so I did my reverence, and kneeled down beside his
bedside; and so he embraced me in his arms, and held me a good
while, and said that I was heartily welcome; and asked me 'how
does mine especial good brother, whom I am so much bound to
love above all the world?'

"And, Sire, I showed his grace that your grace recommended
you to him, as unto your most entirely beloved brother; and further I showed him that you commanded me to give unto him
thanks on your part, for the great honor and love that he had
showed unto the queen, your sister. And upon that, his grace said
that there should [be nothing] that he will spare to do your
grace's pleasure, or service, with as hearty manner as ever I saw a
man; and, Sire, I said unto him that your grace would do unto
him in like case, and he said, 'I doubt it not; for I know well the
nobleness, and trust so much in your master, that I reckon that I
have of him the greatest jewel that ever one prince had of another.'

"And so I rose up, and made my reverence to the queen, and
made your grace's recommendations unto her, and the queen's
also. And, Sire, I assure your grace that there was never queen nor
lady that ordered herself more honorably nor wiser, the which I
assure your grace rejoiced me not a little; your grace knows why.
For I think there was never queen in France that hath demeaned
herself more honorably, nor wiselier; and so say all the noblemen
in France that have seen her demeanor, the which letted not to
speak of it; and as for the king, [there was] never man that set his

mind more upon [woman] than he does on her, because she de-means herself so winning unto him, the which I am sure [will be n]o little comfort unto your grace."[47]

Henry was delighted at this seeming compliance by his sister with his wishes. He was pleased that she no longer urged on him awkward political and domestic problems. With a happy heart he wrote of Mary to Louis:

"And our will, pleasure, and intention is, that in so acting, she should persevere from good to better if she wish and desire to have our love and fraternal benevolence; and thus we gave her advice and counsel, before her departure from us, and we make no doubt that you will, day by day, find her more and more all that she ought to be to you, and that she will do everything which will be to your will and contentment. . . ."[48]

The warning was clear enough. Mary had better mind her complaints as well as her manners or arouse the wrath of her brother and her husband. While Louis sought to entice her daily with gifts of jewels, "and every day he gave her also Rings with stone of great estimation,"[49] Mary's thoughts were occupied with major considerations—the plight of her recently dismissed friends and her forthcoming coronation.

The queen had done all she could about and for Lady Guild-ford. But there were others for whom she demonstrated feelings of responsibility and affection. To her ladies she gave rings and jew-els, rubies, emeralds, diamonds, sapphires, pendants set in gold and silver to the amount of six hundred gold crowns.[50] John Palsgrave, her French tutor, called for special recommendation, and she wrote to Wolsey: "I heartily recommend me unto you, desiring you for my sake to be good lord to my servant John Palsgrave, and provide for him some living that he may continue at school. If he had been retained in my service, I would have done for him gladly myself, but since he was put out of my service, I willed him to come to Paris, partly because I trust verily that you will provide for him [that] he may be able to continue, and also because I intend myself somewhat to do for him. . . ."[51]

Mary wrote to Henry on behalf of another gentleman whose life had become misery: ". . . praying you to accept my recom-mendations in behalf of a poor honest man, Mr. Vincent Knight, who has always dwelt and remained in your kingdom since he came in with our late dearest lord and father, whom God absolve.

This poor man has made several voyages over here during the wars, by command of your privy council, which had promised him a benefice. This they have not granted, but, in lieu of it, have put him into prison. . . . My dearest lord and brother, I pray you earnestly, both for my sake, as a reward of the services he has done you . . . to do him some good. . . ."[52]

Louis, under Mary's continued coaxing shrouded by an outward acquiescence to his will, relented to the point that she was allowed to keep her almoner, her master of horse, her physician, certain ushers, grooms, and pages, and six ladies of the bedchamber: Lady Elizabeth Grey, the similarly named Elizabeth Grey of Wilton, Anne Jerningham, Mary Fiennes, Anne Boleyn, and Lady Jane Bourchier.[53] Harmony was thus restored to the royal circle and Mary's coronation went forward.

On Sunday, November 5, at ten in the morning, Mary Tudor was led into the Cathedral of St. Denis by Francis of Angoulême. As she knelt at the altar, the Cardinal de Brie anointed her with the sacred oil, gave into her right hand the sceptre of mercy and into her left the rod of justice. He then placed upon her head the crown matrimonial. She was led to the left side of the altar to a chair of estate, richly canopied. Near her stood the chief witnesses of the coronation: the Duke of Suffolk, her long-standing friend and companion from childhood; the Duke of Longueville, the prisoner-turned-proxy-husband; and the Duke of Albany, newly appointed Governor of Scotland. Behind her stood Francis of Angoulême, who looked toward his own coronation; and throughout the rest of the service he gently lifted and held the weight of the crown just off her head. In this manner, the small group whose lives were so intertwined with each other and with the destinies of three nations—England, France, and Scotland—were caught in frozen pageantry throughout the rest of the ceremony of coronation and its concluding high mass. King Louis, prevented by etiquette from attending the ceremony, watched these young men and this young woman, his wife, from a secret and quiet place.[54]

CHAPTER FIVE

LOUIS PRECEDED MARY TO PARIS IN ORDER TO WELCOME HER FOR-
mally to the capital; then Mary left St. Denis at nine in the morning. Already she had greeted the sheriffs and burgesses of the town
and assured them—through her interpreter the Archbishop of
Paris—of her good faith and will. Afterwards the citizens of the
town, the guildsmen in their colorful gowns, and the members of
parliament returned her greetings and offered welcome to France.
They then turned toward Paris to lead the procession of Swiss
Guard, the heralds of France and England, and the peers and
princes of France with their liveried entourages. In their midst
rode the queen herself. Dressed in heavy white cloth of gold and
covered from head to foot in jewels, necklaces, collars, and rings,
Mary Queen of France sat in her decorated and embroidered
chariot drawn by horses trapped in cloth of gold. Near her Francis
of Angoulême again sat his horse and kept up a running com-
mentary on people, sights, and events. They were followed by the
princesses and noble ladies on horseback—each with a running
footman at her side. At the gate of St. Denis, Mary entered Paris as
the burgesses came forward to carry the rich canopy of estate—
embroidered with the roses of England and the lilies of France. As
in all such moments of welcome, the city was made even more
beautiful by the hanging tapestries, its finely dressed citizenry,
and the inevitable pageants with their allegorical presentations.
From the rigging of a gigantic boat, "sailors" chanted:

> Noble lady—welcome to France!
> Through thee we now shall live in joy and pleasure,

> Frenchmen and Englishmen live at their pleasance
> Praises to God, who sends us such a treasure!

A magnificent fountain spewed its waters over golden lilies and roses, tended by handsomely dressed figures representing the Three Graces. Another pageant presented the "Queen of Sheba" and "King Solomon"; elsewhere "Justice" descended from the sky, and "Gabriel" saluted the "Virgin":

> Since erst by means of the Virgin Mary,
> > Peace was made betwixt God and Men;
> So now are we Frenchmen relieved of our loads,
> > For Mary is married amongst us again.

The path of entry led to the Cathedral of Nôtre Dame, where Mary knelt before the altar and was raised with welcome and salutation by the assembled clergy of Paris and representatives of all France. Amidst the pealing of bells, the clamor of the organ, the chants of praise and prayer, Mary took leave of the clergy— again assuring them of her love, her devotion, and her goodwill. By six o'clock she reached the city palace, where she held court, ate and drank from the marble table—seat of French government —with the help of Lady Claude and the princesses of France. Her dishes had been prepared not only to please the palate but also to delight the eye: a phoenix, by beating its wings, consumed itself in flames; a cock and a rabbit jousted; and St. George rode on horseback. As the hundreds of dishes passed before her, the queen tasted while courtiers and commoners watched. By nightfall the splendid if exhausting day ended for the queen, and Mary, half-asleep, was half-carried to her chamber. Paris, however, felt extremely pleased with its grand entertainments and the queen's kind reception. Throughout it all, everyone talked of her beauty— her sudden conquest of the French was more thorough than all of the massive artillery of Henry VIII.[1]

The next day Mary joined Louis who rested at the Hôtel des Tournelles. For the rest of the week they were allowed a needed respite from the processions and pageantry which had punctuated the queen's days and nights since her hard and turbulent voyage from England. In spite of fatigue, however, Mary met frequently with the English delegation led by Charles Brandon Duke of Suffolk. To him in particular, the queen felt free to speak her mind and express her fears. She still felt the lack of counsellors and confidants, and she feared Louis' immediate death and her consequent political dilemma.

After Suffolk and Dorset, Mary's cousin, had discussed the queen's "need of some good friends," they approached the Duke of Longueville, the Bishop of St. Paul's, and the General of Normandy. In a letter to Wolsey, Suffolk recalled the conversation: ". . . and showed unto them that the Queen had sent us and desired us that we would send for them, and desire them on her behalf and in the name of the King our master, that they would be good and loving to her; and that they would give her counsel from time to time how she might best order herself to content the King, whereof she was most desirous; and in her should lack no good will; and because she knew well they were the men that the King loved and trusted, and knew best his mind, therefore she was utterly determined to love them and trust them, and to be ordered by their Counsel in all causes, for she knew well that those that the King loved must love her best, and she them. And so we did.

"And when we had showed them all this on the Queen's behalf, they were very well contented, and said that they would make report unto the King what honorable and loving request she had made, the which they said would content him very well. And they thanked her Grace for her good mind toward them, and said that they would do in every thing her request, and to accept and take her as their Sovereign Queen, and to counsel her on every behalf to the best of their powers to do the thing that should please the King their master. . . ."[2]

Mary's political problems were, for the moment, solved, but she knew by now that her marriage with the French king was tenuous at best. Although he doted on her, was demanding of her constant presence, and was generous to excess in his gifts of jewels, he was a pitiful, weak, dying man. He rose late in the morning, attended briefly to affairs of state, and spent most of his time lying on a cot or in his bed. In vain, he sought to recall the strength and vigor of his youth. For hours he talked of his past victories, his exploits in war and game—almost as though by recalling the experiences he could revitalize his sickened body. His feet and legs continued, however, to swell as his neck and face grew thin. The wedding and accompanying ceremony, the pretense at youth, and the physical demands to play lover, husband, and ready host tore heavily at his remaining shreds of strength. Through sheer will he rallied himself to watch the Grand Tournament in honor of Mary on Monday, November 13, 1514.

The tournament conceived by Francis Duke of Angoulême and heir presumptive to the throne had been designed not only to challenge the English in play but also to satisfy his delight in ostentatious display and to demonstrate his own special talents as jouster and master spearbreaker. He was confident that his own abilities surpassed the famed exploits of Henry VIII in the field. As a result, a challenge had been issued with sufficient time to allow the English to send over a select few guaranteed to uphold the honor of England. These best jousters of the realm were led by Charles Brandon Duke of Suffolk, and included Sir Edmund Howard, Sir Edward Neville, Sir Giles Capell, Sir Thomas Cheyney, Sir William Sidney, Sir Henry Guildford—son of the displaced "Mother" Guildford—and Thomas Grey Marquis of Dorset.[3]

The rules of the joust provided for a three-day contest with a total of three hundred five combatants fighting individually on horse with spears, then on foot with lances and swords. On the third day all combatants were to be divided into teams and fight in a general free-for-all at the barriers. For these events the lists were erected at the Parc des Tournelles; its walls were banked with the arms of England and France, shields and escutcheons of the leading contenders, and banners and blazons of all participants.

On Monday, the thirteenth, persons of all estates jostled and pushed into their seats. The trumpeters announced the appearance of the royal party led by Louis, who saluted his people and quickly surrendered himself to the comforts of his couch. Near him stood his wife Mary and his daughter Claude, wife of Francis of Angoulême. There they remained resplendent in the magnificence of royalty—a tableau of youth and age. The dauphin and his aides, apparelled in silver cloth of gold and crimson velvet, first entered the arena. Twice around the ring they went, proudly, disdainfully, in their plumed helmets. As they passed the royal box, the challengers bent so low their plumes swept their horses. In turn all the answerers of the challenge repeated the opening ritual, with Suffolk and Dorset leading the English party. While the French changed from one grand costume to another, the English "had ever on their apparel red crosses [of St. George] to be known for love of their country."

Once the tourney was underway, the sweating charge of horses, the resounding crack of spears, the scream of wounded and dying animals, the grunts and heavy breathing of each man pierced the dust-filled arena. Blood was quick to ooze through the slits of armor or gush through eye and mouth openings of a helmet, and of the three hundred five who fought "divers were slain and not spoke of." What had begun as a game of pageantry in the best Renaissance tradition quickly became a duel for national honor. The crowd was demonstrably partisan in cheering the efforts of the French even though it was clearly apparent that Suffolk and Dorset were the champions of the field. When either seized a spear, spurred down the long lane, galloped full speed at an opponent, both Suffolk and Dorset consistently broke their spears with such force against the breasts of their opposers that both man and horse were knocked to the ground. From the galleries, however, neither English champion received much applause.

Francis was abashed at being so outplayed and overwhelmed in this his own tourney, designed as a framework for his own abilities. And when he was hurt in the hand, he asked Suffolk to take his place as challenger. For answerer to the event, Francis smuggled into the arena an enormous German—the tallest and the strongest man in the entire French court. This hooded figure rode unannounced into the lists. Before the call was sounded, before Suffolk was ready, the German charged full tilt, with his spear aimed at Suffolk's heart. Suffolk, however, rallied sufficiently to stand the blow and return it; and one witness noted that "the judges allowed many more strokes to be foughten than were appointed." With both spears broken, Suffolk and the German fought on foot. Suffolk seized the antagonist by the head and beat and battered him "that the blood issued out his nose." When the judges saw the German stagger and about to fall, they dropped the rail to end the fight. This time no chivalric courtesy closed the contest; instead Francis' henchmen hustled the German from the field so that none would know either his identity or Francis' duplicity.[4]

The French nobility increasingly appreciated the efforts of the

English party, and the unfairness shown to many of the English was generally deplored. But of the tournament, Suffolk wrote only ". . . blessed be God all our Englishmen sped well."[5] Louis, however, delighted in the discomfiture and discrediting of his son-in-law Francis, the inevitable successor, and demonstrated growing admiration for Suffolk's valor in the field and his success in the court. In a letter to Henry VIII, Louis spoke of Suffolk as his "good brother, cousin, and companion," and added, "I beg you to believe that, independent of the place that I know he holds with you, and the love you bear him, his virtues, manners, politeness, and good condition, deserve that he should be received with even greater honor."

Of Mary, the king wrote in the same letter, that she ". . . has hitherto conducted herself, and still does every day, towards me, in such manner that I cannot but be delighted with her, and love and honor her more each day; and you may be assured that I do, and ever shall, so treat her, as to give both her and you perfect satisfaction. . . ."[6]

Thus throughout these early days of Mary's marriage to Louis, Suffolk had been much in the presence of the royal couple. To the queen he had brought certain solace and security. Together they had settled the ticklish matter of counsellors to the queen. Together they had won the affection and interest of the king. Together they had solidified the interests of France and England in a common peace. And in so doing, they had protected English interests in Scotland and inadvertently those of Mary's sister, Margaret Queen of Scots. Louis continued to keep Albany at the French court at least for the moment.

To keep Albany forever was, they knew, quite impossible. The Scots nobility had continued and increased their appeals to Albany to come and to Louis to release him. There was, after all, the "auld alliance" with Scotland as well as the newer one with England to consider. Throughout the days of merriment in France, the government of Scotland continued its rapid deterioration. Since Margaret's marriage to Angus, her power continued to erode and her last vestige of support—popular sentiment—turned against her. That she apparently held English interests above those of Scotland pricked the very heart of Scottish independence and pride. Upon that injury the dissident chieftains played and their rival factions brought the country to undeclared civil war.

Even the allegiances so strongly pledged to Margaret in the woeful aftermath of Flodden now turned to Albany in appeal. If Scotland were to survive, a leader must arise; and Albany was the only figure both by blood and by consent to whom all parties would extend at least token acceptance. Realizing that the dilemma of the Scots could not continue indefinitely, Louis sought to work out a compromise between the English and Scottish factions; he offered advice to Albany and then sent him to Suffolk.

Of this visit, Suffolk wrote: ". . . the Duke of Albany came to my lodging, and said that he was come to speak with me, and that it was the King his master's mind that he should break with me of a matter; and I said that I would be content to hear what the King his master's pleasure was by him, or by any other body; and so, upon that, he began, and said that the King's mind was that he should go into Scotland, and that he trusted that his going should do good, for he entended to reduce them of Scotland to be contented to take such a Peace as should be for the King my master's honor, and for the surety of the children; and because that there should be no suspicion, he had married, and he would leave his wife in France, and also he would come by the King my master, and would return as soon as he might possible, for he must go over the Mountains; with many other words.

"And so when I heard him all that he would say, I showed unto him that I had no commission to meddle of such matters; and then he said that the French King would speak with me in the matter; and I said that if his Grace did, I would make his Grace such an answer that his Grace should be content; and so, since, I heard no more of the matter. How be it, my Lord Chamberlain and Doctor West showed me, that the French King's Council had been in hand with them upon the going of the said Duke; and upon that, we and they took a conclusion to advertise the King thereof in all haste; and if so were that the French King would be in hand with me, I should do all that is in me possible to let [prevent] his going; and I ensure you I will do so, for I promise you he entendeth not well as far as I can perceive. . . ."[7]

Albany was moving reluctantly toward acceptance of the Scots' petition, but he remained a Frenchman at heart. France was his home, and that he tried to make clear. It was Louis, for instance, not James, whom Albany considered "his maister." Consequently it was more as a peer of France than the designated Governor of

Scotland that Albany attended the wedding and coronation festival for the new queen. Perhaps it was with this recognition that the young Queen of France asked of Albany protection for her sister and her nephews. For Mary the Scottish question was a personal issue rather than a political one, and she spoke to Albany more freely than could Suffolk. Moreover Albany was in frequent, if not constant, attendance at court throughout the early days of Mary's reign.[8]

The last of Mary's coronation celebrations was a banquet given by the University of Paris at the Hôtel de Ville—an elaborate dinner party punctuated with even more elaborate speeches and toasts in praise of the French-English union. Although there were occasional snide allusions to the War of the Roses and the usurpation of her great uncle's throne by her father as opposed to the long stability of the French government, Mary failed to respond outwardly. Perhaps she was being tactful; perhaps she was floating in some private euphoria of being a queen; perhaps it was simply that her French was not sufficiently refined to catch nuances that translators gently misinterpreted. But her popularity had grown so quickly and fame of her beauty had circulated so widely that the queen had found it impossible to reach the hall through its main entrance. She and her party had been forced to go a secret way through the porter's lodge and up a narrow winding stairway to reach the banqueting hall. Her final diplomatic touch was when she tasted a certain dessert and enjoyed it with such pleasure that she sent it to the royal nursery at Vincennes for the enjoyment of her four-year-old stepdaughter the Princess Renée.[9]

At the conclusion of the wedding and coronation gaiety, the royal couple retired to the villa at St. Germain—fourteen miles from Paris. Then life settled into a quiet, more scheduled routine in a vain effort to restore the waning strength of Louis XII. Since Mary's arrival he had forsaken the rigid schedule suggested by his physicians. Instead of retiring at six, he had held court until midnight; instead of careful diet, he had indulged in hundreds of rich dishes and sauces. And the rigors of ceremony and the charade of a youthful bridegroom had brought him to utter exhaustion. Now he scarcely left his chambers; when he did, it was to move with aid from couch to couch. But his insistence on Mary's presence was constant, and it was with loving—if anxious—attention that he watched her skill at the lute and listened to the songs she sang.

The rest, however, was to no avail. His precarious health continued to disintegrate and finally broke his will to live. On January 1, 1515, he died. And in the streets the people wept and cried: "Le bon roi Louis, père du peuple, est mort."[10]

The fears expressed by Mary and the English ambassadors were now fully realized. Eighty-five days after his marriage, the body of Louis XII lay in state in the Great Hall of Les Tournelles. After a procession to Nôtre Dame and elaborate obsequies, the body was buried in the Cathedral of St. Denis next to that of his second wife Anne of Brittany. The banners of celebration had given way to those of mourning, and the cheers of welcome had turned to cries of farewell. In England Henry ordered elaborate funereal expression to be held before a costly hearse at St. Paul's Cathedral. In France, Francis of Angoulême prepared to ascend the long-coveted throne as Francis I. He was crowned at Rheims on January 28, 1515. Between the two nations there were numerous letters of condolence, congratulation, and concern. The concern centered on the newly established alliance between the two nations and on the particular vehicle of that alliance—Mary Tudor Dowager Queen of France.[11]

During the preparation for Francis' coronation, Mary—now known as "La Reine Blanche," or the childless widow—moved into enforced seclusion at the Hôtel de Cluny in Paris. There, always dressed in white for mourning, she remained alone, supposedly recovering from her sudden sorrow. Her only companions were French ladies whom she neither knew nor trusted. No sunlight was allowed to penetrate her chambers, no entertainment was allowed to vary the long days and longer nights. Instead she watched the flickering candles as they played upon the smiling Virgins, the bleeding Christs, and the suffering saints. For six weeks she stayed in the virtual solitary confinement of this macabre chamber. For one who had so recently been the center of adoration and entertainment, the harsh realities of this unhappy place brought her to nervous exhaustion, and she begged Henry to allow his chief physician John Veyrye to remain with her.

As Mary's nerves buckled under the rigors of constant surveillance of people she did not trust, as her body and soul yearned for fresh air and freedom, not the least of her concerns was her own future—both political and private.

Francis, with immodest haste, began to urge upon Mary new marital alliances, and he offered her many suitors, from peers of France to the Roman Emperor Maximilian. If Mary were to re-marry in France, the new king hoped to avoid the need of return-ing her dowry and restoring the goods which had formed her vast trousseau.[12]

Wolsey, throughout Louis' last days of illness and Francis' opening days of kingship, however, sent warnings and under-scored the need for caution in all of Mary's words and deeds: "I most humbly beseech the same never to do anything but by the advice of his Grace [Henry VIII], referring all things to him whether fair promises, words, or persuasions shall be made to the contrary, having always a special regard to his common honor and letting nothing pass your Grace's mouth whereby any person in these parts may have [you] at an advantage. And if any motions of marriage or other [offer of] fortune to be made unto you, in no wise give hearing to the [same]. And, thus doing, ye shall not fail to have the King fast and loving to you, to attain to your [own heart's] desire [and come] home again unto England with as much honor as [ever woman] had. And for my part, to the effusion of my [blood and the spen]ding of my goods, I shall never forsake or leav[e you]. . . ."[13]

Nine days after Louis' death, Mary wrote the following letter of assurance to Wolsey:

My own good Lord, I recommend me to you and thanking you for your kind and loving Letter, desiring you of your good countenancy and good lessons that you hath given to me; my lord, I pray you as my trust is in you, for to remember me to the King my brother, for such causes and business as I have for to do; for as now I have no other to put my trust in but the King my brother and you. And as it shall please the King my brother and his Council I will be ordered. And so I pray you, my lord, to show his Grace, saying that the King my husband is departed to God, of whose soul God pardon. And whereas you advise me that I should make no promise, my Lord, I trust the King my brother and you will not reckon in me such childhood. I trust I have so ordered myself so since that I came hither, that I trust it hath been to the honor of the King my brother and me . . . and so I trust to continue. If there be anything that I may do for you I would be

glad for to do it in these parts. I shall be glad to do it for you.
No more to you at this time but Jesus preserve you. Written at
Paris, the x. day of January, 1515.

> By your loving friend,
> Mary Queen of France.[14]

While Louis' health had hung in its final balance and throughout the first weeks of Mary's widowhood, the diplomatic arena
became the center of speculation for Mary's second marriage. She
was too valuable a political commodity and too beautiful a young
woman not to arouse curiosity and renewed offers. Through the
shrouded days in the darkened chamber of the youthful widow
the rumors swirled, and the weakened, sickened woman bent
under the confusion and worry. Would Henry remember the
promise at Dover, the promise that he would allow her to marry
this second time who and when she liked? Would he find the
political and financial offers of Francis, of Maximilian, of that
melancholy Prince of Castile too irresistible? Would she again be
swept into an unhappy marriage—this time to spend what might
remain of all the years of her life? Locked within the walls of
Cluny, the sense of helplessness all but engulfed her and she wrote
urgently to Henry to remember her with brotherly kindness. She
would resist all importunity and asked that he do for her the
same: "Sire, whereas your grace sends me word that I will not give
no credence [to the]m for no suit, nor for no other words that
shall be given me; sire, I promise your grace that I never made
them no promise, nor no other fo[r the]m, nor never will [until]
that I know your [grace's mind] for nobody alive; for [your
grace] is all the comfort t[hat I have] in this world; and I trust
your grace w[ill not] fail, for I have noth[ing in this] world that
I care for but to have the good and [kind] mind that your grace
had ever toward me, [which] I beseech your grace to continue,
for therein is my trust that I have in this world. . . ."[15]

A few days later Mary made an even stronger appeal, reminding
her brother of his specific commitment to her and demonstrating
the strength of the Tudor will for which the family was fast becoming famous. In matters of the heart, neither the Tudor
brother nor his sisters would allow interference. Mary wrote:
"[In my] most kind and [loving wise I] recommend me unto
your grace. I would be very glad to hear that your grace were in

good health and p[eace], the which should be a great comfort to me, and that it will please your grace to send more oft time to me than you do, for as now I am all out of comfort, saving that all my trust is in your grace, and so shall be during my life.

"Sire, I pray your grace that it will please your grace to be so good lord and brother to me that you will send hither as soon as you may possibly hither to me. Sire, I beseech your grace that you will keep all the promises that you promised me when I took my leave of you by the w[ater s]ide. Sire, your grace knoweth well that I did marry for your pl[easure a]t this time, and now I trust that you will suffer to [marry as] me l[iketh fo]r to do; for, sire . . . I assure your grace that [my mi]nd is not there where they would have me, and I trust [your grace] will not do so to me that has always been so glad to fulfil your mind as I have been; wherefore I beseech your grace for to be good lord and brother to me. For, sire, if your grace will have gran[ted] me married in any place, [sav]ing whereas my mind is, I will be there, whereas your grace nor no other shall have any joy of me: for, I promise your grace, you shall hear that I will be in some religious house, the which I think your grace would be very sorry of, and all your realm.

"Also, sire, I know well that the king, that [my so]n [Francis I], will send to your grace by his uncle . . . for to marry me here, but . . . I shall never be merry at my heart, (for if ever that I d[o marr]y while I live) . . . I trow your grace knoweth as well as I do, and did before I came hither, and so I trust your grace will be contented, unless I would never marry while I live, but be there where never [no] man nor woman shall have joy of me; wherefore I beseech your grace to be good lord to him and to me both, for I know well that he hath m[et ma]ny hinderances to your grace of him and me both. Wherefore, if your grace be good lord to us both, I will not care for all the world else, but beseech your grace to be good lord and brother to me, as you have been here aforetime, f[or in you] is all the trust that I have in this world after God. No m[ore from m]e at this [time], God send your grace [long life an]d your heart's de[sires]. By your humble and loving sister, Mary Queen of France."[16]

Although she ordered that "this be delivered, in haste," for the moment she could only wait and hope that her letters to Henry and to Wolsey would awaken the memory of a promise given. In

the meantime, Henry dispatched the Duke of Suffolk, Sir Richard
Wingfield, and Dr. Nicholas West to France to review with the
new king the alliances made with Louis and to settle the affairs of
the widowed queen. In this latter charge, the delegation was to
demand of Francis I: ". . . restitution as well of such jewels, precious stones, plate, apparel and other things that her Grace
brought with her, as also of the charge of traduction, which the
French King received for the value of 200,000 crowns," together
with the securance of Mary's dower lands and their attending
revenues.[17] Francis argued that he must have the town of Tournai as part of any new treaty; furthermore he questioned the
return of all the jewels which Louis had lavished on his bride.

Mary, in a politically astute gesture, responded to the jewel
question by proclaiming: "Be it known to all persons that I, Mary
Queen of France, sister unto the King of England Henry the
VIIIth, freely give unto the said King my brother such plate and
vessel of clean gold as the late King Louis of France the XIIth of
that name gave unto me the said Mary his wife; and also by these
presents I do freely give unto my said brother, King of England,
the choice of such special jewels as my said late husband King of
France gave me; to the performation whereof I bind me by this
my bill whereto with mine own hand and signed with my name
and to the same have set my seal the IXth day of February, the
year of our lord fifteen hundred and fourteen.[18] By your loving
sister. Mary Queen of France."

The gift was an obvious appeal to Henry's acquisitive nature
and a part of Mary's attempt to woo his support and win his aid.
But the gift was aimed at doing more than that. Since the return
of Suffolk to France, Mary had made the most dramatic decision
of her life. She had decided to marry this friend and counsellor—
with Henry's approval if possible, and in spite of his wrath if
necessary. This she made clear to Francis I during one of his not
infrequent visits to the Hôtel de Cluny. In a letter to Henry,
Mary described the interview.

"Pleaseth it your grace, the French [king], on Tuesday night
last [past], came to visit me, and [had] with me many diverse
[discoursin]g, among the which he demanded me whether I had
[ever] made any promise of marriage in any place, assuring me
upon his honor, and upon the word of a prince, that in case I
would be plain [with] him in that affair, that he would do for me

therein to the best of his power, whether it were in his realm or out of the same. Whereunto I answered, that I would disclose unto him the [secre]t of my heart in hu[mili]ty, as unto the prince of the world after your grace in whom I had m[ost trust], and so declar[ed unto him] the good mind [which] for divers consi[derations I] bear to my lord of Suffolk, asking him not only [to grant] me his favor and consent thereunto, but [also] that he would of his [own] hand write unto your grace, and to pray you to bear your like favor unto me, and to be content with the same; the which he granted me to do, and so hath done, according as shall appear unto your grace by his said [letters].

"And sire, I most humbly beseech you to take this answer which I have [made u]nto the French king in good part, the which [I did] only to be discharg[ed of t]he extreme pain and annoyance I was i[n, by reason] of such suit as t[he French kin]g made unt[o me not accordi]ng with mine honor, [the whi]ch he hath clearly left [off]. Also, sire, I feared greatly [lest, in] case that I had kept the matter from his knowledge, that he might have not well entreated my said lord of Suffolk, and the rather [for] to have returned to his [former] malfantasy and suits. Wherefore, sire, [sinc]e it hath pleased the said king to desire and pray you of your favor and consent, I most humbly and heartily beseech you that it may like your grace to bear your favor and consent to the same, and to advertise the said king by your writing of your own hand of your pleasure, [and] in that he hath ac[ted after] mine opinion [in his] letter of request, [it] shall be to your great honor . . . to content w[ith all] your council, and [with] all the other no[bles of the] realm, and agr[ee thereto] for your grace a[nd for all] the world; and therefore I eftsoons requi[re you], for all the love that it liked your grace to bear me, that you do not refuse but grant me your favor and consent in form before re-hearsed, the which if you shall deny, I am well assured to [lead] as desolate a life as ever had creature, the which I know well shall be mine end. Always praying your grace to have compassion of me, my most loving and sovereign lord and [brother, where] unto I have [entreated] you, beseeching [God al]ways to [pre-serve your] most royal [estate. Written] at Paris the 15th day of February.

"[I mo]st humbly beseech your grace to consider, in case that you make difficulty to condescend to the promises [as I] wish, the

French king will take new courage to renew his suits to me; assuring you that I had rather to be out of the world than it so should happen; and how he shall entreat my lord of Suffolk, God knoweth, with many other inconvenience, which might ensue of the same, the which I pray our Lord that I may ne[ver ha]ve life to see."[19]

The letter made clear a number of points. Mary's interest in Suffolk, here so boldly stated, could not have come as news to Henry. Mary, Suffolk, and Henry had spent too many years together, had shared too many happy days, for Henry not to have known of the romance between his favorite sister and his best friend. Secondly, the well-known "water-side promise" must have rested on some knowledge of the unnamed third-party in order for Henry to have given his consent. Thirdly, the weeks in almost solitary confinement were fast wearing the nerves of the French queen. Her tone bordered on despair. She was besieged by Francis to form some alliance not to her liking and to the possible disadvantage of her brother. And finally, the letter demonstrated Mary's desperation at her situation in France, her new widowhood, her fear that she would be forced into another unhappy political marriage.

Francis, of course, leapt at any chance to embarrass the King of England. He revelled in knowing the secret heart of the young queen. No doubt he secretly gloated over the distress which was bound to fall upon Suffolk once Henry learned of the proposed marriage. He delighted in knowing that since he could not use Mary's second marriage to his own political purposes, neither could Henry. Mary's marriage—to one so far below her station— would remove a significant card from Henry's political hand. And it must have been with these thoughts in mind that Francis so eagerly jumped to the support of the marriage. Motivations such as these seem to have been only partially realized by Suffolk in the early days of his winter visit to France.

After visiting Mary, Suffolk wrote to her brother: "So when I had been there awhile I was in hand with her Grace, and asked her how the French King did with her Grace and how she found him. And she said at the beginning he was in hand with her of many matters, but after he heard say that I was come, he said unto her Grace that he would trouble her no more with no such matter, but be glad to do for her as he would do for his own mother, and prayed [her that] she would not be a known of none thing that he had spoken to her, neither to your Grace nor me, for because your Grace should take no unkindness therein.

"A[nd further] he said that wheresoever her mind was [for to mar]ry he would be glad to help her there[to with all] his heart, and so since he never me[ddled other]wise, but as he would be to her as [to his m]other. And so, Sir, I perceive that he had [regard to] your Grace, for I think he [would not] to do anything should discontent [your Grace or your] Grace should think any unkindness, in w[hich I assure] your Grace that I think that you will find him [either] a fast prince or else I will say that he is the most [untrue] man that lives. And not he only but all the [noble] men of France for I cannot devise to have [any] speak better than they do, nor to your honor. . . ."[20]

After a lengthy discussion with the King of France, Suffolk detailed the meeting in a letter to Wolsey: "My lord, so it was that the same day that the French king gave us audience his grace called me unto him and had me into his bedchamber, and said unto me,—'My lord of Suffolk, so it is that there is a bruit in this my realm that you are come to marry with the queen your master's sister'; and when I heard him say so, I answered him and said 'that I trusted that his grace would not reckon so great folly in me to come into a strange realm and to marry a queen of the realm without his knowledge and without authority from the king my master to him, and that they both might be content; but I said I assured his grace that I had no such thing, and that it was never intended on the king my master's behalf nor on mine.'

"And then he said 'it was not so, for then [since] that I would not be plain with him, he would be plain with me,' and showed me that the queen herself had broken her mind unto him, and that he had promised her his faith and truth, and by the truth of a king that he would help her, and to d[o what was possib]ly in him to help her to obtain [this that she did desi]re, 'and because that you shall not th[ink that I do] bear you this hand and that [she has not spo]ke her mind, I will s[how you some wor]ds that you had to her [grace privily]'; and so showed me a ware-word,* the which none alive could tell then but she. And when that then

* word of caution

I was abashed and he saw that, and said 'because for [that] you shall say that you have found a kind prince and a loving, and because you shall not think m[e other], here I give you in your hand my faith and truth, by the word of a king, that I shall never fail unto you but to help and advance this matter betwixt her and you with as good a will as I would for mine own [self].'

"And when he had done this I could do none less than to thank his grace for the great goodness that his grace intended to show unto the queen and me, and by it I showed his grace that I was like to be undone if this matter should come to the knowledge of the king my master and then he said, 'Let me alone for that: I and the queen shall so instance your master that I trust that he would be content, and because I would gladly put your heart at rest, I will when I come to Paris speak with the queen, and she and I both will write letters to the king your master with our own hands, in the best manner that can be devised.' "My lord, these were his proper words. . . ."[21]

Although Henry assured Suffolk through letters by Wolsey that ". . . his grace marvelously rejoiced to hear of your good speed in the same, and how substantially and discreetly you ordered and handled yourself in your words and conversation with the said French King, when he first secretly broke with you of the said marriage . . . the [English] King continueth firmly in his good mind and purpose toward you for the accomplishment of the said marriage, albeit that there be daily on every side practices made to the let* of the same, which I have withstood hitherto, and doubt not but so to do till you shall have achieved your intended purpose. . . ."[22]

The implications were clear. Henry had given his consent to Suffolk's marriage to Mary. This statement from Wolsey verified an understanding made between Henry and Suffolk at Eltham Palace before Suffolk's coming into France. His commission as ambassador was to return the French queen and her dower to England.[23] Upon that accomplishment, Henry would allow the marriage. Apparently Suffolk promised Henry to take no advantage and not to marry Mary Tudor until their return to England.

Mary, however, forced his hand. Perhaps she was afraid Henry

---

* hindrance

would find the foreign offers too irresistible and a new foreign alliance too attractive. He would then appeal to her patriotism and sisterly devotion and force her into another foreign marriage. That had happened once, and once was enough. Perhaps, too, she was afraid of what Henry's council would say. There were many—especially the Duke of Norfolk—who were afraid of Suffolk's influence and the heightened impact he would have through a royal tie. Already Norfolk had sent a rather foolish priest, Friar Bonaventure Langley, to Paris to gain Mary's confidence and warn that Suffolk and Wolsey worked hand in glove with no one less than the Devil himself and "by puissance of the said Devil" subjugated Henry to their own will and private advancement.[24]

Perhaps Mary had reached the brink of despair through the constant pressures of Francis, the seemingly endless delay of negotiation, and the quixotic personality of the brother she knew so well. Maybe she merely meant to have her way in a marriage Henry had already sanctioned. Perhaps she was willing to gamble that her brother's initial anger would soon give way to forgiveness.

At any rate, Mary knew that Henry loved them both—Suffolk the best of friends and she the best beloved of sisters. As she had earlier threatened to enter a convent, she now offered Suffolk an ultimatum. He must marry her within four days or never see her again. The challenge was too much for Suffolk, and whatever protestations he might have made fell by the way. The two were married in the early morning hours in the chapel of the Hôtel de Cluny. The witnesses were few—only some waiting women to the queen.

With the marriage now an accomplished fact, Suffolk stood clearly in violation of the royal authority. And he wasted no time in trying to avoid the royal wrath of Henry VIII. Rather than braving that wrath directly, however, Suffolk took the circuitous route and wrote immediately to Wolsey and spoke of the wedding and asked for guidance. The archbishop's answer did little to calm the fears of Suffolk.

"My lord," the cardinal wrote, "With sorrowful heart I write unto you . . . that I have to my no little discomfort and inward heaviness perceived by your letters, dated at Paris the 5th day of this instant month [February], how that you be secretly married unto the king's sister, and have accompanied together as man and wife. And albeit you by your said letters desired me in no wise to disclose the same to the king's grace, yet seeing the same toucheth not only his honor, your promise made to his grace, and also my truth towards the same, I could no less do but, incontinent upon the sight of your said letters, declare and show the contents thereof to his highness, which at the first hearing could scantly* believe the same to be true.

"But after I had showed to his grace that by your own writing I had knowledge thereof, his grace giving credence thereunto took the same grievously and displeasantly, not only for that you durst presume to marry his sister without his knowledge, but also for breaking of your promise made to his grace in his hand, I being present, at Eltham; having also such assured affiance in your truth that for all the world, and to have been torn with wild horses, you would not have broken your oath, promise, and assurance made to his grace, which he doth well perceive that he is deceived of the constant and affirmed trust that he thought to have found in you.

"And for my part, no man can be more sorry than I am that you have so done, and so his grace would I should expressly write unto you, being so incholered† therewith that I cannot devise nor study by the remedy thereof, considering that you have failed to him which hath brought you up of low degree to be of this great honor, and that you were the man in all the world he loved and trusted best, and was content that, with good order and saving of his honor, you should have in marriage his said sister. Cursed be the blind affection and counsel that hath brought you hereunto, fearing that such sudden and unadvised diligence shall have sudden repentance.

"Nevertheless, in this great perplexity I see no other remedy but first to move your humble pursuits by your own writing, causing also the French King and the Queen and other your friends to write, with this also that shall follow—which I assure you I write unto you of my own head without knowledge of any person living, being in great doubt whether the same shall make your peace or no—notwithstanding of *any* remedy but it shall be by that way. It shall be well done that with all diligence possible you

* scarcely   † enraged

and the Queen bind yourselves by obligation to pay yearly to the King during the Queen's life four thousand pounds of her dower, and so you and she shall have remaining of the said dower six thousand pounds and above to live withal yearly. Over and besides this you must bind yourselves to give unto the King the plate of gold and jewels which the late French King had. And whereas the Queen shall have full restitution of her dot,* you shall not only give entirely the said dot to the King, but also cause the French King to be bound to pay to the King the 200,000 crowns which his Grace is bound to pay to the Queen, in full contentation of the said dot, *de novissimus denariis,* and the said French King to acquit the King for the payment thereof, like as the King hath more at large declared his pleasure to you by his letters sent unto you.

"This is the way to make your peace, whereat if you deeply consider what danger you be and shall be in, having the King's displeasure, I doubt not both the Queen and you will not stick, but with all effectual diligence endeavor yourselves to recover the king's favor as well by this means as by other substantial true ways which by mine advice you shall use and none other towards his Grace, whom by colorable drifts and ways you cannot abuse. Now I have told you mine opinion hardily. Follow the same and trust not too much to your own wit, nor follow not the counsel of them that hath not more deeply considered the dangers of this matter than they have hitherto done.

"And as touching the overtures made by the French King for Tournai, and also for a new confederation with the King and him like as I have lately written unto you, I would not advise you to wade any further in these matters, for it be thought that the French King intendeth to make his hand by favoring you in the attaining to the said marriage. Which when he shall perceive that by your means he cannot get such things as he desireth, peradventure he shall show some change and alteration in the Queen's affairs whereof great inconvenience might ensue. Look wisely therefore upon the same, and consider you have enough to do in redressing your own causes, and think it shall be hard to induce

* dowry

the King to give you a commission of trust which hath so lightly regarded the same towards his Grace.

"Thus I have as a friend declared my mind unto you, and never trust to use me nor have me in anything contrary to truth, my master's honors, profits, wealth and surety, to the advancement and furtherance whereof no creature living is more bounden, as our Lord knoweth who send your Grace to look well and deeply upon your acts and doings, for you put yourself in the greatest danger that ever man was."[25]

Many of the directives of Wolsey would be followed by both Mary and Suffolk, but there were also other pressures at work in France. The clandestine marriage had, in short, accomplished more harm than good except perhaps in the shared conscience of the bride and groom. No one who knew specifically of the marriage spoke of it, and to this day no one knows precisely when it took place. Instead, rumor piled upon rumor as the growing intimacy between the queen dowager and the English ambassador became embarrassingly obvious. Hints, insinuation, knowing looks and glances became so profuse that Mary's international reputation bordered on the scandalous. Disgust at being the butt of bawdy jokes was compounded by Mary's fears of pregnancy in these early days of marriage. Her fears worked on Suffolk so that he again begged Henry to allow publication of the news of the marriage.

With great anxiety Suffolk seized his pen and in a letter to Wolsey spilled forth a second, more detailed description of the anxiety-filled days and the precipitous events they marked: "My lord of York, I re[commend] me unto you, and so it [is that I know] well that you have been the chief man [before al]l that has been the helper of me to that I am [now] next God and my master, and therefore I will never hide none thing from you, trusting that you will help me now as you have always done.

"My lord, so it is that when I came to Paris, I heard many things which put me in great fear, and so did the Queen both. And the Queen would never let me be in rest till I had granted her to be married. And so, to be plain with you, I have married her heartily, and have lyen with her, insomuch that I fear me lest she be with child. My lord, I am not in a little sorrow lest the King should know it, and that his Grace should be displeased with me, for I assure you that I had rather have died than he should be miscontent. And therefore, my own good lord, since you have brought me hitherto let me not be undone now, the which I fear me I shall be, without the special help of you. My lord, think not that ever you shall make any that shall be more [forwa]rd to you, and therefore, mine own good lord, give me help. My lord, as me-thinks th[ere is no] remedy in this matter but that I m[ay ob-tain] another letter from the French K[ing, and a let]ter from the French Queen, and a [letter from the King's] mother to the King my [sovereign lord], desiring his Grace that . . . the which should be m[ade known] to all France, and that his Grace should thereby perceive that they would be glad to see it [done] most honorable that could be, and m[ight now] specially because all the noblemen of France be here. My lord, I doubt not b[ut that] they will write this for me or how ye shall think best they should write. . . . For I beseech you to instruct me in all haste possible.

"My lord, they marry as well in Lent as out of Lent with licence of any bishop. Now, my lord, you know all, and in you is all my trust, beseeching you of your assured help, and that I may have answer from you of this or all my other writings as shortly as it may be possible, for I ensure you I have as heavy a heart as any man living, and shall have till I may hear good tidings from you."[26]

The only response from England was silence. At Mary's insis-tence, Suffolk petitioned Francis for permission to marry publicly the "French queen," as Mary was now styled. According to the diary of Francis' mother, Louise of Savoy, the second marriage—a semiprivate affair—was held in Lent on March 30. Among the witnesses was Francis I, who must have stood and smiled at this triumph over Henry and what seemed to be the ultimate downfall of Suffolk—the rival who not long ago had shamed him in the lists and tourney in celebration of the wedding he did not want.[27] This present marriage he liked very well.

In the meantime, the Suffolks were following Wolsey's advice in one particular. They began to buy their way back into England as Suffolk wrote to Wolsey: "My lord, for to induce the Queen's matter and mine unto the King's grace, I think best for your first entry you should deliver unto him a diamond with a great pearl, which you shall receive with this from the Queen, his sister, and require him to take it[s] worth, assuring his Grace that whensoever she shall have the possession of the residue, that he shall have the choice of them according unto her former writing. My lord, she and I remit this matter wholly to your discretion, trusting that in all haste possible we shall hear from you some good tidings touching our affairs, wherewith I require you to despatch this bearer and that he tarry for no other cause."[28]

The "diamond with a great pearl" was no less a jewel than the famed Mirror of Naples. It had been Louis' first wedding gift to Mary, and with it he had sought to win her favor. Now she thought of it as her own and with it hoped to win Henry's good-will. Of all the jewels Louis had given her, of all the jewels of France, indeed of all the jewels of Christendom, the Mirror of Naples was among the finest. It was obviously much cherished by the French and much coveted by the English. Francis had insisted many times that the Mirror, as well as the other jewels with which Louis had bestrewn his bride, were hers only as Queen of France. With Louis' death, Francis demanded the return of the jewels to the crown. Mary disagreed and secretly sent the great Mirror into England.

When neither Henry nor Wolsey responded to this grand gift, Mary wrote to Henry and sought to share the responsibility for the marriage—not with Suffolk—with the king's council. She went to great lengths to alleviate any responsibility from her husband. While she was the king's sister, Suffolk was considered by many to be a foolish upstart, and he had at court many enemies, especially amongst the older, more established aristocracy. Mary could imagine the plotting of those enemies even as she wrote to Henry.

"Pleaseth your Grace, to my greatest discomfort, sorrow and disconsolation but lately I have been advertised of the great and high displeasure which your Highness beareth unto me and my lord of Suffolk for the marriage between us. Sir, I will not in any wise deny but that I have offended your Grace, for the which I do put myself most humbly in your clemency and mercy. Nevertheless to the intent that your Highness should not think that I had simply, carnally, and of my sensual appetite done the same, I having no re[gar]d to fall in your Grace's displeasure, I assure your Grace that I had never done [against your] ordinance and consent, but by r[eason of the grea]t despair w[herein I was put] by the two fr[iars . . .] which hath certifi[ed me] in case I came [to] En[gland] your Council would never consent to the mar-

riage between the said lord and me, with [ma]ny other sayings
concerni[ng] the same marriage; so that I verily [thought] that
the said friar[s] would never have [offered] to have made me
like ove[rture] unless they might have had charge from some of
your Council.

"The which put me in such consternation, fear, and doubt of
the obtaining of the thing which I desired most in this world, that
I rather chose to put me in your mercy by accomplishing this marriage, than to put me in the order of your Council, [knowing
the]m to be otherwise [minded]. Whereupon, Sir, I put [my
lord of Su[ffolk in choice w[hether he woul]d accomplish th[e
marriag]e within f[our days, or else that he should never have]
enjoyed me; whereby I know well that I constrained him to break
such promises he made your Grace, as well for fear of losing me, as
also that I ascertained him that by their consent I would never
come into England.

"And now that your Grace knoweth the both offences of the
which I have been the only occasion I most humbly, and as your
most [sorrow]ful sister, requiring you to have compassion upon
us both, and to pardon our offences, and that it will please your
Grace to write to me and my lord of Suffolk some [comfor]table
words, for it sh[all be] the greatest comfort for u[s both.]"[29]

Suffolk was more than willing to let his wife take either blame
or credit for the marriage. It was not that he lacked courage but
rather that he was a plain, blunt man who could tell things only as
they were while he suspected the duplicity of others. He lacked
subtlety and he lacked intellect, but he never lacked honor. He
wrote to Henry in the only way he knew, with straightforward
directness.

"Sire,—So it is, that when I came to Paris the queen was in hand
with me the first day [after], and said she must be short with me,
and [show] to me her pleasure and mind, and so she b[egan]
unto me and show how good lady she was to me, and if I would be
ordered [by her] she would never have none but me, [and so]
she showed me that she had verily und[erstood a]s well by friar
Langley . . . that if ever she came in Eng[land she shou]ld never
have me, and therefore she [told me plainly] that if I would not
marry her, [then, she should neve]r have me nor never come
[into England. An]d when I heard her say so I showed [her that
she] said that but to prove me with. And she [said 'that] I would

not you know well:' that [at] my coming [to Paris h]ow it was showed her, and I asked her [what that wa]s, and she said that the best in France had been unto her, that if she went into England she should go into Flanders, to the which she said that she had rather to be torn in pieces than ever she would come there, and with that weeped.

"I never saw woman so weep. And when I saw [that], I showed her grace that there was none such thing by my faith with the best words I could, but in no wise I could make her believe it; and when I saw that, I showed her grace that, as her grace would be content to write unto your grace and to obtain your good will, I would be content, or else I durst not, because I had made unto your grace such a promise: whereunto in conclusion she said: 'If the king my brother is content, and the French king, both the one by his letters and the other by his words, that I should have you, I will have the time after my desire, or else I may well think that the words of them in these parts and of them in England are true. And that is, that you are come to [en]tice me hence, to the intent that I may be married into Flanders, the which I will never to die for it, and so [I promi]sed the French king ere you came: And th[us if so be] you will not be content[to follow [after my mi]nd, look, never after this day [shall you have] the proffer again. And, sire, I saw me in that case, and I thought . . . rather to put me in y[our mercy] than to lose all, and so I granted thereunto, and so she and I was married."[30]

The "she and I was married" summarized Suffolk's predicament. Both bride and groom suspected pregnancy, and they wanted to insure the lawful status of their child by a public ceremony. This Henry refused. Encouraged by the council now acutely aligned against Suffolk, Henry reminded his childhood friend that the essential part of the ambassadorial mission had yet to be achieved. Francis had not renewed the treaty between the two nations. Furthermore, Henry added, there were rumors in the council that Suffolk had promised the return of the city of Tournai for Francis' help in the marriage.

To this charge, Suffolk responded: "Yet, Sir, I insure your Grace that I have not put the French King in none hope of it [Tournai]; insomuch [that I have] caused him to leave it out of his instructions given to his ambassadors to the inte[nt] he should not manner anything that should not be to your contentation, but to refer it [to your] pleasure."[31] In the midst of his personal trial, Suffolk had continued to go about the business of his king. It was Francis who was playing for time and hoping to make the best of the bargain regarding Mary's return. The deliberations over Tournai and Mary's revenues would in fact continue for years.

In the end Francis and his council conceded, and the jointure offered originally by Louis XII was granted to Mary together with payment of two hundred thousand gold crowns—restitution of half of her original dower. The gold and silver plate and most of her jewels, however, were considered the property of queens of France. Those riches were to remain in France. In a gesture of pleasantry, however, Francis allowed Mary to keep twenty-two diamonds, sixteen pearls, one ruby, and a large emerald even as he continued to demand the return of the Mirror of Naples. For that magnificent pride of the French crown, Mary eventually was forced to give a written receipt. She knew that Henry would not return it.

Now that her accounts were squared with France, Mary was more anxious than ever to leave the French court. She wanted to go home, and she was willing to sacrifice the hard-won dower and all of her jewels to do so. She again made the point to Henry: "[Please it y]our Grace to understand [that wh]ereas I wrote unto your Grace touching my jewels and plate which I promised your [Gr]ace, such as I have shall be at [yo]ur commandments ever while [I live]. Howbeit 'tis not so well [as] I would it had been, for there is much sticking thereat. Howbeit I doubt not but I [s]hall have it at the link with the good help [of] your Grace and your [Coun]cil that be here.

"Sir, I think my lord of Suffolk will wr[ite m]ore plainlier to your Gra[ce tha]n I do of these matters. Then when you and the[y be] agreed with your Gr[ace, and] I have them, I will [give] you my part of th[em]. Sir, the French King speaks many ki[nd word]s unto me, a[nd doth affirm] that he ha[th a] special mind to ha[ve] peace with your Gra[ce be]fore any prince in Christendom. And, Sir, I would beseech your Grace that it may be so, if it [might] stand with your favor [and] pleasure, for by the means and favor of your Gr[ace] I have obtained as much honor in this realm as was possible to any woman to have, which causes me to write to your Grace in this matter. Over and ab[ove] this I most humbly beseech your Grace to write to the[e Fr]ench King and all [yo]ur ambassadors here [that they] make all sp[eed] possible that I m[ay come] to your Gra[ce for my] singular de-s[ire] and [co]mfort [is to see] your Grace, above [all thi]ngs in this world. As knoweth our Lord, who [ev]er preserve your Grace."[32]

To this and all appeals, the king continued his silence. How much of this reticence was part of the regal pose, how much was seated in the royal anger was uncertain. That he had not placed any real or legal barrier to the Suffolks' return was clear. Neither had he made any overt gesture of welcome. He simply left the negotiations in the hands of Wolsey, who alone of Henry's council supported Suffolk's cause. Everyone of import, whether in England or France, knew that Suffolk's enemies were many. Those enemies were fast seeking the destruction of Suffolk through the inopportune marriage. Therefore, Wolsey carefully directed the negotiations on both sides of the Channel. To make Mary's and Suffolk's letters of supplication more palatable to Henry and less offensive to the council, Wolsey told the truants what to say and even went so far as to modify what they said. The following letter of Suffolk to his king was typical of many: "Most Gracious Sovereign Lord. —So it is that I am informed divers ways that all your whole Council, my lord of York excepted, with many others are clearly determined to tempt your Grace that I may either be put to death or be put in prison and so to be destroyed. Alas, Sir, I may say that I have a hard fortune, seeing that there was never none of them in trouble but I was glad to help them in my power, and that your Grace knows best. And now that I am in this none little trouble and sorrow now they are ready to help and destroy me.

"But, Sir, I can no more but God forgive them whatsoever comes to me, for I am determined. For, Sir, your Grace is he that is my sovereign lord and master, and he that has brought me up out of nought, and I am your subject and servant and he that has offended your Grace in breaking my promise that I made your Grace touching the Queen, your sister. For the which, with most humble heart, I will yield myself unto your Grace's hands to do with my poor body your gracious pleasure, not fearing the malice of them, for I know your Grace of such nature that it cannot lie in their powers to cause you to destroy me for their malice. But what

MARGARET TUDOR

Courtesy H. M. The Queen

MARGARET TUDOR'S LETTER TO HER FATHER HENRY VII
(see pages 3–4)

Cotton MS Vespasian F XIII, f. 134.
Reproduced by permission of the British Library Board

MARY TUDOR

Courtesy Bibliothèque Municipale de Lille

ELIZABETH OF YORK

Courtesy National Portrait Gallery, London

HENRY VII

Courtesy Victoria and Albert Museum, London

HENRY VIII

Courtesy H. M. The Queen

CATHERINE OF ARAGON

Courtesy National Portrait Gallery, London

MARGARET TUDOR QUEEN DOWAGER OF SCOTLAND
AND JOHN STEWART DUKE OF ALBANY

Courtesy Lord Bute

MARY TUDOR QUEEN OF FRANCE AND DUCHESS OF SUFFOLK,
AND CHARLES BRANDON DUKE OF SUFFOLK

Courtesy His Grace the Duke of Bedford

JAMES IV

Courtesy National Galleries of Scotland

JAMES V

Courtesy National Galleries of Scotland

ARCHIBALD DOUGLAS EARL OF ANGUS

Courtesy H. M. The Queen

LOUIS XII

Courtesy H. M. The Queen

CHARLES V

Courtesy Cliché des Museés Nationaux

FRANCIS I

Courtesy Cliché des Museés Nationaux

THOMAS CARDINAL WOLSEY

Courtesy National Portrait Gallery, London

punishment I have I shall thank God and your Grace of it, and think that I have well deserved it, both to God and your Grace. As knows our Lord, who send your Grace your most honorable heart's desire with long life, and me, most sorrowful wretch, your gracious favor, what sorrows soever I endure therefore."[33]

Mary sent another appeal by the same messenger. It too had already gone through several drafts and been improved and approved by Wolsey. As a result, it was much more restrained than her earlier outbursts to her brother: "My most dear and entirely beloved brother, In most humble manner I recommend me to your grace.

"Dearest brother, I doubt not but that you have in your good remembrance that whereas for the good of peace and for the furtherance of your affairs you moved me to marry with my lord and late husband, king Louis of France, whose soul God pardon. Though I understood that he was very aged and sickly, yet for the advancement of the said peace, and for the furtherance of your causes, I was contented to conform myself to your said motion, so that if I should fortune to survive the said late king I might with your good will marry myself at my liberty without your displeasure. Whereunto, good brother, you condescended and granted, as you well know, promising unto me that in such case you would never provoke or move me but as mine own heart and mind should be best pleased; and that wheresoever I should dispose myself, you would wholly be contented with the same. And upon that, your good comfort and faithful promise, I assented to the said marriage, which else I would never have granted to, as at the same time I showed unto you more at large.

"Now that God hath called my said late husband to his mercy, and that I am at my liberty, dearest brother, remembering the great virtues which I have seen and perceived heretofore in my lord of Suffolk, to whom I have always been of good mind, as you well know, I have affixed and clearly determined myself to marry with him; and the same [I] assure you hath proceeded only of mine own mind, without any request or labor of my said lord of Suffolk, or of any other person. And to be plain with your grace, I have so bound myself unto him that for no cause earthly I will or may vary or change from the same. Wherefore my good and most kind brother, I now beseech your grace to take this matter in good part, and to give unto me and to my said lord of Suffolk your good will herein. Ascertaining you, that upon the trust and comfort which I have, for that you have always honorably regarded your promise, I am now come out of the realm of France, and have put myself within your jurisdiction in this your town of Calais, where I intend to remain till such time as I shall have answer from you of your good and loving mind herein; which I would not have done but upon the faithful trust that I have in your said promise. Humbly beseeching your grace, for the great and tender love which ever hath been and shall be between you and me, to bear your gracious mind and show yourself to be agreeable thereunto, and to certify me by your most loving letters of the same, till which time I will make mine abode here, and no farther enter your realm.

"And to the intent it may please you the rather to condescend to this my most hearty desire, I am contented and expressly promise and bind me to you, by these presents, to give you all the whole dot which was delivered with me, and also all such plate of gold and jewels as I shall have of my said late husband's. Over and besides this I shall, rather than fail, give you as much yearly part of my dower, to as great a sum as shall stand with your will and pleasure; and of all the premises I promise, upon knowledge of your good mind, to make unto you sufficient bonds. Trusting, verily, that in fulfilling of your said promise to me made, you will show your brotherly love, affection, and good mind to me in this behalf, which to hear of I abide with most desire; and not to be miscontented with my said lord of Suffolk, whom of mine inward good mind and affection to him I have in manner enforced to be agreeable to the same, without any request by him made; as knoweth our Lord, whom I beseech to have your grace in his merciful governance."[34]

As Mary noted, the Suffolks had again taken the initiative and moved from Paris to Calais—the English city on the coast of France. In doing so they placed themselves specifically in Henry's domain and under his control. Still no word from England was forthcoming as the Suffolks moved into the so-called King of England's House. There they soon found themselves virtual prisoners. Although Henry had made no open move against the marriage, he was still to make an open move for it. The English citizenry of Calais, however, exercised no such restraint. Suffolk found himself mocked in the streets for what was felt to be his impudence in undertaking the royal marriage and depriving the English of another good marital alliance. The cries of derision and insult would not be put down. Neither the wardens of the house nor the enclosure of the garden could keep away the mobs, quiet their shouting, or guard against the rotted foods which slapped against the building. And as Suffolk and Mary lived out their nightmare, they could only wonder if this were a foretaste of their reception in England.[35]

CHAPTER SIX

THROUGHOUT THE BRIEF REIGN OF MARY TUDOR AS QUEEN OF France her mind had been occupied by many things, including her concern for those who had served her and those she had come to love. For those who had so joyfully attended her to France only to be dismissed abruptly by Louis, Mary had already provided elaborate gifts of gold and jewels and sought for them positions at court or service with her friends. For those for whom she had especial regard, such as Dr. Denton her almoner, John Palsgrave her tutor, and Nicolas West her advisor, she continued to solicit help. In their behalf, she petitioned the two most important men of England, Henry and Wolsey, to secure benefices of substantial worth.[1]

Mary's appeal for Denton was typical of the others which she made, and in this instance she wrote to Wolsey: "My lord, you remember, I doubt not, that, at my last being at Guildford, you desired the king my brother to give unto my trusty and well-beloved almoner, doctor Denton, the prebend in St. Stephen's, which as then the dean of his chapel, and now bishop of Lincoln, had in possession, as then the king's grace showed me in your presence that he should have it, and also you promised me the same, and to solicit the king my brother for the performance of his promise. Nevertheless, I am credibly informed that my almoner is disappointed of the said prebend, and that your chaplain hath it, of the which I marvel greatly; forasmuch as my said almoner hath done me good service in this country, to the great honor of the king my brother, and mine also, and that the promise was made undesired of my behalf, for you were the person that only moved the king to give it unto my almoner, and I am assured that his grace would not have varied without he had been persuaded to the contrary.

"My lord, forasmuch as I see you benevolent unto me in all my matters, and ever hath been since our first acquaintance, and now especially, I pray you, therefore, to do so much at mine instance and request, to desire your chaplain to resign the said prebend to the behoof and use of my said almoner; and I promise you that I will not cease until I have gotten some promotion of the king my brother, or else of some other person, for your said chaplain, which I trust shall be worth do[uble] the value of Saint Stephen's; and, besides that, I shall help that he may have the next prebend hereafter in Saint Stephen's. I pray you, my lord, send me word of your mind, and that [there be] none excuse made; for, I assure you, my lord, [my promise] shall be without any excuse if God send me life; I [will not] say that word that I would not wilfully per[form, as] knoweth his grace. Amen."[2]

Here as elsewhere Mary revealed herself as a woman of her word, secure in the knowledge of herself, secure in herself. She was forceful, not arrogant; gracious, not subservient. When she saw injustice, she sought to right it—but not at the sacrifice of the innocent. She was a princess and a queen who never forgot the kindnesses large and small of those she served and those who served her. And in the harried days with Louis and the early ones with Suffolk, no one served her better than Wolsey. Although she was a daughter of a king and he the son of a butcher, she saw the man as a man and valued him for what he was; and she was grateful for what he had done.

Throughout the final days of Louis' life, it had been Wolsey who ventured careful, thoughtful advice to Mary. Even when she had violated that advice, he had remained her steadfast friend and constant champion in the heated discussions of the king's council. Throughout the awkward days of secret marriage, it had been to Wolsey that the prodigal bride and groom had first turned. It was to him alone that they left the difficult task of bargaining and discussing, of finding the way by which they might return to England. And although Henry VIII seemed to have been disposed to allow the marriage of Mary and Suffolk, Wolsey had been left to answer the opposing voices of the English nobility. In that endeavor, he had never wavered. For his pains, Suffolk

had secured—sometime in March—from Francis I the bishopric of
Tournai for Wolsey. Although a lucrative post, the payment it
brought with it was actually small in proportion to the enormous
amount of diplomacy he managed in the Suffolks' behalf.[3] Mary
never forgot that, and in the years ahead she remained his friend
and champion.

By the end of April, Wolsey's arguments succeeded in placating
the council, and the financial offerings of Mary and Suffolk as-
suaged the sore feelings that had resulted from the violation of
royal authority. The couple was called home and sailed for Dover
on May 2. This time there were no storms and no tempests, and
they reached the opposite shore the same day. This time Mary
sailed with greater hope and less fanfare than she had seven
months earlier. Although she kept for the rest of her life the
courtesy title of Queen of France, she was never again to find
herself a center of political influence. Unlike her brother and
sister, power was never a major interest of the youngest Tudor.
To be married to Suffolk and to enjoy the affection of her brother,
the king, were enough.

At Dover the couple was welcomed by a large escort of the
nobility sent especially from London to usher them home. The
day after their arrival, they were met by Wolsey who brought
them to the royal manor of Barking in Essex where they met
privately with Henry VIII. Although there was a marked absence
of welcoming celebration, there was no absence of warmth in his
greeting. He was glad to have his old companion and his young
sister home again. His court would be the merrier and the more
beautiful with them. And as Henry accepted the jewels, the gold
and plate, the dowry, and their promise to pay one thousand
pounds a year for twenty-four years, the royal pride was eased and
the royal heart was opened. He assured them both of his good
love.[4]

As anxious as Mary to guard her honor, Henry welcomed one
final petition of the returning pair—that they be publicly married
". . . and performed in due form and manner with the publication
of banns and all other ceremonies. . . ." On Sunday, May 13, in
the presence of Henry VIII and his Catherine and all other nobility of the realm, Mary Tudor Queen of France and Charles Brandon Duke of Suffolk were married at Greenwich. In an attempt to
squelch all rumor, the wedding was published widely and Francis

and his court were asked never to mention the two earlier marriages.[5] To celebrate the event, Suffolk commissioned their bridal portrait and had inscribed upon it:

> Cloth of gold do not despise,
> Though thou be matched with cloth of frize.
> Cloth of frize be not too bold,
> Though thou be matched with cloth of gold.

This slight bit of verse, apparently Suffolk's single poetic effort, was to become a definition of his marriage, which was based on the rarest of commodities in royal life—love and mutual understanding. Much to the amazement of the rivals of Suffolk, he never sought to use this marriage as a political tool, and Mary seemed never to have regretted her hysterical persuasion in the darkened chambers of the Reine Blanche. Instead she was anxious to establish her own household and urged Suffolk to call home his daughter Lady Anne Brandon long in the court of Margaret of Savoy. And so he did. In a letter to the archduchess, he wrote: "I had intended to leave her permanently with you, since I know no place where she could better be, but the queen has so urged and prayed me to have her, that I could not contradict her."[6]

Suffolk's daughter came home to Suffolk Place, a vast and wooded estate on the southern banks of the Thames in Southwark. There during the spring of 1515, Mary established her household. In later years, she came to prefer the country retreat of Westhorpe Hall in the county of Suffolk. It was there and in the religious houses near Ely and Bury St. Edmunds that she would spend her days unless specifically called to court. Although she never lost her love of ostentation and courtly splendor, she learned too of the pleasures of the country; for hers was a quiet and retiring nature not unlike that of her mother Elizabeth of York. And perhaps that was one reason Henry VIII loved this sister best.

There were many, however, who marvelled at the ease with which the Suffolks reentered England and moved into the circles of influence; for Suffolk's mission into France had been largely a diplomatic failure. French and English relations were again strained. Francis I had wasted no time in betrothing his young sister-in-law, the Princess Renée, to Charles of Castile—the young man whom nobility and commoners alike believed to be the rightful bridegroom for Mary Tudor. France had succeeded in an alliance where England had failed.

It was, however, in early May—amidst the pleasantries surrounding the third marriage of Suffolk and Mary that the most shattering news of all burst upon the English court. Francis had moved quickly to reestablish the "auld alliance" and had given leave to Albany to go forth as Governor of Scotland. Somehow Albany had evaded the English spies hounding him in France and the English navy searching for him at sea. By mid-May he was welcomed by nearly everyone but Margaret and her few friends.

Margaret had spent the long winter months and the chilled spring mornings pacing the corridors of the castles of Stirling and Perth. Many were the days and often were the evenings when she would stand at her window and gaze southward, awaiting the help that never came. She knew that politically Henry's hands were tied by his treaty with France, but the point was difficult to remember as she stood a prisoner within her castle in the land over which she had once reigned. What monies she had, she had long ago spent. What jewels and plate were hers, she had long ago pawned. What strength she had seen in Angus had begun to pale— he was so often away waging ineffectual warfare. She called for help, but help seemed never to come. And now having withstood the long months of siege, the supplies of the castle were disappearing. Want was replacing plenty much as despair had long ago replaced mirth.

Throughout the winter of 1514–1515, Henry's main suggestion had been that Margaret and her sons, James and Alexander, escape their assailants and seek refuge in the south. What might follow could only be hypothesized. With the King of Scots in his hands, Henry might then deal more forcefully with the Scots as a whole. He could give substance to the belief that he had long held—that Scotland was and should be a fiefdom of England. At other times, as Catherine of Aragon gave him children who did not live, Henry VIII proposed that James of Scotland become James of England and the young Alexander have Scotland for his own. While Margaret preferred these suggestions to her own present state, she could only write: "Right excellent, high, and mighty prince, and dearest brother, I commend me to you with all my heart.

"I have received instructions from the lord Dacre by my servant, sir James English, this 21st day of January, made by the advice of you and your council, wherein I consider the great affection and love that you have to me, my children, my husband, and his friends, whose counsel I would be gladder to do than to make me the greatest lady of the world. Yet it comforts mine heart to hear your fraternal desire; but it is impossible to be performed by any manner of fashion that I, my husband, or his uncle can devise; considering what watch and spies there is daily where I am, and I dare disclose my counsel to none other but God.

"If I were such a woman that might go with my bairn in mine arm, I trow I should not be long from you, whose presence I desire most of any man. I trust, dear brother, to defend me from mine enemies, if I had sufficient expenses till the coming of your help; but I am so super-expended that I doubt that poverty shall cause me to consent to some of their minds, which I shall never do without your counsel, as long as I have a groat to spend. Wherefore I pray you to send me some money, as you think necessary; for it is not your honor that I or my children should want.

"Also, brother, I have sent to you in this other writing, how the bishop of Dunkeld is deceased, whose benefice I have given to the apostolate, my husband's uncle; for the bishop of Murray has purchased all the other benefices of this country. I have written to the pope for the said apostolate, and I beseech you to farther the same at the pope's hands, for I am right much beholden to him. All other things as occurs in the country Mr. Adam Williamson can show you, to whom you shall give credence; and the Holy Trinity have you in keeping."[7]

Escape, as Henry described it, was impossible; and in spite of Margaret's continued appeals for English invasion, invasion was, because of the treaty with France, equally impossible. Her constant advocacy of the invasion of Scotland by English troops merely underscored Margaret's inability to think herself other than an English princess who happened to be the Queen Dowager of Scotland. That narrow vision worked not only to the betrayal of her adopted country but also to her own undoing. She was her own worst enemy.

When, however, Albany entered the harbor of Ayr on May 17 with his fleet of eight ships, Margaret attempted to adjust herself to the inevitable. As Albany approached Edinburgh, she moved to

Holyrood. There she waited and listened to the growing cheers of the multitude and so was able to mark his progress through the pageants of welcome until he came before her at the gates of the palace. There she greeted him with all honor, courtesy, and respect, and Albany with all courtliness returned her greeting.[8] For the time she retained the custody of her children, and Albany made no move to intervene.

Whatever concern the Scots may have had about Albany's abilities and interests was quickly dispelled as he set about the enormous task of quieting the seemingly endless disputes and quarrelling factions. His first act was to seek the advice of John Hepburn Archbishop of St. Andrews, Margaret's most implacable enemy. In so doing, however, he inadvertently offended the pride of the fiery Hume who turned in almost instant support of Margaret. Not realizing the extent of Hume's displeasure, Albany proceeded directly against the supporters of the queen. Lord Drummond, grandfather of Angus, had violated protocol in a fit of anger and struck the Lion herald who represented Albany. For that offense, Albany imprisoned Drummond in the castle of Blackness. Gavin Douglas Bishop of Dunkeld was imprisoned in the sea tower of St. Andrews.[9]

On July 12 parliament convened. The Earl of Arran bore the sword of state before Albany who was then presented with the sword and sceptre and became the Regent of Scotland. Angus and Colin Campbell, Earl of Argyll and chieftain of the Western Highlands, then placed the coronet upon Albany's brow and he became Protector, a position he could hold until James V was eighteen years old. As a gesture of reconciliation to the pro-English faction, Albany took the occasion to pardon Drummond but retained his lands and possessions in the name of the king.[10]

Parliament under Albany's direction ordered that the king and his brother be placed in the care of eight lords: four to be chosen by lot; three to be chosen by Margaret. Albany, as next of blood to James and Alexander, was seeking to quiet the rumor that he would play the role of Richard III and seize the crown for himself.

Margaret, however, was leaving little to chance. She had once again removed herself to Stirling to be with her sons—she was determined to keep them in her care. When in late July she learned that the four emissaries from parliament were approaching the castle, she ordered the gates of the fortress thrown open. Then Margaret appeared holding the little king by the hand; behind her stood Angus and a nurse with the child Alexander. The gathered citizenry tore the air with cheers and huzzahs of acclamation before their king; but as the lords labored the steepness of the hill, the cheers diminished and quieted.

When the men approached the summit, Margaret, "with an air of dignity, and a voice, whose full tones all could distinctly hear, . . . bade them stand and declare their errand." The spokesman answered. They came in the name of parliament to take away the king and his brother. Upon those words, Margaret ordered the portcullis to drop. The massive iron gate slammed with sudden heaviness to the ground; and before the ringing of the bars ceased, she spoke to the astonished lords: "I hold this castle by the gift of my late husband, your sovereign, who also entrusted to me the keeping and government of my children, nor shall I yield them to any person whatsoever; but I respect the parliament, and require a respite of six days to consider their mandate." Angus openly fretted at the consequences of refusing the parliamentary request and urged Margaret to concede. Margaret refused and listened with fire in her heart as Angus weakly spoke to the peers through the bars to remind them that the opposition was not his. The representatives of parliament withdrew, and Margaret's finest moment was over.[11]

What Margaret hoped to accomplish in her six days remains conjecture. Confronted by the lack of will in Angus she knew she could not carry alone the burden of defiance. Her only hope lay, as she saw it, in continued appeals to Henry. Still bound by the French treaty, the King of England had only one course open to him—insurrection. With sudden urgency he ordered Lord Thomas Dacre to renew the border raids and to work upon the latent hostilities and inherited hatreds of the border chieftains of Scotland. From Berwick to Carlisle, Dacre rushed to his business with relish. As he raged, burned, and pillaged the villages and farms, the barns and fields, as he slaughtered the cattle and sheep, he wooed Hume the chamberlain into becoming the chief rival of the Duke of Albany. Hume, while not betraying any English interests, entered the border raids with delight and waged angry destruction on his own land and against his own people with English arms and munitions.

Albany, however, was not to be swayed from his initial purpose. Possession of the king and his brother was of prime importance—they gave substance to his rule. Without them he could not continue to act in the king's name. As a result he ordered the siege of Stirling Castle by the earls of Lennox, Borthwick, and Boswell. Nor was Angus, in this instance, overlooked. He too was ordered with his men to Stirling and there to help prevent any relief and any substance to reach either the queen or her sons. On August 4, Albany himself appeared before Stirling with seven thousand armed men. Dacre, however, had not been out of touch with events. He had arranged for Angus and Hume with a company of sixty men to ride to Stirling with the intent of smuggling the two boys into England. The plan was doomed from the beginning. All that Hume and Angus could manage was to speak with Margaret and smuggle inside the castle Angus' brother George Douglas. When the regent and his men appeared at the gate, George Douglas disappeared. Margaret knew that all—for the time being—was lost. She had exploited all possibilities and they had brought her only to this moment of capitulation.

For this dramatic moment, Margaret dressed James in his tiny robes of estate and placed the crown upon his head. She placed the keys of the castle in his hands and walked with him to the gate. The little king offered the keys to the kneeling Albany, and Margaret gave over her sons. As she did so she asked Albany for the favor of seeing her boys, the right to the dignities of queens dowager, and pardon for Angus her husband. To these requests Albany, with all courtesy, answered that "to herself and his infant sovereign, he was animated by no feelings but those of devoted loyalty; but [not so] for Angus, whose opposition to the will of parliament and dangerous correspondence with England amounted . . . to treason."[12] The governor turned to the earl marshal and Flemming and Borthwick and gave into their keeping the custody of James V. John Erskine was appointed governor of the castle and left with seven hundred soldiers to guard the person of the king. Margaret, with courtesy, was escorted to her apartments at Edinburgh.[13]

Although Margaret was now stripped of even token authority, Albany remained ever-gracious to her and seemed to have no desire to trample further upon her dignity. He was not a malicious man. To avoid any question or suggestion of threat to the young king, Albany rarely went near him and never visited him alone. As a result Margaret, while not totally trusting the regent, at least tried to reach a certain agreement, a certain understanding with him. She had no other course. When Henry heard of Margaret's capitulation and seeming acceptance of the new government, the King of England was furious and informed Margaret in no uncertain terms of his displeasure. By releasing custody of her sons, Henry's plans to kidnap the boys were blasted. His hopes of seducing and subjugating Scotland were more impossible than ever. Rage and frustration poured from England, and Margaret could offer only vague assurance.

"Right excellent, right high, and mighty prince and dearest brother, I commend me unto you with all my heart. I have received your writing from Unicorn Herald, wherein you reproved me of certain things that I have done which is not to your pleasure. Verily, brother, I wrote to you as I found cause, and trust that I and my cousin the duke of Albany, governor, shall continue in that fashion, that unity and peace may persevere betwixt both the realms. It is ordained in this realm, with consent of the governor, in plane* parliament, that three lords which were most convenient therefor should have the charge and keeping of the king and his brother, my sons; which lords I consented to receive. Nevertheless I have presence of my children at my pleasure, and enter to them when ever I will.

"Brother, I am determined that I and my said cousin shall take one part, for I know it is most for my profit. Therefore I pray you send some wise man to see and know the state, and to make a sure way betwixt me and him, and write your letters to him thereupon to entreat me and my children honestly; for I know that he will do the better to me for your sake. And if I find otherwise, I shall advertise you by the said wise man that you shall send. My cousin, the king of France, has sent me writing by this bearer, and prays me that I will entreat and do my diligence to keep the peace betwixt the realms, the which I pray you to do in like wise for my request. Brother, I purpose, by the grace of God, to take my chamber and lie in my palace of Linlithgow within this twelve days, for I have not past eight weeks to my time; at the which I

* full

pray Jesu to send me good speed and happy deliverance, and to have you, dear brother, eternally in his keeping. At Edinburgh, the 20th of August."[14]

This reply did nothing to satisfy the King of England. He wanted Scotland, he wanted control of his nephews; and he decided that the best way to handle this new situation was to talk with Margaret in person. He consequently ordered Dacre to increase the border-burning, to continue to inflame the independent border chiefs to the distraction of Albany, and to work an escape for Margaret and her sons. These things he wanted immediately.

Dacre approached Hume with the plot, and the surly chieftain took the opportunity to war with Albany. He victualled his border stronghold at Flint Castle, roared and raged up and down the borders, drew Albany's men in pursuit, and disappeared over the English border. Whenever Albany's men withdrew, Hume would renew his maniacal revenge—even to the point of burning Flint, levelling its walls, and damming "up the well forevermore." Dacre had succeeded in drawing Hume into irrevocable alliance against Albany. The English Lord of the Marches then proceeded to harness Hume in a grand act of defiance against Albany—a rescue (or kidnapping) of Margaret. Together they plotted and seized upon the ambiguity of Margaret's "good speed and happy deliverance." On September 1 Dacre wrote to Margaret and asked her to change her place of lying-in from Linlithgow to Blacater near the English stronghold of Berwick.

Thus the basis of an escape plan was laid. In the meantime, Margaret apparently had certain misgivings about leaving Scotland at this particular moment. For her part she had established something of a working relationship with Albany. Although they did not totally trust each other, each was moving toward a sympathetic appreciation for the other's predicament. Albany, never captivated by the desire to rule, was already anxious to return to his wife and more comfortable life in France. He hinted that he would relinquish the government to Margaret and Angus once they ceased their pro-English bias. For Margaret such an idea was preposterous and impossible. She could not conceive of herself other than a daughter of England. On the other hand, severe restriction on her movements had eased, although she knew that any untoward action was looked upon with suspicion and reported by spies. If she were to leave Scotland, she would not only lose touch with events and give weight to the accusations of her enemies, but also remove the focal point of any pro-English sentiment. Moreover, she was pregnant. None of her pregnancies had been easy; indeed each had brought her near death. Yet she knew too that whatever aid Henry might offer would be more readily forthcoming if she herself might argue her case. Like all the Tudors, Margaret placed great faith in her persuasive powers and her own personal charm. After weighing all the choices, she decided to hazard all. She would flee to England; she would face her brother in his own court; she would kneel before him in irresistible plea; and he would send her home with arms, munitions, and soldiers to take again the government for her own.

By mid-September Margaret feigned illness and prepared to leave, ostensibly for Linlithgow. However, once on the road with Angus and a few servants, she met the chamberlain, Hume, with his "forty and well striking fellows." The party made a hell-bent ride for the border.

Once there Dacre allowed only Margaret into the stark and unaccommodating chambers of the castle. He wanted to offer no opportunity for reprisal or to allow Margaret any second thoughts. His plan to move her quickly southward was, however, interrupted. The fears of flight and capture, and the strenuous horseback ride through the silent days and dark nights brought on early and prolonged labor. Margaret was forced to her barren chamber, and there—poorly attended—gave birth to her daughter Margaret Douglas.

Seeing the birth as an event which brought him only inconvenience, Dacre refused to send a special messenger to Henry. Instead he wrote the following disdainful description of all that had transpired: "Please it your most noble Grace to know, that the third day next and immediately after the date of our Letters last sent unto your Highness by post, being the eighth day after that the Queen of Scots your sister came and entered into this your Realm, her Grace was delivered and brought in bed of a fair young Lady, and, with such convenient provisions as could or might be had in this barren and wild country, was christened the next day after; and everything done accordingly as appertained to the honor of the same, the sudden time, by God's provision so chanced, well considered. Glad would we have been to have ad-

vertised your said Highness of the Queen's said deliverance, but
our causes here were so entricked with much combersomeness and
business, as hereafter ensuing it doth appear, that we could not
ascertain your Highness of the same till this time, unless we
should have sent up a post purposely for the Queen's said deliverance, which we thought was not greatly requisite but if there
had been further matter touching your causes to have been sent
up unto your Highness. . . .

"Forasmuch as the Queen's lying here is uneaseful and costly,
by occasion of far carriage of everything, we be minded to move
her Grace to remove to Morpeth, as soon as conveniently she may
after her Grace have sought the Church and be purified. It may
like your Highness to signify your mind and pleasure unto her
said Grace how ye think ye will have her further to be ordered
that we may motion and move her accordingly.

"Sir Christopher Garneys came to Morpeth immediately upon
the Queen's deliverance and by our advice hath continued there
with such stuff as your Grace hath sent to the said Queen your
sister, till Sunday last past, which day he delivered your Letter,
and disclosed your credence, greatly to the Queen's comfort. And
for so much as the Queen lieth as yet in childbed, and shall keep
her chamber these three weeks at the least, we have advised the
said Sir Christopher Garneys to remain at Morpeth till the Queen
is coming thither.

"And then her Grace may order and prepare every part of the
said stuff after her pleasure, and as her Grace seemeth most convenient. And Almighty God have you our most dread Sovereign
Lord in his most blessed preservation. At Harbottle the xviiith
day of October."[15]

"The stuff" which Henry had sent his sister were costly fabrics
and twenty-two handsome robes and gowns with jewels and furnishings so that she might enter the kingdom in a manner befitting the sister of the King of England. They could not have
arrived at a better time. Margaret's physical health again hung in
delicate balance, and her mental health was scarcely better.
Wrenched by the twisting situations of the past two years, and
now scorched with fear at her break with Scotland, Margaret
Tudor writhed upon her bed of pain.

Sir Christopher Garneys remained with Margaret during those
days of anguish, and it was he alone who spoke of her with sympa-

thy. He wrote to Henry of Margaret: "I think her one of the lowest-brought ladies with her great pain in her right leg[16] that these three weeks she may not endure to sit up while her bed is a-making; and when her Grace is removed, it would pity any man's heart to hear her shrieks and cries that her Grace giveth." Upon hearing, however, of the rich gifts from Henry, Margaret had herself carried into the great chamber the better to see her presents and to exhibit them. "When she had seen everything, she bid the chamberlain [Hume] and the other gentlemen come and look at them; exclaiming, with an air of triumph, 'So my Lords, here ye may see that the King my brother hath not forgotten me, and that he would not I should die for lack of clothes!'"[17] Her estimation of herself was reckoned through Henry's estimation and the gifts he sent, and only underscored her lack of self-worth, her insecurity, her need to establish her own value in the eyes of others.

The dresses and shining fabrics symbolized what had been and the hope of what might come—the single bright moment in the dark days of pain. Little wonder that she called often for the gowns to be held before her eyes, to be placed in her hands. She was a tortured and lonely woman reaching out to the glories which ever seemed to escape her grasp.[18] It was a sad if not pathetic scene.

The pathos was compounded by those who knew what Margaret did not. No one had the courage to tell her that her favorite child, the infant Alexander Duke of Ross, had died December 18. Garneys wrote again: "If it comes to her knowledge, it will be fatal to her. These four or five days of her own mind it hath pleased her grace to show unto me how goodly a child her younger son is, and her grace praiseth him more than she doth the king her eldest son."[19] The news could not, of course, be kept from her indefinitely. When it came, her grief was so strong that it would be April before she could renew the journey southward.

In the meantime, when Albany heard of Margaret's escape, he quickly promised to restore her possessions and return Angus to favor. Margaret rejected both offers—she wanted the government. In her answer she demanded the custody and governance of her children. The council answered with scorn and heaped upon her their reasons: her right had died with James IV; Albany had been appointed with her consent; her second marriage had forfeited custody of the children.[20] Albany, however, pleaded with many persons for Margaret's return. He wrote to her sister, Mary the French Queen, to the Duke of Suffolk, to the Archbishop of York, and to the King of England.[21] But peace was not part of the English plan, and Albany's letters were in vain.

Margaret's behavior was for the Scots impossible to understand. One chronicler, for instance, wrote: "To league herself . . . with England, against the independence of that country of which her son was sovereign, whilst Albany, with much earnestness and sincerity, offered her a complete restoration to all those rights and revenues, as queen-dowager, which she had not forfeited by her marriage, was an excess of blindness and pertinacity difficult to be understood. . . ."[22]

Based upon many of the facts of Margaret's behavior, the Scots' assessment was understandable. The flaming notoriety of her sudden marriage to Angus and the impetuous flight from Scotland were foolish acts. Her so-called intrigues with England smacked of treason from the Scots' point of view. But her letter to Henry, indicating resignation to her fate and reconciliation with the new government of Albany was signed in accordance with the prearranged code—the closing of "Your loving sister." That letter must be accepted as a valid statement of Margaret's assessment of her situation and a true expression of her feeling. Then she was called to England, and she went. It was as though Margaret was unable to separate her role as a woman from her role as queen. She could separate neither from her Englishness and the mission to which her father had assigned her.

Margaret's weakness lay in the fact that she was never secure in what she was or perhaps even in what she wanted to be. And there was no one who would help her to that understanding. Her brother sought to use her and, through her, to dominate her kingdom. He wanted her dependent on him. Her council, that rough-knuckled group of swaggering, ambitious chieftains, feared a strong monarchy because it limited their own self-centered interests. Their general hatred of England surpassed only their hatred of each other. They could not and would not subordinate themselves to any but the strongest of kings. They had no intention of subordinating themselves to a queen—especially one of English birth. Consequently Margaret's policies floundered whichever way she went; for she defined herself in terms of the men she knew, never in terms of her own.

That lack of definition had forced Margaret into the arms of Angus and his private ambitions. Now that husband and wife had come to the brink of disaster, the husband had all but completely disappeared. Throughout the months of Margaret's confinement and recuperation, Angus had spent much of his time dodging about the borders, toying with a reconciliation with Albany, and coming only occasionally to Morpeth to visit. It was apparent to most observers, and gradually apparent to Margaret, that the "Earl of Anguish," as the English called him, came to visit his new daughter rather than his ailing wife. He was having second thoughts about self-imposed exile in England. By spring he had changed his mind; he had made his peace with Albany and fallen in love with a young woman, Lady Jane Stuart of Traquair, to whom he had once been betrothed. He turned his back on England and Margaret "like unto the nature of his Country," reported the London chronicler, "and went home again into Scotland taking no love. . . ."[23] The man for whom Margaret had chanced and lost her crown, her throne, her children, and her heart, had left her. He had stolen away to make his peace with her enemies. Margaret was left with her anger, her injured pride, and her chagrin at meeting Henry and his court as a deserted woman.

In the last days at Morpeth, there were surely moments when Margaret reconsidered her own course. The petitions from Albany grew increasingly persuasive and attractive. Perhaps she had been wrong to flee; perhaps Albany would be true to his word—he had always treated her well. Only at the insistence of his council did he ever appear harsh. And though Angus now was gone, perhaps she could persuade him to return, to come back to her. Then too there was the young James, her only son; would she ever see him again? He needed her protection and vigilance more than ever now that Alexander was dead. Dacre, her guardian, watched her growing confusion and wrote: ". . . for by occasion of the daily messengers that come to her out of Scotland, she is troubled at some times in her mind, and put in study to imagine and cast what . . . is best for to do."[24] As a result, he dictated her letters to Scotland and succeeded in widening rather than healing the many ruptures. He was anxious to complete the already lengthy mission.

Margaret had not been the easiest houseguest and had been an even more impossible patient: "Her long confinement has destroyed her appetite, nor at any time heretofore would she take coleses, morterons, almond milk, good broths, pottages, or boiled meats, but only roast meat with jellies, and that very scantily."[25] Dacre urged—he insisted—that she go; he played upon her promise to Henry, and in April he placed her on the road to London.

Although there was little of the fanfare and pageantry that marked the long-ago trip northward, Margaret's return to London was not unpleasant. The gifts of her brother made her handsome and elegant. The kindly welcomes of villages and cities made her proud and helped to remind her that there were many who beheld her with awe. On April 27, she joyously wrote to Henry from Stony Stratford: "Dearest brother, as heartily as I can I recommend me unto you, and let you know that yesternight I came hither, so being comforted of you in my journey in many and sundry wises that, loving be to our Lord God, I am in right good health, and as joyous of my said journey toward you as any woman may be in coming to her brother, as I have great cause, and to have sight of your person, in whom next God, is mine only trust and confidence. . . ."[26]

On the third of May, the long-awaited day came. Margaret entered London on Catherine of Aragon's white palfrey. At Tottenham she was greeted by Henry VIII, no longer the boy to whom she had said good-bye thirteen years ago. He was handsome, virile, magnificent, in the prime of his manhood. Together they rode through the streets of London with a vast host of ladies and gentlemen of rank. The city had not changed; to Margaret it was still as lovely as when the Scots poet, who had helped to lead her northward so long ago, had written:

> Strong be the walls that above thee stands
>   Wise be the people that within thee dwells;
> Fresh be thy river with his lusty strands;
>   Blythe be thy churches, well sounding be thy bells;
>   Rich be thy merchants in substance that excells;
> Fair be thy wives, right lovesome, white and small;
>   Clear be thy virgins, lusty under kellis[a]
> London, thou art the flower of cities all.[27]

[a] gowns

The city glittered in the light of the spring day and sang its welcome from every spire—how different from the darksome gloom left behind in Edinburgh. And as Margaret was led to her apartments at Baynard's Castle on the banks of the swan-thronged Thames, she must have felt great pleasure in this so fine a home-coming. From there she took a barge richly hung with banners of England and Scotland, and musicians sang her way past London and down to Greenwich.

The songs of men and birds reverberated through the lush parks of lovely Greenwich; only happiness filled this favorite home of the Tudors so rich with childhood memories. It was a fitting place for reunion between the two sisters, Mary and Margaret, and their childhood friend Catherine of Aragon. None of them had expected this reunion. Royal brides rarely returned home. But reunion was not the only cause for joy. It had been also a year for royal births, and the nursery was filled with Tudor infants. The oldest was Margaret's little daughter, on whom Henry immediately bestowed his affection and nicknamed Marget. The youngest infant, not yet two months old, was little Henry Suffolk.

Born March 11 at Wolsey's estate of Bath Place, young Suffolk's christening at Suffolk Place had been nothing less than an affair of state. Amidst the exquisite pageantry of the sixteenth century, with chambers hung in tapestry and gold, the infant was baptized in the presence of his godmother, Lady Catherine—daughter of King Edward IV and sister of Elizabeth of York—and his godfathers Wolsey and Henry VIII, who gave the child his name. Among his christening gifts were cups of gold, flagons of gold and silver, pots of silver and gilt—gifts fit for a prince. And great was the speculation at the grandeur of the ceremony and the affection and love of his kingly uncle. If Henry were to have no sons, perhaps this little Henry would become his heir.[28]

The third infant of the royal nursery was the daughter of Henry VIII and Catherine of Aragon. After so many miscarriages, so many stillbirths, the king and queen produced a child who would live. This child of necessity was born February 18, 1516, and was named for her aunt—Mary.

Henry's joy at the birth of his daughter, while diminished because she was not a boy, was heightened by the fact that she was living proof of his own virility and Catherine's fertility. He was confident now that time would bring him sons, and he rejoiced. His personality was so strong that when the king rejoiced, the nation rejoiced. And this year of royal births seemed to epitomize the springtime with its glorious excess and its promise of hope. To manifest his feelings and to celebrate the coming of the Queen of Scots, the King of England ordered tournaments—his favorite pastime. And he summarized his philosophy in one of his frequent outbursts of poetic ejaculation:

> Pastime with good company
> I love and shall until I die;
> Grudge who will, but none deny,
> So God be pleased, this life will I
>   For my pastance,
>   Hunt, sing, and dance,
>   My heart is set;
>   All goodly sport
>   To my comfort;
>   Who shall me let?*[29]

On May 19 and 20, Henry, Suffolk, the Earl of Essex, and Nicholas Carew challenged all comers. As they stood in the lists, richly harnessed and dressed in black velvet embroidered with gold branches of honeysuckle with "every leaf of the branches moving," they were marvelous to behold. Once the battles began "every man did well, but the king did best." The second day was finer than the first, and "the king and his aides . . . ran *volant* at all comers, which was pleasant to see," and all was in honor of Margaret. It was splendid to be reminded of the glories of a princess, of a queen. It was grand to be appreciated and adored. And it all made Scotland seem very distant indeed.[30]

Such tourneys, pageants, and stagings were expensive, however, and Henry asked Wolsey—now Cardinal of York and the Lord Chancellor of England—to look to the accounts.[31] Among those whose indebtedness to the king seemed ever to increase was Suffolk, although both he and Mary had made extensive efforts to meet their financial pledge. They paid what they could, but it was

* hinder me

never enough. When at court, their obligations always increased, for they were charged for their expenses and those of their entourage. Even the tourney, itself a command performance, gouged still further into the Suffolk resources. In order to control rising debt and to gather past due revenues, Suffolk and Mary retired from court and went to their country retreats.

Margaret took up temporary residence at Baynard's Castle and later moved into Scotland Yard, the ancient residence of the kings of Scotland who visited England. Henry, in the meantime, "in flame and fury" sent letters, petitions, and directions to the lords of Scotland urging the cause of his sister and the interests of his nephew. Those interests were, of course, those which coincided with his. He ordered that his letters be placed before the Council of Scotland and "that, laying all their heads together, they deprive the Governor of all authority, and banish him from the Realm." The council rejected the "foul scheme" and righteously declared that it was treason to James V and "perdition and dishonor of all the Realm."[32] Moreover both Angus and Hume had made their peace—at least for the moment—with Albany. Disgusted with this latest turn of events, Henry encouraged Dacre to a renewal and intensification of border warfare. Dacre was happy to be about his bloody business, and with joy in his heart he wrote to Henry: "I labor and study all that I can to make division and debate, to the entent that if the Duke will not apply himself, that then that debate may grow that it shall be impossible to him to do justice: and for that intended purpose in that behalf I have the Master of Kilmawers kept in my house secretly, which is one of the greatest parties in Costland. . . . And also I have secret messages from the earl of Angus and others, which I trust shall be to the pleasure of the King's Grace if the said Duke apply not himself; and also hath cccc.[th] outlaws (and giveth them rewards) that burneth and destroyeth daily in Scotland; all being Scots men which should be under the obeisance of Scotland. . . ."[33]

As event piled upon event, Margaret found that a return to Scotland with dignity, let alone authority, was nearly impossible. Nor did she feel totally at ease in England. Once the festivals of reception ended, Henry's warmth and brotherly compassion seemed to dissipate. He refused to give his sister any reliable income and her revenues from Scotland were anything but dependable. The Queen of Scotland found herself in no less a position than that of a poor relation. She and Henry were too much alike in personality, too imperious, too fiery in temper, too anxious to assert themselves, to be long on friendly or close terms. Moreover, Margaret had not even the advantage of the appearance of youth or beauty. Seven pregnancies and the trials of living had left her stout, dumpy, and prematurely old at age twenty-seven. In short, Henry did not urge her presence at court and began to wonder at the vast expense of keeping her in England.

Summer turned to autumn, and autumn to winter, and Margaret found her situation increasingly precarious. As Christmas neared, her situation became more intolerable. Unable to get from Henry necessary monies, Margaret wrote to Wolsey: "I commend me to you, and know [how] that I have spoken to you, and caused master Magnus to speak to you, for some money to me. My lord, I am very sorry to put the king's grace to so great cost and charges as I do, howbeit that I have been in times past, I shall not be so in time to come; nevertheless I think I should be like his sister, to his honor and mine. Now, my lord, you know the time of Christmas is near, and part of things I will need both to me and my servants, and I trust to get part of [my] money out of Scotland, for you may see they are owing much, and say they will cause me to be paid, which, if it be not, I have as great wrong as is possible; but my trust is that the king's grace my brother will see me have reason, and therefore I pray you my lord to let me borrow so much as 200 £. English, and I shall give you a writing of mine own hand, to cause my lord Dacre to take off as much of mine of the first that is gotten now, and I shall trouble you no more for no money, for I trust to get mine own, and I shall do the best I can with it. I pray you heartily my lord to put me off no longer, for the time is short, and if you will do so much for me at this time, I pray you send me word, for I will trouble you no more with my sending, for then I will speak to the king my brother, for I trust his [grace] will do so much for me and trust me for a greater thing. As our Lord knoweth, whom keep you."[34]

One begging letter was not enough. Margaret was forced by circumstance to write again to Wolsey: "My Lord Cardinal I commend me to you, and I would fain have spoken with you but ye were gone ere I could come to you and therefore I must write to you my mind. My Lord, I beseech you to show your good mind to me, as ye have done ever, but specially now, for now is the time. My Lord, I pray you heartily to get me some money against New Year Day for ye know well I must give part of rewards and other needful things both for the king my brother's honor and mine: and I shall not put you to no more trouble but I beseech you heartily my Lord that I may have it tomorrow at night at the farest: for else I will be disappointed. But I put my whole trust in you, and this bearer shall wait upon you for your answer as our Lord knoweth whom keep you."[35]

Henry, however, had no hesitation in spending money for his own Christmas entertainments. Provoked by vanity rather than affection, he invited Margaret to the Twelfth Night festival at Greenwich Palace. After banqueting to the point of bursting, the king and queen and Margaret seated themselves in the Great Hall. The doors flew open and in rolled an artificial garden—the Garden of *Esperance*. Towered at every corner, the garden was railed with bars of gilt. Its banks "were set with flowers . . . of silk and gold, the leaves cut of green satin, so that they seemed very flowers. In the midst of this Garden was a pillar of antique work, all gold set with pearl and stone, and on the top of the pillar, which was six square, was . . . an arch . . . crowned with gold; within which stood a bush of Roses red and white, all of silk and gold. . . . In this garden walked six knights and six ladies richly apparelled, and then they descended and danced many goodly dances, and so ascended the garden again, and were conveyed out of the hall."[36]

The splendor, the extravagance, the sheer magnificence of it all was enough to make the heart of the Queen of Scots ache. Despite all that ostentatious display of wealth, her "dearest brother" could spare nothing for her. When the banquet renewed itself and the two hundred dishes began to pass, Margaret found each delicacy salted with bitterness.

Notably absent from the Christmas festival were the Suffolks. They too were out of favor, and the problem was again one of money. Saddled with tournament and christening expenses, Suffolk was now twelve thousand pounds in debt to the king, and invitations to come to court stopped. Earlier in the year, while on progress, Henry had condescended to stop at one of Suffolk's manors at Donyngton; and after much correspondence, he had been gracious enough to allow the master of the house into the

kingly presence. Although the visit was of huge expense to the
duke and his wife, Mary wrote to thank Henry for his attention:
"My most dearest right entirely beloved lord and brother,—In my
most humble wise I recommend me unto your Grace, showing
unto your Grace that I do p[erceive] by my lord and husband
that you are pleased and contented that he shall resort unto your
presence, at such time as your Grace shall be at his manor of
Donyngton, whereby I see well that he is marvellously rejoiced
and much comforted that it hath liked your Grace so to be pleased,
for the which your special goodness to him, showed in that behalf, and for sundry and many other your kindness, as well to me
as to him, showed and given in divers causes, I most humbly thank
your Grace, assuring you that for the same I account myself as
much bounden unto your Grace as ever sister was to brother, and
according thereunto I shall to the best of my power during my life
endeavor myself as far as in me shall be possible, to do the thing
that shall stand with your pleasure.

"And if it had been time convenient and your Grace had been
therewith pleased I would most gladly have accompanied my said
lord in this journey. But I trust that both I and my said lord shall
see you, according as your Grace wrote in your last letters unto my
said lord, which is the thing that I desire more to obtain than all
the honor of the world. And thus I beseech our Lord to send unto
you, my most dearest and entirely beloved brother and lord, long
and prosperous life with the full accomplishment of all your honorable desires, most humbly praying your Grace that I may be
humbly recommended unto my most dearest and best beloved
sister, the Queen's Grace, and to the Queen of Scots, my well
beloved sister, trusting that [I?] be ascertained from your Grace
of the prosperous estate and health of my dearly beloved n[iece]
the princess, to whom I pray God send long life."[37]

Since the royal visit, however, the Suffolks had been ignored by
their patron and kinsman. And royal dismissals did not go un-
noticed. By the new year, Suffolk found himself harassed by cred-
itors large and small, by royalty and the lesser nobility. In
February he journeyed alone to London to meet with Wolsey and
review the financial morass. Henry remained aloof, sent no word
of invitation, and Suffolk felt compelled to write his master: "Sir,
—In the most humble wise I commend me to your Grace. And,
Sir, so was it at the last time I was with your Grace I went through

with my lord Cardinal for such debts as the Queen your sister and I are in to your Grace, for the which it was thought by your Grace's Council learned that your sister and I both must confer divers things before your judges according unto the law.

"And, Sir, I beseech you that she may come up to the intent that she may do all such acts, according as be devised or shall be devised most for your Grace's surety, to the intent that whatsoever shall happen of me that your Grace may be in surety, and that it shall not be said but it is her deed and free will the which your Grace shall well perceive that it is done with good mind and heart. And, Sir, the coming up of her to see your Grace shall rejoice her more than the value of that if it should be given to her. Sir, it is so that I have heard by my lord Morley and others that your Grace intends to have some pastime this May and that your Grace's pleasure is that I shall give mine attendance on your Grace, the which I shall be as glad to do as any poor servant or subject that your Grace has living. Howbeit, Sir, I am somewhat unprovided of such things as belong to that business, wherefore if it may stand with your Grace's pleasure I would bring up the Queen, your sister, against Easter to both plays, and then remain till she and I may know your Grace's further pleasure, to the which she and I shall obey with humble heart, according to her duty and mine. As knows God, who preserve your Grace in long life with as much health and honor as your noble heart can desire, which is both her and my daily prayer."[38]

The letter was followed by Mary's payment in jewels to the value of one thousand pounds as the first of seemingly endless installments.[39] With this in hand, the royal demands eased, and subtle signs of forgiveness began to appear. Queen Catherine, pregnant once again, travelled to the shrine of Our Lady of Walsingham to pray for a son. The queen interrupted her journey to visit the Suffolks. It was a happy visit, and Catherine assured her friends that they would soon be called again to court. They must be patient; Henry held no grievance, but the council's opposition to Suffolk remained. The king was doing the best for all by seeming to withhold his favor. Patience was the Queen of England's counsel; indeed it was her watchword, her way of life. By May, Henry would call them to court. The queen left to pray for the son who never came, and the Suffolks remained behind and prayed that the days would not be long before Henry called them into his presence. The royal silence, however, did not break until spring.

By then there was a worse, more sinister fear—an outburst of the sweating sickness swept through England. With the warming of the days, the open sewers of cities and towns proved fertile breeding ground for the infection which emptied villages and left no one to bury the dead. Infection bred infection, and nobleman and commoner alike sought the fresh air of the countryside. Henry swiftly moved his court from place to place. Even so, his pages of the royal bedchamber itself were seized by the fever, suffered wracking pain, sweated away their life juices, and died within eight hours.[40] The plague would continue to rage, abating only in the colder months, for nearly a year.

As fearful as Henry was of the sickness, neither his disposition nor his desires would allow him to forgo his own love of grandeur and magnificent display. In the spring he moved his court back to London for a carefully staged demonstration of the royal magnanimity.

On St. George's Day, the king gathered his court about him. Before him stood the prodigal apprentices of London who had risen against their masters. The prisoners—each with a halter about his neck—were brought in solemn procession to their king. Henry sternly rebuked each man and boy and spoke as a wise, judicious patriarch. His lecture continued; it rolled and swirled in splendid tones over the kneeling prisoners. The king's voice was majestic, rhetorical, raising the question of duty and obedience until suddenly three women threw themselves at his feet. Kneeling before him were the three queens of his family—Catherine of England, Mary of France, and Margaret of Scotland. In one voice they pled for mercy, they petitioned for pardon of the wretched boys. Their prayer was irresistible. In sweeping gesture, Henry capitulated. He could sentence, but he chose to pardon. The hall erupted in prayers and huzzahs of thanksgiving as the forty men and boys ripped away the halters and grabbed each other in impromptu dance.[41]

When the scenario played to an end, it marked the end too of the reunion of the Tudor sisters and brother. As Henry gathered his current favorites and rode laughingly into the countryside to escape the stench of plague, Mary returned to her role of wife and mother. By mid-July she would again have a child—Frances

named for the saint on whose day she was born. Although both
Queen Catherine and her infant daughter, Princess Mary, were
named godmothers, neither attended the christening. Instead they
sent two proxies, one of whom was the queen's waiting woman—
Lady Anne Boleyn.[42]

In the meantime, Margaret had grown weary of her role as poor
relation. In matters financial, Henry had never yielded, and Margaret's revenues from Scotland were still undependable. Moreover
Henry's supercilious attentions to her made it patently clear that
he was bored by her needs, her problems, and her very presence.
Since writing letters and sending messengers were less expensive
than keeping Margaret at court, Henry had not totally ignored his
sister's political situation. In March he had formed a new treaty
with Scotland which opened the door to Margaret's return. It was
time for Margaret to return to her unwanted home. Not welcome
in either country, with few friends in either place, she really had
nowhere to go. But to stay longer in England she knew was impossible. On May 18 she left Baynard's Castle for the last time and
carried with her manifestations of Henry's goodwill. Perhaps out
of relief over his sister's departure, or perhaps out of fear that her
impecunious state would cast a derogatory reflection across his
own image, Henry heaped rich gifts upon the departing Margaret.
In addition to gowns and robes, he gave her jewels and plate,
tapestries and cloths of arras, monies, horses—in short, all things
necessary for the long trip home.[43]

By the first of June, Margaret reached York and received not
only hearty welcome but welcome news. Albany had left Scotland
in the charge of the archbishops of St. Andrews and Glasgow and
the earls of Huntley, Arran, and Angus. As for Albany, he was
finally on his way to France, relieved to be free from the impossible problems of Scotland. Upon hearing of his departure, Margaret immediately sat down, seized her prolific pen and wrote to
Henry: "In my most humble wise I can I recommend me to your
grace. Pleaseth you to wit* that upon Tuesday, Canter came to
me to York from the duke of Albany, with writings which I send
to your grace, the very copy word by word, because I keep his
letter myself; and he hath sent writings to your grace to show you

* understand

of his departing out of Scotland, and that the council of Scotland would not suffer him to pass through England, as your grace will perceive by his writings.

"Howbeit methinks he has taken this purpose very hastily, for I know well he thought it not within this short while. But I may thank your grace and no other, or else it had not been; beseeching your grace as humbly as I can, now, since he doth depart, to look well upon it for my surety and that he may not come to trouble me after, as my special trust is in your grace, for he proposeth to come again into Scotland. Sir, I am sure the duke hath written to your grace how he hath ordered everything now at his departing, and what persons shall have the rule, both the wardens of the borders, and within the realm, or else I would have written all at length. For he hath sent me word of everything, and how I shall be received into Scotland, and how I shall be answered of my conjunct feoffment, as is made between your grace and him, with the council of Scotland.

"Howbeit I will be plain to your grace if you will not be displeased, for I say it not for no displeasure to your council, for I think they know not that I know in this matter. Sir, your grace knoweth it is concluded between your council and Scotland that I shall have all that I have right to pertaining to me, with one clause in it, that is, I giving again it that I have pertaining to my son, not declaring plainly what it is; which may be hurt to me in time coming, for the king my husband, whose soul God pardon, ere he went to the field [of Flodden], gave me a letter of his hand, commanding to deliver me 18,000 crowns of weight, that the French king did send; which was without the council of Scotland's consent. And also they may claim any other things that I have that the king my husband gave me, which were wrong. And I spent the most part of it ere I came to your grace, for I was not answered of my living since the field, to hold my house with. And, therefore, I beseech your grace to command my lord Dacre to see a sure way for me and master Magnus, ere I go in.

"But now the duke goeth away, I set not much by the remnant that is behind: for I know them and their conditions; with fear that they have of your grace they will be glad to please me. I desire this to be done in adventure that the duke come again, that I be not troubled with him. I would not show this to none but to your grace, beseeching your grace to continue good and kind

brother to me, as you have been ever, and that I may hear from
your grace; which will be to my great comfort, as God knoweth,
whom preserve you. Written at York the 3rd day of June.

"Sir,—Since I ended this letter, Canter, this bearer, said to me
in the duke's name, that he prayed me to write to your grace that
the peace might be continued longer than Saint Andrew's Day.
Sir, I trust you do remember that I spake to your grace when I
went to Windsor this last time, that it should not be long continued without my desire, for causes,—but do to me as your grace
thinks best for me, so that I may know it before him when it is
continued, so that I may have thanks of Scotland."[44]

The truth was that Margaret, in the frantic days following
Flodden Field, had absconded with the national treasury of Scotland. No doubt she had meant to secure it for her son's government. But the days had not been easy, the years had been long,
her revenues had not been forthcoming, her needs both political
and private had been persistent, and little by little the treasure
had dribbled away. Always before, she had managed to dodge the
embarrassing issue. Indeed in the early days of regency none but
James IV, Francis as Duke of Valois and Count of Angoulême, and
Margaret had known of its existence. Now Scotland knew, and it
was best that Henry know. Sitting at her writing table at York,
amidst the trappings of her estate, Margaret could only worry and
wonder at the new floodgate of dangers that waited the other side
of the border to engulf her. Yet she must go home; there was
nowhere else.

Slowly, reluctantly, she renewed her journey. Once at the border, she loitered away her days. The ravages of war, the scars of
Dacre's outrages and those of his Scots outlaws were everywhere.
The land was scorched, houses and barns, ricks and cribs lay in
broken ruin. Magnus, Henry's agent, encouraged her onward, but
he was forced to write the English king: "Her Grace considereth
now the honor of England, and the poverty and wretchedness of
Scotland, which she did not afore, but in her opinion esteemed
Scotland equal to England."[45] But Scotland was not England. It
lacked England's political stability, its loyalties to the crown, its
great wealth. In England eighteen thousand pounds would supply
an evening's entertainment; in Scotland, it might prove to be
worth all that life might hold for her.

At Berwick Castle, Angus came out to meet his wife. He was all humility, filled with ingratiating and winning phrases. He seemed happy to take her home, and Margaret seemed willing enough to go. She did not know, however, of his continuing affair with the Lady Jane Stuart of Traquair.

So Margaret Tudor Queen Dowager of Scotland reentered the land she could never love and rode by the side of the man who could never love her. At Edinburgh she was cordially received by commons and nobles alike. But in no way was her authority restored, and she found her influence even less than it had been before.

Of Margaret's old allies, only Angus remained in power. Hume had been attainted by parliament, then restored briefly to favor. His duplicity and that of his enemies, however, had eventually led him to the block. Hume's head had been placed on the Tolbooth of Edinburgh, and birds of prey had eaten away the rotting flesh. In revenge, Hume's clan trapped in a bog the agent of Albany and the ambassador of France, the accomplished de la Bastie. He too was executed and his head tied by its hair to the saddle of George Hume. When word reached France, Francis I was infuriated and demanded execution of the Humes. The Scots parliament immediately declared all of the Humes outlaws, their goods attainted, their holdings forfeited. Some were caught, some fled into England, but they would never again be of help to Margaret and her passion for power.[46]

THE
FINAL YEARS

CHAPTER SEVEN

Dearest brother the king,

In my most humble wise I can I recommend me to your grace, desiring greatly to hear of your good health and prosperity, which would be to my great comfort. And if it please your grace to wit* how the king my son, your nephew, he is in good health, I thank God. As touching to myself, if it please your grace to wit how I am done to since my departing from you, it hath been very evil; howbeit, I was very loath to trouble your grace, and would not while I may no further that I see. I can get no reason, for I am not answered nor obeyed of my living, whereof I have not gotten two thousand pounds of Scotch money since my departing from your grace, which should be every year to me nine thousand pounds, and this is not to me to live in honor, like your sister, nor like myself; which I beseech your grace to look well upon, and give no more credence to the fair words of the lords of Scotland, for it is to none effect.

And, as for me, I have put off so long that I must give my jewels and such things as I got from your grace, for fault that I have nothing to spend, which will be great dishonor to me, and no honor to your grace, for I have no other to help me but you. And now it stands to me upon this point, I beseech your grace to help me, and to give me license to come into your realm; or else I will be put to the point to give my living at the pleasure of the duke and the lords, and they to give what they please, which would be of little value to me. And please your grace to remember, the last writing I got from you, you bade me that I should not give over my conjunct feoffment for a sum of money, which I have

* know

kept. And your grace knows that you may of reason cause the ships of Scotland to be taken, and the goods in them, when they fail me that I be not answered; which I have suffered too long, considering that your grace hath forborne so long to do any evil, and I am nought the better.

Dearest brother the king, I trust your grace will not let me be overrun; and I wit well I will never get good of Scotland or fairness, nor I will never with my will bide here with them that I know well loves me not, which proves daily; and therefore do to me as ever your grace will, for all my weal is in your hands. Also please you to wit that I am sore troubled with my lord of Angus since my last coming into Scotland, and every day more and more, so that we have not been together this half-year. Please your grace to remember that, at my coming now into Scotland, my lord Dacre and master Magnus made a writing betwixt me and my lord of Angus, for the surety of me, that he might not have no power to put away nothing of my conjunct feoffment without my will, which he hath not kept.

And the bishop of Dunkeld, his father's brother, and others his kinsmen, caused my lord of Angus to deal right sharply with me, to cause me to break the bond that he made to me, which I would not do; and upon that he went and took up it that I live upon, and would not let none answer to me, and took my house of the new work, within the forest of Ettrick, which should be in the year to me four thousand marks, and I get never a penny; with much more evil that I shall cause a servant of mine to show your grace, which is too long to write.

And I am so minded that, if I may by law of God and to my honor, to part with him, for I wit well he loves me not, as he showeth to me daily. Wherefore I beseech your grace, when it comes to that point, as I trust it shall, to be a kind prince and brother to me; for I shall never marry but where you will bid me, nor never to part from your grace, for I will never with my will abide into Scotland: and to send me your pleasure, and what your grace will do to me, for all my hope and trust is in your grace. I durst not send by land to your grace, for such causes as I shall cause you to understand, and I beseech your grace to write me your mind with this bearer, and God preserve you. At Edinburgh.

Your humble sister,
Margaret.[1]

In spite of the multiple promises of the Council of Scotland and of the conciliatory greetings of Angus, Margaret's plight in Scotland was more hopeless than ever. Whatever control she had once wielded over her husband had, in her absence, totally dissipated. He had learned to live without her and now was determined to rule in spite of her. Archibald Douglas Sixth Earl of Angus was no longer the impetuous youth who had been urged by a determined grandfather into the seemingly powerful marriage with the Queen of Scots. Now Angus was a man more confident in his own abilities, ambitious in his own right, and powerful enough to bring his dreams to fruition. He considered himself the sole head of the pro-English faction in Scotland. The power of his family and the strength of his following gave him the necessary impetus so that few could challenge his authority. Moreover, he was in love with the fair Lady Jane Stuart of Traquair, and he lived openly with her on the estates of his wife and supported the mistress on the revenues of the queen.

Margaret was both hurt and angered by such insolence. As a girl, she had been forced to accept the infidelities of James IV. She had then had no choice. But to accept such insult from a subject was beyond any Tudor's comprehension. Her royal blood boiled; it raged in torrents of stinging verbiage and fits of hysteria. By the time it settled to a simmer, her course was determined. She would have a divorce. She would sue to Rome, petition the pope, have her brother and his agents write in her behalf, and she would have her divorce.

Henry VIII was appalled by this latest foolishness of his most untoward sister. For weeks he could not bring himself to consider so sacrilegious an act. He turned to his wife Catherine for consolation; together they were scandalized. How dare Margaret besmirch the house of Tudor? How could she bring infamy upon herself? He urged her to remember ". . . the divine ordinance of inseparable matrimony, first instituted in Paradise. . . ." He ordered his wayward sister to "return to God's word and the lively doctrines of Jesus Christ . . . for ye are yet carnal. . . ."[2] He denounced her ideas as ". . . wicked delusions, inspired by the father of evil, whose malice alone could prompt you to leave your husband, Lord Angus, or unnaturally to stigmatize the fair daughter you had by him."[3] These and other letters of self-righteous indignation, consternation and remonstration poured from the pens of Henry, Catherine, and Wolsey, and fearing that the written word was not enough, they sent priests as messengers and counsellors. This heavy bombardment of chastisement brought temporary reconciliation. Angus wrote letters of contrition and thanksgiving to Henry, tolerated Margaret's beratings, and went home to her estates and the more consoling arms of his mistress.[4]

Margaret listened to the upbraidings and wondered that her brother should show such concern for her immortal soul and so little for her earthly needs. In the midst of the flurry of correspondence nothing was said of her rents, her revenues, or how she should sustain herself in the manner in which she had been trained and that tradition demanded.

In spite of Angus' token reconciliation, he would not share his new resources—his money, his power, or, for that matter, his heart or his custody of the young king. He simply did not need Margaret any more. She, on the other hand, had great needs which she could never fill alone. Neither Henry nor Angus seemed willing or able to answer her particular demands. So with the full force of Tudor impetuosity, Margaret turned to the pro-French party in Scotland. First she made overtures to the Earl of Arran, kinsman to the king; then she wrote fervent letters to Albany, asking him to come home. Albany responded in warm, glowing terms. He not only welcomed Margaret, but he also offered her control of the government with the consent of council. Margaret returned his compliments, urged him home, and added that she had always been satisfied with his government.

When news of this latest coalition reached Henry, the royal hands flew up in frustration, anger, and dismay. He and Wolsey were fighting to keep Albany in France on the thesis that Scotland could never unify without him, that the country would continue to rot from within, and that internecine wars would finally destroy even fragmentary leadership. Neither Henry nor Wolsey believed that Margaret could not be persuaded from this latest of what they considered a long series of foolish acts. They decided to turn over the business of persuasion to Dacre. The desolation of Scotland had, after all, been his long-cherished dream. He thrived on the ruin he had wrought and on the fires yet to burn, the churches, homes, villages yet to be levelled, the people yet to be robbed and slaughtered.

In letters more fitting an equal than a subject, Dacre raged at

Margaret, reminded her of Henry's good feeling and bountiful aid, accused Albany of murdering the child Alexander, threatened Margaret with the heavy displeasure of English arms, and called her traitor to the policies and treaties of her native land.[5] As the Queen of Scots penned her own reply to these harsh and bitter accusations, she exercised a restraint that was surprising. No Tudor brooked defiance from subordinates. Yet she went to certain length to explain her course to Dacre and knew full well her explanations would be repeated in the court of England if not in France. She wrote:

"My lord Dacre, I commend me heartily to you, and wit* ye that I have received your writing from John Simpson your servant and understand it at length; and where ye remember me in your writing of my labor and desire made unto the King's Grace my brother, and to my lord Cardinal, and their Council, upon sundry considerations to them declared, and specially for the weal and surety of the King my Son, and for the recovering of my authority of this Realm and Tutrixship of the King my Son, according to the testament of the King my husband; and that the Duke of Albany then being in Scotland should be removed into France again, and not return into Scotland.

"My lord, all that I did there I thought for the best, as the King's Grace my brother and his Council knows; for I trusted that the Lords of this realm and I should have agreed well, and I to have broukyt† peaceably my own as they are bound to do by their writings and seals; and then they might not have no cause to excuse them to the duke.

"Howbeit I am not the better, for I was never so evil answered nor obeyed of my lands as I am since my last coming into Scotland, as I have often times written both to the King my brother, and to my lord Cardinal, and You. Howbeit I got no remedy, and I did show you, my Lord, in my writings, that I did write to you which ye have, that if I got not shortly help that I must do what the Duke and the Lords of this realm will have me to do; for I have none here that will help me of my complaint, nor do me justice; so that I may not live to my honor; if my living is here, I must cast me to please this realm.

* let you understand   † abided by

"Also, my Lord, where ye write to me to know if I have sent any writing to the King of France for the furthering of the Duke of Albany's coming into Scotland, my Lord there was a letter written into France to the King of France from me by the special desire of the Duke and the Lords, which I might not deny; for they said it was for the weal of the King my Son and his Realm; my Lord, I pray you remember that if ye were in another Realm where ye should live your life, ye would do that ye might to please them so that they should not have any mistrust of you; and so must I, for if I should refuse to have written when I was desired, the Duke and the Lords would have thought that I had stopped his coming, and there through I might get evil; and thus I trust my lord that the King's Grace my brother, and my lord Cardinal, will remember as I stand in this realm. And in last writing that I had from the King my brother he commanded that I should do nothing that the Lords might have any occasion to complain of me, which I trust I have done.

"My Lord, I pray you to remember that I did write to you, I was at such a point that I must a-layd* my jewels for fault of money, for I am not answered of no part of my living; and had [it] not been [for] the Comptroller Robert Barton I had been shamed before now, for I have not to find the expenses of my house, and I am as sober as can be. And suppose it be evil to me, it is dishonor to the King's Grace my brother as well as to me. But the unkindness that I find doth me more evil nor any thing in the world, for I see well what point that ever it stand me on, I will get no help but fair words. My lord, ye must pardon me that I write so sharp, for it touches me near. And God keep you."[6]

When Dacre challenged her on the question of divorce from Angus, Margaret responded: "My lord, also you write right sharply to me in your last article, saying that I do dishonor to myself that bideth from my lord of Angus, and that I follow them that will be my destruction, and cannot stand with the pleasure of the king's grace my brother, and that I may not look for any favor at the king's grace my brother's hand; for it is thought that I am sore abused under color of fair promises, which should bring me to the displeasure of God and my dishonor and undoing at length.

* give up

"My lord, these is sore words and unkindly; if this be the king my brother's mind,—I being his sister—that evil and false folk shall make such report of me, and so lightly credence to be given to the same, it is right heavy to me; and I may think it strange that my lord of Angus may make the king my brother so displeased at me, without any fault making as shall be well known; wherefore it is no marvel suppose others be unkindly, considering that I took my lord of Angus against all Scotland's will, and did him the honor that I could, wherethrough I lost the keeping of my sons, my house of Stirling, my rule of the realm which I had by right, that might not have been taken from me, and all this for his sake; and now himself hath shown him as unkindly to me as is possible, which all the realm knows hold my living from me as far as he may. And above all things, he spake openly dishonor of me, which is no token of love, and I did neither displeasure nor dishonor to him, as is well known.

"My lord, this [is] not a good way that should cause me to come to my lord of Angus; since I took him at mine own pleasure, I will not be boasted* to take him now; and thus I must do the best I may to get my friends, since his grace, that I trusted most in, may be put by me without fault, which I shall never make to his grace. . . ."[7]

Margaret had settled her course for political and personal reasons. It was clear that neither Henry nor Wolsey wanted her in England; she was too expensive to maintain there, and she was still a vehicle—albeit an unwieldy one—to political control of Scotland. As a result, she could not go home to stay or visit. Her brother and his minister demanded her presence in Scotland, but they failed in the visible support of money and arms which would give substance to her presence. The ineffective "fair words" had for years sustained her only hopes; now she sought something more substantial. And substantial backing, as she needed and defined it, lay solely with the pro-French faction, with Albany, Arran, the men who controlled her revenues, her sons, and ultimately her future. Henry's obstinate approach to Margaret's divorce from Angus only drove her farther into the Albany camp. Albany promised help and pursued her cause in Rome. Although

---

* compelled

Rome would take years to review and finally allow the divorce, Margaret would be free of Angus. On that point she would have no turning. He had insulted her, been unfaithful to her, mismanaged her lands and revenues, and in the end deserted her. She would not have him back.

Margaret's future was tied too to that of her son James V. When she first returned to Scotland, access to the six-year-old monarch had been denied her. By August, however, when fear of plague caused his guardians to move the boy to Craigmiller, Margaret was allowed to visit him whenever she liked. She was greatly pleased with the boy, his quiet seriousness, his studious manner, and his delight at seeing her. But wherever Margaret went, rumor was quick to follow; and it followed her to Craigmiller. There were many who said that her frequent visits with her son were merely a prelude to another escape attempt to the south.

Any suspicion of a possible English kidnapping of the Scottish king was excuse enough to close the doors on Margaret and to whisk the boy back to the stronghold of Edinburgh Castle. If the castle could not keep out the plague, at least it would keep out the English.[8] The lesson for Margaret, however, was clear. If she were to have any contact with her son, if she were to see him, if her fortune were to be with his—and she would have it so—she must sever the ties with England and give herself over to those whom she had always opposed. Henry's plans had failed; now she must try her own in these matters which "touched her near."

Letters from England and Scotland bombarded the court of France, and messengers and ambassadors elbowed each other in the crowded corridors for Francis' attention. While England urged the detention of Albany, Scotland demanded his release.[9] So matters continued through 1518 and 1519.

Henry and Wolsey were also seeking faster ties with the Continent. Wolsey, whose political rise was based on the series of treaties with France, was especially anxious that the alliance continue for both political and personal reasons. Neither he nor his cause was popularly supported. If France and England were to war, if the alliance collapsed, so would Wolsey's influence on Henry diminish and the base of his power and influence fold. Henry had so long tied his fortunes to those of France that he considered no other alternative. War with France meant war with Scotland. In 1513 when he had wrested victory from both nations, he had been lucky. He had proved to his satisfaction his prowess on the field of battle. He had brought home the laurel. But he had learned too that war was expensive. Were it cheap, he might have indulged himself further. And given the choice, Henry preferred to indulge his pleasures rather than support armies of questionable success.

In consequence, the King of England and his Lord Chancellor pushed toward closer alliance with France. To secure it, they utilized the oldest political ploy—a marriage alliance. This time the bride was Henry's own daughter, the two-year-old Princess Mary. Her groom was the infant son of Francis I.

For the betrothal, Henry once again ordered the decoration of his favorite home of Greenwich, and to it came the ambassadors and Suffolk and Mary the French Queen. Mary, of course, found there many of her old French acquaintances from the brief days of trial and glory. And she entered the festival with all energy as though to show herself gloriously to her former subjects.

Throughout the first week of October, 1518, every day was filled with pageantry, parties, games, and festival. In all of these events Mary took first place, for her sister-in-law Catherine of Aragon was guarding her health against her latest pregnancy. Foremost among the entertainers was Wolsey, whose hopes seemed crystallized in this latest Anglo-French marriage. At his home in Westminster he gave a banquet unequalled, it was said, by either Cleopatra or Caligula. The halls were filled with vases of silver and gold. The sweetness of the musicians was matched by the gaming of the minstrels, the headiness of the ever-flowing wine and the superabundance of dishes of beef, mutton, pork, capon, swan, crane, pigeon, lark, geese, peacock, peachicks, dates, almonds, prunes, raisins large and small, marmalade, pears, apples, quinces, and comfits. After the banqueting, the mummery began and twelve masked couples "in the richest and most sumptuous array possible" danced before the French guests, and about each couple there danced a handsome knight holding high a single burning torch. When the dancing was over and the vizors were lifted, the lead dancers were discovered to be Henry VIII and his lovely sister Mary.

On the fifth of October, the two-year-old bride, dressed in gold and black velvet, her head shining with flaming jewels, stood before her royal parents. When Henry and Catherine gave consent for her to marry, Wolsey blessed the tiny ring of gold with its diamond of great value, and the Lord High Admiral of France, Bonnivet, proxy for the Dauphin, put the ring upon her finger. Wolsey blessed the bride, blessed the groom, and celebrated the nuptial mass. That evening there was more magnificent banqueting and pleasure, and the chronicler wrote: "All that day were the strangers feasted, and at night they were brought into the hall, where was a rock full of all manner of stones, very artificially made, and on the top stood five trees, the first an Olive tree, on which hanged a shield of the arms of the church of Rome; the second a Pineapple tree, with the arms of the Emperor; the third a Rose with the arms of England; the fourth a branch of Lilies, bearing the arms of France; the fifth a Pomegranate tree, bearing the arms of Spain; in token that all these five potentates were joined together in one league against the enemies of Christ's faith. In and upon the midst of the Rock sat a fair lady, richly apparelled with a Dolphin [Dauphin?] in her lap. In this Rock were ladies and gentlemen, apparelled in Crimson satin, covered over with flowers of purple satin embroidered on with wreaths of gold, knit together with golden laces, and on every flower a hart of gold moving. The ladies attire was after the fashion of India, with kerchiefs of pleasance, hatched with fine gold, and set with letter of Greek in gold of bullion; and the edges of their kerchiefs were garnished with hanging pearl. These gentlemen and ladies sat on the nether part of the Rock, and out of a cave in the said Rock came ten knights, armed at all points, and fought together a fair tourney. And when they were severed and departed, the disguisers descended from the rock, and danced a great space; and suddenly the rock moved and received the disguisers, and immediately closed again. Then entered a person called *Report*, apparelled in Crimson satin full of Tongues, sitting on a flying horse with wings and feet of gold called Pegasus. This person in French declared the meaning of the rock and the trees at the Tourney."[10]

The pageant was typical of the many which marked the wedding festival and the treaties of peace. On the lighter side they gave vent to Henry's and Mary's love of game and magnificent display. On the more serious side they underscored the close alliance between England and France which meant that Mary's rents should be more regularly paid. In the broadest sense they underscored the three-way alliance between Henry, Francis, and Charles the Emperor. Each king swore peace for his lifetime, and promised that any violator would be subject to war waged by the other two.[11] As part of the treaty, Henry agreed to return to France possession of the city of Tournai, but there were many in England who resented, not only the treaty as a whole, but the return of this city which had cost so many English lives.[12]

The celebration with France had marked the return of the Suffolks to the courtly arena, and there they stayed in rather constant attendance to the king. While Mary often played the role of hostess for her brother, Suffolk was ever ready to joust and tourney, to play tennis or cards, to sing and dance for his friend. But as always these delights carried heavy costs, and the Suffolks were forced to occasional retreats to rest their purses as well as their bodies.

Mary's health from childhood had never been robust. Her widowhood and all its tensions had drawn heavily upon her strength. By 1520, although she was only twenty-five years old, her illnesses became more and more frequent. For days she would lie weeping because of the ague and the great pain in her side. At such times, she was loathe to have Suffolk leave her for his duties at court, and he was forced to explain to Wolsey: "My lord, whereas I, of a certain space, have not given mine attendance upon your lordship in the King's council, according to my duty, I beseech your lordship to pardon me thereof. The cause why, hath been that the said French queen hath had, and yet hath, divers physicians with her, for her old disease in her side, and as yet cannot be perfectly restored to her health. And, albeit I have been two times at London, only to the intent to have waited upon your lordship, yet her grace, at either time, hath so sent for me, that I might otherwise do but return home again. . . ."[13]

In spite of her weepings and her pain, Mary insisted upon going to court. Therein lay her pleasure and her hope of recovery. She appealed to Henry: "Sire, so it is that I have been very sick, and ill at ease, for the which I was fain to send for Master Peter the [court] physician, for to have holpen me of the disease that I have. Howbeit, I am rather worse than better. Wherefore I trust surely to come up to London with my lord, for and if I should tarry here, I am sure I should never aspear the sickness that I have. Wherefore, Sire, I would be the gladlier a great deal to come thither, because I would be glad to see your grace, the which I do think long for to do; for I have been a great while out of your sight, and now I trust I shall not be so long again; for the sight of your grace is to me the greatest comfort that may be possible. . . ."[14]

By May Mary was sufficiently recovered not only to participate in the usual court festival but also to undertake the extended demands of travel and royal receptions. The newly elected Holy Roman Emperor, the melancholy Charles of Castile, was to stop in England en route to his new empire. Ostensibly his purpose was to seal his latest treaty with England and to visit his aunt Catherine of Aragon. Mary, however, sought to make of this visit of the man to whom she had long ago been betrothed a personal triumph.

When Wolsey and Henry met Charles at Dover, they encouraged him to visit Canterbury where Mary, Catherine, and hundreds of the nobility waited to receive him. Charles agreed, and hungry English eyes watched with fascination his meeting with Mary. She had decked herself and her ladies in their splendid costumes, and it was rumored that Charles was so smitten by her beauty and so disquieted by his loss that he refused to join any of the festival. Instead he sat moodily and talked only with Wolsey and Henry.

The visit was of necessity a brief one, however. Charles was anxious to take formal possession of his new dominions, and Henry was prepared for the most splendid outing of his reign. On June 1, 1520, the two rulers sailed to their differing destinies— Charles to new kingdoms and Henry to the grandest spectacle of the century.[15]

Since the previous March, the king's master mason, the master carpenter, three hundred masons, five hundred carpenters, one hundred joiners, painters, glaziers, tilers, smiths, and builders "to the number of two thousand and more" had worked steadily, even frantically, to build the castle of gold at Guines to house the English king.[16] The palace, squarely built, was three hundred twenty-eight feet long. Its windows, clerestories, posts, and mullions were overlaid with gold. Statues of gold flanked its gates, guarded its corridors, and seemed to suspend the silken coverings of the ceilings, "which showed like bullions of fine burnished gold." Everywhere the hangings, bosses, statuary, and colonnades glittered with gold and flashing jewels. In the courtyard, a statue

of Bacchus spouted claret, hippocras, and water into silver cups.
Opposite was a pillar of gold supported by four golden lions, and
above all stood the figure of Cupid, the blinded child of love, with
his golden bow and arrows. Profusion of riches was everywhere;
even the chapel of the palace was covered in the blue hangings
which Henry VII had given to Westminster Abbey. And throughout the days and nights, thirty-five priests and numerous singing
boys filled the air with the chants of prayers and hymns while the
golden images of the Twelve Apostles stood and watched.

In the kitchens two hundred cooks sweated over smoking cal-
drons and daily prepared hundreds of dishes. In the yards, grooms
and stablemen swarmed amidst the growing confusion of horses,
mules, the heaps of armor and weaponry, the banners and shields
of the combatants. In the fields beyond, two thousand eight hundred tents spread in the morning light, flaunting the banners,
pennons, and badges of their occupants. Beyond the tents were
the makeshift bedrolls of the less opulent, the hangers-on, the
spectators, the beggars who hoped to grab scraps of glory and
pieces of gold from the brilliance of the setting and its central
figures.

Mary and Suffolk had their apartments near those of Henry,
Catherine, and Wolsey in the golden palace. There they entertained Francis—Mary's old acquaintance to whom she had once
turned in desperation but never with fondness. Now she turned to
him with pride in her marriage and the love which bound it; and
Henry's obvious joy in Mary and Suffolk showed that he had
forgiven. Francis' plan had backfired; and Suffolk and Mary had,
in the long run, won. But there was little talk of the past with so
much to occupy them in the present.

The "Field of Cloth of Gold," as the tourney was to become
known, was designed to demonstrate martial prowess, breaking of
spears, swordplay, horsemanship, the gallant exploits of kings and
their subjects against a backdrop of ostentatious magnificence. It
was, in short, the frame for picturesque manly pursuits. The
women were to be part of the backdrop, part of the splendid color
which set the scene, or as one observer wrote: "To tell you the
apparel of the ladies, their rich attires, their sumptuous Jewels,
their diversities of beauties, and the goodly behavior from day to
day since the first meeting, I assure you ten men's wits can scarce
declare it."[17] The women, especially Claude Queen of France,

Catherine Queen of England, and Mary Queen Dowager, were the chief spectators, the leaders of applause, and principal dancing partners. They entertained and were entertained according to the strictures of etiquette of the ancient courts of love.

Only once throughout the days of festival was Mary to play a leading part. Etiquette prevented the queens of England and France from visiting each other, but Mary's days of queenship were over and her movements were more freely made. When the two kings exchanged courtesy visits, Mary and nineteen ladies, in handsome satin gold and red, mounted their horses trapped in velvet white and yellow, and joined the King of England and nineteen knights all in matching costume. Once on the road, they passed Francis in a chariot accompanied by twenty-eight persons going in the opposite direction to visit Queen Catherine. Since, however, the visits were supposedly impromptu and everyone was disguised, each party pretended ignorance of the other and so passed on the road like ordinary travellers.[18]

The two monarchs were fast turning what should have been a celebration of truce into an exploitation of one-upmanship. When the two hosts faced each other across the open plain, it was with jealousy and suspicion that they eyed the splendor of the other. When the two kings raced alone onto the field to embrace each other in brotherly love, it became a curious dance of "after-you" as each sought to be more gracious than the other. When they knelt together at mass to adore the Host, both were too well-bred to be the first to kiss the Host. The queens of France and England solved their own dilemma by kissing each other instead. When the combatants met in the field of jousting, both sides kept score and saw the little victories as points of national honor and evidence of national strength. When the magnificent charade was over, and the kings and queens bid affectionate farewell, their minds were already set on another course. Francis contemplated continental victories, and Henry was off to Calais to entertain Charles of Castile, Emperor of the Romans, to sign a new treaty to the disadvantage of France.[19]

For the meeting with Charles and his aunt Margaret of Savoy, Henry erected an enormous banqueting tent held by masts, and "within the said house was painted the elements of stars, sun, and moon, and clouds, with divers other things made over men's heads . . . and many ships under sails and windmills going . . . and about the high piece of timber that stood up right in the midst was made stages of timber for organs, and other instruments for to stand in, and men for to play upon them, and for clerks singing . . . but on the same morning the wind began to rise, and at night blew off all the canvas, and all the elements with the stars, sun, and moon, and clouds, and the same rain blew out above a thousand torches and tapers . . . and all the king's seats that was made with great riches that could be ordained, besides all other things, was all dashed and lost."[20]

On July 5, Henry went to Gravelines to visit with Charles, and three days later returned with the emperor to Calais. Although great secrecy shrouded their meetings, one of the chief topics of conversation was the breaking of the young Princess Mary's engagement to the Dauphin of France, and giving her instead to the emperor. Charles, as was his custom, was hesitant to make a new marriage treaty or to break his standing one with Princess Renée of France.[21]

When his visit with Charles was over, Henry returned to England and his rounds of hunting and progresses from estate to estate. Mary and Suffolk returned to the country to nurse their bruised finances and await the next call to court. As far as England was concerned, the splendid outing had changed nothing. No new treaties were really secured, no firm alliances had been established. Moreover Francis had been particularly vague about prohibiting the return of Albany to Scotland. Dacre, in the meantime, had continued harrowing the Scots border, and Margaret— feeling especially left out of the events of splendor across the sea —had grown increasingly firm in her desire to divorce Angus and in her support of the pro-French faction in Scotland. Her letters to Albany implored his return and offered total cooperation.

English monies poured northward to help Dacre and to buy Scots' loyalties. English letters, especially from the pens of Henry and Wolsey, lectured and threatened Margaret to reverse her position. They served only to fire her anger and to strengthen her tenacity of purpose. She was determined to make her own way in the best, most expedient manner, and that now lay with the Duke of Albany. In France, Albany was shadowed by English agents and English spies. A year later, he somehow slipped by them all, shot around the English ships alerted to his escape, and landed in Scotland in late November, 1521. With a sense of triumph, Margaret gave vent to her spleen and her injured pride, and in words of smoldering wrath dashed off the news to Lord Dacre:

My lord Dacre, I commend me to you, and wit ye that my lord duke of Albany, governor of Scotland, is come for to do service to the King my son and to the realm, and to help me to be answered and obeyed of my living, the which I have great need of; for there was never gentlewoman of my estate so evil intreated, and my living holden from me, as I have written often times to you of before. Suppose ye rather hindered me than furthered me, which had not been your part to do: not the less, since my lord Governor is come into this realm for the good of it, and will for his part help to entertain the amity and peace betwixt the King's grace my brother's said realm and this; wherefore I trust it will be truly the King my brother's mind to do the same, as I trust it has not been his mind otherwise. Suppose his servants have not done their part in the keeping of the same, but as yet I pray you my lord to do it that ye should do of reason for the King's grace my brother's and your master's honor, for he should keep it that he promised, and specially to this realm, considering the King my son is so tender to his Grace, and I never failed to him nor shall not.

I would have thought to have had thank of the King's grace my brother, and of the realm of England, that I have kept a good part to this realm, both for his honor and mine; or else all the world might have spoken evil of me to have done the contrary to the King my son and the weal of this realm, which could not have been well guided without the duke of Albany [being] governor of this realm, for my son the King is not of age to do it himself.

But, my lord, I know well ye have done your part to hinder me at the King's grace my brother's hand. Why may ye not fail to me, when ye fail to the King's grace my brother? And better mend in time not to be worse. Which if ye do not, it will be occasion to this realm and my lord Governor to do such like as ye have done; which is receiving of rebels and maintaining of them; which if ye do not mend, it will be laid to your charge hereafter by the King's grace my brother.

My lord, I write sharply and plainly to you, for I have good cause, both for the King my son's sake and mine own; for ye have fortified my lord of Angus against me, and counselled him to trouble me, in the contrary of the band that ye caused me to take of him, which ye would break again; which ye should not have done to your master's sister. And your answer, what shall be your part, that I and this world may depend on; and God keep you. Written at Edinburgh, 4 Dec.

Your friend,
Margaret R.[22]

Dacre's response rained abuse, listed Margaret's so-called infidelities, charged her with grievous faults, accused her of insubordination if not outright treason. Margaret complained to her brother, asked that Dacre be corrected for keeping poor order on the borders, and stated her clear alliance with Albany as totally consistent with her loyalties to her son and to Scotland and ultimately to England. For their purposes, in Margaret's mind, were all leading one way—to peace and prosperity on both sides. Henry wanted peace and prosperity on his side, but he wanted Scotland to be a fiefdom under the combined authority of Angus and Margaret. Albany's return thwarted that dream. In quick succession he and the lords branded Angus a traitor and condemned him to death. But at Margaret's intercession, the sentence was commuted to exile in France. Meanwhile the King of England's irritation with these unwieldy events chafed and itched him into sullen fury. With Angus' departure, his supporters in both Scotland and England were again leaderless and looked at Margaret and her alliance with Albany with unabated disgust. The pro-English faction, once more politically impotent, vented its rage through slander and accusation. Margaret's feelings for and dealings with Albany were born, it was said, not of necessity but of sexual intimacy. Upon hearing this news, Henry roared and raged and sent his herald to Scotland with a smoking declaration:

> . . . he was the king's mother's brother, wherefore the King of Scots his life, health, honor, riches and kingdom should depend upon the English king; all this appears in danger when the king is in the Governor's hands who next would be king himself. But here [is] one thing worst of all, that the Governor intends to allure the Queen his sister and draw her into a dishonest love, which is likely now after the banishing of her husband. Wherefore in respect of his honor, as king, by nature his uncle, he is forced to expel the Governor by a Herald, either that with good words he depart pleasantly, or bide the brunt of battle. But if he respects his country and his own honor, he bids them depart in pleasure and peace.[23]

Albany endured this outpouring of rage and insinuation, before the Council of Scotland, and answered with "a constant countenance and a manly voice . . . that he knew nothing what promise or kind of condition was between the kings of England and France, when they met: but he knew perfectly, that he was not so bound to them as to live under their servitude, of such manner, that he may not visit his country. . . . [Furthermore] when he [Henry VIII] says our King is young and in danger of death, let not that . . . vex your king, for I had such respect of his years, his nature, my conscience, and honor, that when he was an infant, I suffered him not in one jot to be wronged uncorrected; insofar that who will pursue him, or his kingdom anywise, he shall in haste meet him with all force, resist and drive him back. Touching the Earl of Angus, was that, thinks he, a great pain, when he was condemned to die, to be banished for a short space, at request of the Queen, whom I ever honored, and yet shall do as our king's mother? Your king therefore has no occasion of suspicion, or *clenning any clag* to the Queen's honor, unless he be tempted with a wicked spirit."[24]

The answer raised Henry's anger to such a pitch that he sent invitation to Angus to come to the English court and to Dacre to raise an army to scourge again the borders of Scotland. Simultaneously Margaret and Albany doubled their efforts to secure Margaret's divorce. It was based largely on three accounts: that James IV had not died at Flodden as she had supposed but had lived for three years after the battle; secondly, that unbeknownst to the queen, Angus had entered a pre-contract of marriage with the Earl of Bothwell's daughter before he had married Margaret; and thirdly, that Angus was guilty of adultery. The suit of divorce, however, was drawn to protect the Lady Margaret Douglas so that "by the ignorance of the Mother [the Daughter] should not suffer any loss, damage, or disadvantage."[25] Neither Margaret nor Albany expected a speedy response from Rome, but both expected the eventual decree.

Gossip and rumor of Albany's and Margaret's intimacy gushed from the pro-English faction and washed about the eager ears in the court of England. But it was gossip born of malice and of the frustration of those who saw only a dwindling cause for England in the northern reaches. The rumors and Henry's mandates to the

Council of Scotland only served to bring unity and increased support for the government of Albany and acceptance of Margaret. At this uneasy impasse matters rested while both sides, through the early 1520s, talked of war.

France encouraged Scotland to invade England but sent neither money nor supplies. England mustered armies and prepared again to send Dacre against the Scots. But neither country could afford another war, and neither country really wanted war. Yet both were encouraged to it by those who hoped to gain. France increased its demands to the point that the Scots parliament began to consider peace with England. A message was sent to Francis I stating that "the Scotch lords say that the war is merely for the advantage of France, and unless the King of France will issue a bold declaration, and send sufficient assistance, they do not care to stir, as they are weary of fighting for others."[26] France, however, was on the verge of war with England and sought to divert the English force or at least divide its effort. Consequently France sent military aid to Scotland in May, 1522. The Scots agreed to fight. By then the timing was totally confused—Margaret, Albany, and Dacre had entered informal negotiations for peace.

Albany found himself twisted between two mighty opposites. He had opted for peace with England and found himself now forced to war. His armies formed and he took command and led them in a half-hearted search for the enemy. As a result he lost the advantage of a surprise attack and allowed the initiative and energies of his force to slip away. He frittered away the summer in aimless marches, aroused anger within his own ranks, and strained the loyalty of those who looked to him for leadership. When he agreed with Dacre to a cessation of hostilities, he lost his own strength and gave the English time to muster theirs. In order to explain what had happened, Albany sailed for France on October 27.[27]

Throughout all of these maneuverings, Margaret had played an insistent—if not pivotal—role. She had ultimately brought Albany close to her own thinking. She had come to see that the well-being of Scotland lay in peace rather than war with England. To secure that end, Margaret herself had ridden onto the field of battle to negotiate between Albany and Dacre. It was the role she had always wanted, had always hoped to play. Hers, however, was a moment of fleeting glory. As soon as the treaty was signed, Margaret was betrayed by both sides and ultimately betrayed herself.[28]

With Albany in France, Henry, Wolsey, and Dacre set upon Margaret with beratings, promises, and hopes of the fulfillment of her dream of power. They found her an easy target. Ever subject to flattery, ever anxious to be loved and respected, ever desirous of being the mediator between the two nations, Margaret capitulated. She began again her old undermining of Albany's strength, and inadvertently found herself in the old familiar position of being trusted by none and tolerated by few. Her revenues again were either withheld or were slow in coming, and it was with the old desperation that she wrote in December to Wolsey, "For there is few in this country that will do for me any good; howbeit that I have done that was possible to me to have them my friends, for I have made their good cause, as God knows; and since I see that it will not be for me in time coming, I will trust no more unto them, and fain would be amongst them that I might trust.

"Item, where you bid me in your writing to take good regard for certain knowledge to be had, as well what diligence shall be done in the advancement of mine affairs, and to ensearch and know what speed is like to ensue therein, and as I shall perceive to advertise the lord Dacre; my lord, as to that they have made no redress, nor no good is like to ensue hereafter to me in this country; and I wrote my mind plainly to you, and sent it to the lord Dacre for to have sent the same up to you, trusting that you would have informed the king's grace my brother, and through your good counsel his grace would have put me out of trouble. The lord Dacre would not send my said writing to you, but he sent it again to me, and refused all utterly to send it; of the which I think strange, considering that the king's grace my brother gave command to the lord Dacre, when I was present, to send any writings up to his grace and to you, whensoever I should send any. It is not marvel that Scotchmen be unkind to me, when Englishmen are so unthankful. . . .

"I am plain to you, therefore I beseech you to help me out of sorrow. . . . My lord, if it please you, you shall recommend me heartily to the king's grace my brother, and thank his grace of his diamond that his grace sent me; and beseech his grace to be good brother unto me, as his grace was ever. And that his grace and you, my lord, must need have me excused that I wrote not to his grace and to you with my own hand at this time, for because my hands and all my body are so full of the small-pox, that I might neither write, nor sit, nor scantly speak; and hereafter, when I may, I shall write with my own hand at length. . . ."[29]

Margaret's smallpox brought her again near death, but somehow her body rallied. She lived in spite of illness, disease, and the curses of her maligners. She gained her health only to find that, though Scotland was content to maintain the peace, England was determined on war. The Earl of Surrey, son of the commander of the Flodden victory and ablest of English generals, mustered an army and raided Scotland. In quick and bloody succession he devastated Eccles, Ednam, Stichell, Kelso, and prepared to sweep the border "that there is left neither house, fortress, village, tree, cattle, corn or other succor for man; insomuch as some of the people which fled from the same, and afterwards returned, finding no sustentation, were compelled to come into England, begging bread, which oftentimes when they eat they die incontinently for the hunger past; and with no imprisonment, cutting of their ears, burning them in the face, or otherwise, can be kept away. Such is the punishment of Almighty God to those that be the disturbers of good peace, rest, and quiet in Christendom."[30]

In Scotland, all was confusion. While Albany remained in France, the Scots could in no way be brought under single authority. The French faction, which the governor left behind, took refuge in the castle of Dunbar and wrote frantic letters begging Albany to return. But the ships of England scoured the coasts and blocked his passage. The governor was trapped on the opposite shore.

In the meantime Dacre flattered Margaret into believing she could lead a faction of her own, seize the reins of government, and control the person of the king. Once again she presented herself as the leader, the rallying force, but the Scots lords were unwilling to follow her. Although they rejected war with England, they feared the yoke of English government.

Margaret tried a different tactic. James V, now eleven years old, asked the counsel to set him free to govern in his own right. He would, he maintained, keep peace with England. As his government seemed willing to follow the proposal of the young king, the French ambassadors stepped in to assure Albany's return within six days.[31]

Albany of course did not, could not, come, and James remained in custody of the counsel. Margaret went unheralded, and the state of Scotland wallowed confused and leaderless. The uneasy months of summer passed into fall when in late September, Albany took the great risk, escaped capture by the English navy, and landed in Scotland. Immediately the lords of Scotland rushed to his banner. They were ready for war at last. For six months Surrey and Dacre had burned and scorched the borders. The city of Jedburgh was ravaged. The skeleton of its ancient abbey still stood against the sky, but the city itself lay in smoking ash.

As Albany planned for war, he again found Margaret torn between allegiances. Her earlier suggestions to Surrey to assault Edinburgh had gone unheeded, her pleas for guidance and relief from Henry produced only words. Albany was solicitous, he flattered her, he encouraged her; and she gave herself again to his cause. Many called her fickle, which she no doubt was. But she was also a driven woman who spent her life casting about for security, strength, and the need to be needed. If her vision were shortsighted, her hopes nevertheless were long-lived. She believed in the necessity of cooperation between the two nations. Unfortunately that belief seemed to be based on only a self-serving interest; yet in the long run she was proven right in her dreams.

Although Margaret acquiesced to Albany's government, she endeavored to keep abreast of activities on both sides of the border. She sent to Surrey information about the Scots and gave to Albany information about the English. She still hoped to be the great mediator. While Surrey amassed his host, Albany gathered the greatest force since that which had marched to Flodden Field.

Surrey, however, had done his homework. He thought he knew his man and wrote to Wolsey of Albany: ". . . and by many ways I am advertised that the Duke of Albany is a marvelous wilfull man, and will believe no man's counsel, but will have his own opinion followed. And because the French King hath been at so great charges by his provoking, having his wife's inheritance lying within his dominions, dare not for no Scottish counsel forbear to invade this realm. I am also advertised that he is so passionate that if he be apart among his familiars, and doth hear anything contrarious to his mind and pleasure, his accostumed manner is to take his bonnet suddenly off his head and to throw it in the fire; and no man dare take it out, but let it to be burnt. My Lord Dacre doth affirm that at his last being in Scotland he did burn above a dozen bonnets after this manner. And if he be such a man, with God's grace we shall speed the better with him."[32]

Wolsey tempered Surrey's fears about Scots invasion. The cardinal spoke of the great barrenness of the borders, the lack of supplies for Scots troops, the near impossibility of feeding soldiers far from home. Time was on the English side. Wolsey ordered Surrey to delay, to worry the Scots without engaging in a pitched battle, to exhaust their limited foods and munitions, and to remember the earlier campaign when the English had taken the field. Wolsey insisted that the Scots, regardless of Albany's desire, threats, and leadership, would refuse to cross the border. The sagacious cardinal added: "Besides it is not unknown that King James, whom your father and you slew, was a man of great courage, well beloved and in great estimation amongst his subjects; and yet was it not little difficult for him to bring the Scots, the King's grace [Henry] being then out of the realm, and the King of Scots having great treasure, victual, harness, ordnance, and provision made of a long season before in the best and most convenable time of the year, to condescend unto the invasion of England; wherein what fortune and success they had may percase be a remembrance and example to those which at a more unmeet time would think to attempt the same."[33]

Wolsey's prediction was on the mark. Albany aroused the lagging spirits of the Scots. He called upon the memory of Flodden Field, he entreated the unquiet dead, and he closed by appealing to national pride and ancient hatreds: "A mighty neighbor may be a cruel enemy. I affirm this, if we would keep amity with the realm of England, we were out of all these dangers. God forbid . . . that Scotland ever should seek a new friend . . . to the destroyers of their country and nation, but you my lords of Scotland are sufficient to maintain your lands, liberty, and freedom against your common enemies the Englishmen. And therefore now let us together revenge the hurts done to us and our country. And I on mine honor shall go with you, and therefore I have brought with me both treasure, men, and artillery unto this realm. I think not but we shall so do that all Christendom shall speak of our noble consent."[34]

Although the lords of Scotland applauded and cried agreement to this appeal, Albany was forced to move in slow march. And Margaret was careful to write Surrey of Albany's movements, his soldiers, his arms, for "I can do no more for my part but advertise you of all things that I know, and that I shall not fail."[35]

On November 2 Albany began the siege of Wark Castle on the southern shore of the Tweed. While keeping his main force on the northern shore, he sent one thousand Frenchmen to the attack. When news came of Surrey's advance, the governor forced the French to recross the river, and the entire army retreated.[36]

As the Scots army moved again to Edinburgh, Margaret wrote to Surrey: "I commend me heartily to you, and wit you that I have received your writings, with other writings written out of France, which methinks are right good, and I pray God bring them to a good end, to the pleasure of the king's grace my brother. Also, my lord, I thank you of your good remembrance and kind writing, which I pray God that I may quit.

"And as touching the king my son, thanked be God he is in good health, and I am with him into Stirling, and think not to be far from him for any danger that may come, if that I be not put from him by force. I beseech God if that you saw him, so that nobody knew of you but I, and I trust you would be right well contented of him.

"Also wit you, my lord, that the governor is in Edinburgh, and I saw him not since he came from the unhonest journey; but he thinks no shame of it, for he makes his excuse that the lords would not pass in England with him, and that is my lord of Arran and my lord of Lennox, with other lords, and says that they would have sold him in England, and therefore he hath begun the parliament this Tuesday next coming, and hath sent for all the lords again. I trust to do little good to them, as they are well worthy; for if they had done as they should, we had been quit of this cumber.

"As to all matters, I have sent my plain mind before to you with my servant, master John Cantley; wherefore, my lord, I pray you heartily to do so to me, that I need not to set by the displeasure of the duke, or else I must be content to follow his pleasure, whether it be against the king my son or not; for there is none here that will contrary his pleasure, suppose he do never so evil; and this I assure you. And you know well, my lord, that my living that I should live upon is here, and he may do with it as he pleases. As I have been intreated since my last coming out of England, it is well known; and hath lived [not] like a princess, but like a sober* woman, and fain by force to take any money that the duke would give me: as I have written to you of before, and hath gotten no answer of effect.

"Also you write to me to take good heed to the keeping of the king my son. As to that I shall do that is in me, with part of support of the king's grace my brother, that I need it not to set by the duke, nor his displeasure; you shall see me take it well upon me, and not set by him; and if it be not thus I dare not displease him, for I have nothing to hold up my honest sustentation to find me. Wherefore, my lord, I pray you consider my part, and show it to the king's grace my brother, and beseech his grace to have regard to me; for the better that I be, the king my son will be the better, and I may the better do the king's grace my brother honor and pleasure. And right in short time. I trust the king my son may be serviceable to his grace; and therefore, for a little cost and cumber, his grace may not leave it now, but be his defender and mine: for we have no other to trust in. And I shall deserve it the best I can, and shall advertise you of all things that I may know, so that you keep it secret. . . ."[37]

Contrary to Margaret's understanding, Albany's strength of leadership was eroding, and there were many who questioned his retreat, his "unhonest journey." What actually provoked his retreat remained unclear: perhaps the Scots lords had again refused to follow him into England; perhaps he responded to the prodding of France to make a show of force against England. Whatever the situation, upon his return to the capital, he charged Margaret with duplicity, and in Margaret's words: ". . . of force put [me] away from the king."[38] She appealed to Albany: ". . . and seeing since you, my lord, and the rest of the lords has ordained that I shall not abide with the king my son, but whiles† to come and see him. And if this be reasonable or honorable I report me to the deed; and I believe in God that hereafter you shall have cause to

---

* poor   † at times

bethink you of the good and true part I have kept to you, praying God to keep the king my son from evil: for the appearance is not when his mother is put forth of his company, and they put about him that sets nought by to put his life in extreme danger for good or profit to themselves. For one of them, my lord Flemming, as in times bypast he has not governed him well, as is known in Scotland, and as I have shown of that before to the lords, notwithstanding it is force that I suffer for a little time.

"And where you say, my lord, I should not give credence to them that says evil of you to me, now you show by your deeds that I have cause to give them credence touching myself; for the most displeasure that I might have in this world, all excepting my life, you and the lords has done to me now, to put me from the company of the king my son. But if there happens any evil, as God keep him, I desire not to be with him. But if the appearance be good of them that is about him, I shall be of good will, the which I pray God give you grace to do for your part; and for my part, I assure you, my lord, that at the departing of master John Cantley I was in all so good will to do for you and your pleasure as was possible to me. . . . But now I see well my reward, trusting firmly that God shall help me and my just quarrels and cause. . . ."[39]

Six weeks later she wrote again to Albany urging much the same point: "And you shall know, my lord and cousin, hereafter, that it is and shall be in my power to do good and honor to you and this realm, if I were well entreated; and one truer than me you shall never find, and have so evil a reward as I. I think also that for the good part that I have kept to the French king, that I should not be thus entreated; as I will ask, if it be his pleasure. For, my lord, you said to me that he commanded you to do for me, and to treat me well, which had been to his honor and yours. It is force that I speak for myself, when I am put from the thing that I love best in the world; as God knoweth, whom give you better counsel, for the good of the king and your own honor."[40]

How much Margaret believed in what she said in these and similar appeals raised, then as now, immediate questions. Surely the heavy irony was unintentional. Did she believe that she had played to Albany "the good and true part," that "one truer than me you shall never find"? Did she underestimate the network of spies which constantly surrounded her and reported her every movement, her every sentiment to the governor? Could she possibly expect that he did not know of her sliding loyalties, her inconsistent support, her intrigues with Henry, Surrey, and Dacre? Did she believe, as she waited for her erratic revenues and pawned her jewels and plate, "that it is and shall be in my power to do good and honor to you and this realm"? Did she see strength in the veiled threat "if I were well entreated"? Could she honestly say that France had found her loyal, that the pro-French faction held her in respect?

As question piles upon question, the answer to each of them seems to be "yes." There is logic in the long list of seeming duplicity and conflicting action. For years she had seen the fortunes of Scotland tied to those of England; that had been the purpose of her marriage. Consequently for years, English policy had dictated Margaret's policy. But Henry's policy had as its goal supremacy through conquest—war from without and conflict from within. Henry used Margaret to that end; and believing him to be right, she allowed herself to be used. When, however, that policy brought separation rather than unity of purpose, she changed her course. The course of stability, as Margaret saw it, was in the security of her son's throne. Thus through him the ultimate goal would be a uniting of policy between the two nations. But there was the real problem of his youth. Somehow he must be safely brought through the hard years of minority; his throne and whatever strength it might possess must be held intact until it was in actuality, as well as in theory, his own. The single thread of consistency to Margaret's policy was "the thing that I love best in the world," James V her son. Through him the policies of England and Scotland might recapture the harmony which the years of her marriage to James IV had achieved. To that end her endeavors were bent; and although her means were often contradictory, although she grabbed after straws in the wind, her goal was ever the same. While she was quick to change her tactics, she never changed her mind.

Margaret ceased to be the pawn of Henry as she became more the mother of James. She was not, as one has called her, "a rather silly woman."[41] She was more complex than that. She had a purpose which she sought to fulfill, but her counsellors—in England and in Scotland—were self-seeking and ambitious men. They played upon her vanity, and she was weak enough to believe them. She put her trust in a few and found herself betrayed by all.

She turned one way, then another, seeking security and fulfillment of promises. Neither ever came.

It is perhaps most curious of all that the man who had most to lose was the one who forgave Margaret most readily; and he always treated her with the greatest courtesy. Albany, whose allegiances too were often at cross-purposes, apparently understood Margaret's dilemma more clearly than she ever did. Shortly after his retreat from the border wars, he came with the council to tell her of the new course which must be followed. This interview Margaret described at length when she wrote to Surrey: "I will advertise you of such things as hath been done at this time. As to the first point, I sent you the letter that the lords sent to me, with a letter of the governor's, that you might understand their minds toward me; and now I send you with this writing my answers again that I sent to them. . . .

"Secondly, my lord, the governor came here to Stirling, and the lords with him, the 9th day of December, and came that same day to the king my son, and I was there present; and after he had spoken to the king he came to me, and excused him to me, saying, that I was displeased at him; and I answered I had no other cause as farther I would show before him and the lords.

"Then the next day after, he and the lords came to the council, and I was present, and said to them that I understood the ordinance and rule that they had made, that I should not remain with the king my son, and that they have put the earl of Murray, the earl of Cassilis, and the lord Flemming, and the lord Borthwick to be about the king my son's person, which I thought not needful, seeing that his person hath been surely kept hitherto with good, true, wise lords, and that they have not failed in nothing; and as to my part, I had never made no cause of suspicion to be put from the king my son: wherefore I had great marvel they should do that to me, but I perceived well that it was done for hurt to the king my son: wherefore I have them in great suspicion that should be about his person, seeing that they will not take the charge upon them, I being with the king my son; wherefore I dissented to their innovations, and if any thing happened it should lie to their charge.

"And I discharged me with many other sharp words that were too long to write. And the governor took an instrument after mine, and said that if that the lords would not fulfill it that they had done, that they failed, and that he laid the charge upon them if any inconvenience came thereafter. And thus we departed that night.

"The next day the governor came himself to the king my son, and desired him that he might speak with him and me: and then he showed to the king and me the order that was devised by the lords and him, touching such persons as should be about him, and prayed him and me to be contented therewith. The king said, if that was for his good he would be contented with; and I answered that I had shown my mind before him and the lords, and therefore I could say no more then.

"I was warned that the governor had sent to fetch eight hundred of his Frenchmen, which should have passed to the west sea, and that he was in purpose to take the king to another place, and to have put me from him. Wherefore, to eschew more evil appearing, I thought for that time I would not contrary them as to the lords that should be about him; but I said before the lords then, that if that was for the good of the king my son's person I would be contented with, and that I should be a good Scotswoman. And then I departed, and I took an instrument before witness that I revoked any thing that I did at this time, for it was to eschew a greater inconvenience that was appearing in the time toward the king my son's person.

"After this, the governor desired at the lords, I not being present, that they would give him license to pass his way into France, not speaking of his returning again. And he had made him ready and his ships to pass; but the lords, both spiritual and temporal, would not condescend to it for nothing that could be done; but said that he should not pass, for if he did they would discharge their bonds to him, and the authority that he hath: and if he would abide with them, they would give him the profits of all the benefices with their own, and the temporal lords would abide continually with him, and spend their goods with him in his service, and by this they would find the governor as much to spend as I should have. Not the less he would not be content with this, but he would pass his way.

"And upon this they sat three days, and yet the lords would not consent to his passing away; and now he will abide while Candlemas, and will hold his Christmas into Edinburgh. And the cause of this is about the benefices, for the governor hath named them to sundry persons, but he hath not made them no surety, but holdeth them in his hands: wherefore they think, if he pass away, that he will dispose them otherwise at his pleasure, and that hath caused them to do this for their profit, and not regarded to the weal of the king my son nor his realm. And part of their benefices spiritual men hath, another part to temporal lords for their friends, as the earl of Arran, the earl of Argyll, which I trusted should not have come to the governor, but to have bidden forth at this time, which made me to be the stronger at my opinion: but I had not one person that took my part, nor that would displease the governor for the weal of the king my son.

"Therefore, my lord, I pray you consider this well, and show it to the king's grace my brother, that there may be remedy seen for the same, seeing that I advertise you of all things. And as to my part, touching the biding with the king my son, I shall not fail as long as I may bide, and that I may get any thing to hold my expenses with. But the lords showeth well by their doings to me, that they would that I were from my son the king: for one way they have ordained me, as you may see by their writings that I sent to you, and another cause they will not answer me of living; in so far as I desired them to see a way for me how I should be answered of my living conforming to their own bonds, or else that [they] would see some other good way for me, that I might live to my honor, or else that they would give me leave to coin gold or silver to make my expenses. As to the answering of my conjunct feoffment, they say that they cannot help me for the war that the king's grace my brother makes on this realm; and as to any other help, they know not where it may be gotten; and as to let me strike any money, either gold or silver, it will do great hurt: and thus they will not consent to nothing how that I may live with my son.

"Therefore, if the king's grace my brother will that I abide with the king my son, he must help me with part to sustain me, as his grace hath done in a part, whereof I thank his grace right humble; and I shall do as he commandeth me as long as [I] may and shall rule me as soberly as I can, with part of servants as I may bear, that there shall be no fault in it that I may do: and therefore my special trust is that his grace will not fail me, for the good of the king my son and me.

"Wherefore I pray you heartily, my lord, to cause me to be

advertised of the king's grace my brother's pleasure touching these matters; for I promise you, my lord, on my honor, that I have written nothing in this letter but that hath been done and said at this time, or else let me never have credence, which I would think right heavy.

"Also, my lord, when that I came before the governor and the lords, when they sat at parliament, I asked at them wherefore I was holden suspect to be with the king my son: and they said, it was the lords that was ordained to be about his person, they said that I was your sister, and that peradventure I would take him into England, thinking that I did for his weal; and that they knew perfectly that the king my son would do more for me than for any other, wherefore they would take no charge on them: and the governor himself, with the lords, said this same language to me. And I answered to them that my deeds had shown otherwise, wherefore that was but of malice and evil will, as I should cause it to be proved with as good as any there.

"And this I get for the king's grace my brother's sake; wherefore his grace should help me and defend me, and let them wit that his grace knoweth this, but not by my rehearse, and that he is not contented that such things should be laid to my charge for his sake; and send to me plainly, and ask if they have done thus to me, and that he marvels that I will not advertise his grace of these doings; saying that he will defend me, and that he will not let me be wronged. And, this being done, it will cause the governor to pass away for fear, and cause the lords to fall from him and his purposes for very fear. For I ensure you that the duke is as afraid of England as can be possible; and another thing, he dare never give trust to Scotsmen to fight against England, for he dreadeth that they will betray him.

"Therefore, my lord, I pray you consider all this weal, and help to labor a good way for the weal and surety of the king my son and me, as you have shown largely for your part to us, the which I pray God that I may acquit and do you pleasure for the same; for, next the king's grace my brother, I am most beholden to you of any. . . .

"Also, my lord, I have received two hundred angel nobles . . . that the king's grace my brother sent me; whereof I thank his grace humbly: for if it be not his help, I am constrained to leave this realm for fault of my honest sustentation. But the duke and the French ambassador that is here hath proffered me, in the French king's name, five thousand crowns of the weight in pension, so that I will help to keep the band betwixt France and this realm; which I have refused, because I will do nothing contrary the king's grace my brother's pleasure, as he shall find.

"Praying you, my lord, to haste me answer of these my writings, and that they be secretly kept, for they may do me great hurt, as my trust is in you. . . ."[42]

On May 20, 1524, Albany gained his wish. The lords of Scotland let him go home. Although he promised on forfeiture of the regency to return in September, he never came again to Scotland. Like Margaret, the governor had never felt at home in the land of warring chieftains. He was weary of the indecision, the backbiting, the disloyalty, the petty enmities. As he left, he gave over the control of government to the pro-French faction headed by the Earl of Arran and James Beaton, now Archbishop of St. Andrews and Lord Chancellor.[43]

No sooner had Albany's sails disappeared over the horizon than a whirlwind of events were set in motion. Margaret, seeing the regency once more obtainable, turned the full blast of Tudor charm upon Arran. He was flattered, he was pleased, he would share the government with her. The two worked to take control. Unbeknownst to Margaret, Henry VIII had developed his own designs. He called to England the Earl of Angus from his enforced exile in France; and these two worked to take control of Scotland. Margaret was taken by surprise. Angus had been out of her life, and she had no desire, no intention of allowing him in again. In spite of Henry's protestations of Angus' maturity, his newly acquired civilities, his popular appeal and powerful following, Margaret knew him to be a ruthless man. He was ambitious, would stop at nothing to take what he wanted, and he had embarrassed and insulted her. Moreover, she had found a lover in her Master of the Horse, Henry Stewart, a charming, handsome, stout-talking but weak-minded youth. But there was no need to speak of him as Margaret responded strongly to Henry's plans for Angus.

"Dearest brother, I have seen your writing touching my lord of Angus, which, as your grace writes, is in your said realm, and that you purpose to send him shortly here, and that you find him right wise and hath ruled him well, and that he hath desired that there may be a peace labored betwixt these two realms, and that he will do his labor and diligence to the same with his help, with many other good words of him; and praying me to have him in my favor, and that he is well-minded to me, and beareth me great love and favor.

"Dearest brother, as to my lord of Angus and me, where your grace desireth me to take him in my favor; as to that, he hath not shown, since his departing out of Scotland, that he desired my good will and favor, neither by writing nor word, but now that he hath desired your grace to write to me, knowing well that there is none that I will do so much for as your grace; but I trust, dearest brother the king, that your grace will not desire me to do nothing that may be hurt to me your sister, nor that may be occasion to hold me from the king my son, both for his weal and mine.

"And now your grace understandeth in what state I stand in, and how the king my son is and will be ruled by me, and that I have labored and broken many lords from the ways of the duke of Albany to his way, that he may be put out of danger, and that he and his lords may rule this realm with the help and assistance of your grace, wherein is all my trust. Wherefore, seeing all matters standing on this sort, I would not your grace gave any occasion in the contrary to put it aback, but rather to forward it.

"And as to my lord of Angus coming here, it is not unknown to your grace, that there is great breach and disfavor betwixt him and great lords of his realm, which will not be contented with him, nor with me, if I go his way, but all utterly be contrary me, and do that they can to have me from the king my son, and will put them from the good purpose they are in now; which will be great danger to the king my son's person if this time be overlooked. Wherefore I beseech your grace humbly to consider my part in this behalf, and bid me not now do the thing that may destroy the king my son and me, seeing that I show your grace plainly as it is.

"And when your grace hath helped to bring the king my son out of danger, and that he and his lords may rule this realm, and that there may be good peace betwixt your said realm and this, then your grace shall find me ready to do any thing that may be pleasure to your grace. And while that I see this come to a good end I can say no more, for your grace must pardon me to look for the weal and surety of the king my son afore the pleasure of my lord of Angus; for when I am put from the king my son, he will not be the more set by, and I shall not desire to bide in Scotland when I am out of the company of the king my son.

"Thus, dearest brother the king, I beseech your grace to look well upon these matters, and now, since they may be brought to a good end, let it not be undone for your grace's part, for I assure you that the king my son hath great hope in your grace and in your help, and especially since he saw your grace's writing to him, and saith on his part he shall not fail to take upon him as your grace would that he do, you doing to him for your part, and as your writing beareth to him; and for my part I assure your grace that I may and will cause him to do your counsel afore any other, your grace doing for the weal of him and his realm, as my trust is your will.

"And thus it is in your grace's hand, and I refer it to the coming of my lord of Norfolk, as your grace hath bidden me do; and therefore I can say no more. But touching a point that is in your grace's said writing, saying that my lord of Angus hath labored for the peace, and that he will help with his authority; as to that, methinks, dearest brother the king, methinks that he nor no other should be heard in that matter so well as I your sister, nor that you may get so much honor to do for their request as for me. And therefore I beseech your grace that such thing be not in your mind, but that it be I that does it, for the love and favor that you bear to the king my son and me. And if it be through others, I trust I shall not be so thankfully taken here. Pray your grace to pardon me that I write so plainly to you; but I write nothing but as your grace will find. I beseech your grace to pardon me of my evil hand, for I am something not well disposed, and therefore I have caused my hand to be copied, in adventure if your grace cannot read my evil hand; and God preserve you. Written the 14th day of July.

"Dearest brother, please your grace, touching my lord of Angus coming here, I would beseech your grace to be well advised in the same, as I have written of before; and as touching to my part, if he will put hand to my conjunct fee, I will not be contented therewith, for I have but right sober thing to find myself with, and hath shown your grace that divers times, and got but little remedy. Wherefore now, if I be troubled with the lord of Angus, it is your grace that doth it, and then I will be constrained to seek other help; for I will not let him trouble me in my living, as he hath done in times past."[44]

Not waiting for a response, Margaret and Arran brought the young king from Stirling to Edinburgh on July 26. Within a few days, Margaret demanded a meeting of the parliament at Edinburgh.[45] Since there was no reason to believe that Albany would not return in September, there was need for haste. Having baited Beaton to Edinburgh, Margaret deprived him of his authority and imprisoned him. She and Arran thus took the essential control of the government and led James V before the assembly. The twelve-year-old boy was proclaimed *de facto* King of Scots.[46]

James, described by his mother as the wisest child on earth, was indeed accomplished for his years.[47] Under the careful tutelage of the gentle poet Sir David Lindsey, James' childhood had had more stability than circumstances seemed to allow. Like his father and uncle, he was an able horseman skilled in the military games of tourney and joust. Like his mother, he was a talented musician, who loved to sing and dance. But it was Lindsey who encouraged, nurtured, and cultivated the pursuits which would make him something of a philosopher king. One observer wrote: "All which his princely acts and doings be so excellent for his age, not yet xiii years till Easter next, that in our opinions it is not possible they should be amended. And much more it is our comfort to see and conceive that in personage, favor, and countenance, and in all other his proceedings his Grace resembleth very much to the King's Highness [Henry VIII]. . . ."[48] Henry set out immediately to win the boy. Along with personal letters, gifts of hawks and hounds, Henry sent funding for an honor guard of two hundred men. Then he began to talk of marriage between his daughter Mary and the young King of Scots.[49]

Margaret welcomed both pieces of news, but she wondered if Henry would be as conscientious in paying the guard as he had been in establishing it.[50] She welcomed the suggested marriage although she must have questioned Wolsey's remark ". . . that such a marriage may be found for your son as never King of Scots had the like."[51] For once she did not respond to the slight; perhaps she worried that the honor guards, marriages, acts of parliament did not change the basic fact. James V was still a boy. He was still a figurehead and a signature. And until that fact changed, there was still the problem of regency.

In letter after letter she begged that Angus be forbidden to return. Her demands, her tears, her threats went unheeded. By August 31, he was at Newcastle-on-Tyne, and Margaret wrote again ". . . and as to my part, if [Angus'] desires to be more regarded than mine, I will not labor no more to the pleasure of the king my brother, but look the best way I may for myself. And, if it be the king's grace's pleasure to send in the Earl of Angus, yet he cannot cause me to favor him, nor to let him be in my company. And therefore insofar his grace so doing, doeth greatly to my dishonor and displeasure, which I trust I have not deserved."[52] For once Henry listened. Perhaps he noted that since gaining the regency this second time, Margaret's letters were less confused, more controlled, more authoritative. At any rate he recalled Angus to London.

Margaret's hold upon the government was tenuous at best, and she knew it. Her alliance with Arran was, however, slowly gaining confidence. That delicate balance Margaret knew would be immediately destroyed if Angus were to return. Her husband was a popular man. His clan rivalled in strength and public appeal that of Arran's, and between them lay ancient, ever-sensitive rivalry. Moreover her personal attachment to Henry Stewart was growing. All the court talked of the young man who had so captured the queen's attention and heart. She appointed him Treasurer of Scotland and promised him more, once she obtained the elusive divorce. But whatever happened in Scotland, if Angus were to return, both her private and public plans would crumble. She wrote again to Norfolk, her intermediary with Henry.

"I commend me heartily to you, and have understood your writings delivered to me by Williams Hals, your servant, together with his credence thereby shown to me in your name, purporting that agreance and amity to be treated betwixt me and my lord of Angus was good and necessary to the weal of the king my son, me, and this his realm; and that the king's grace my brother may not lawfully detain the said earl of England, as is, with others divers persuasions and sharp reports to that effect, to the apparent pleasure of the said earl, in your said writings and credence aforesaid rehearsed.

"My lord, as to the weal of the king my son, I am so desirous thereof that if I believed the said agreance was necessary thereto, I would not only (discharging the many divers displeasures done to me by the said earl), accomplish the same, but also therewith—as naturally by tender entire motherly affection I am constrained— would procure and do whatsoever other things to me possibly believed, to the surety and weal of the king my best beloved only son: whose prosperity is, above all other earthly thing, to me most acceptable comfort, consolation, and pleasure; in such manner that, secluding and removing all others my private desires and pleasures, I will thereunto expend myself to the uttermost and ex- termining of my life, without any dread or fear of the same.

"But I firmly know that the said desired agreance, color of amity, and thereby coming of the said earl in this realm, should rather be to the king my son's great apparent damage, making of break and trouble within this his realm, contrary to his erection, reducing of his person from liberty to captivity and thraldom of his mortal enemies, from perfect surety to apparent imminent danger and destruction, and consequently amoving of me, not only from my authority and rule which I now have, but also secluding of me from the keeping, presence, and company of my dearest son's person, and therewith impediment to all other things now well devised and beginning for the weal of both these realms, as I have amply shown by the last articles sent by me to my lord cardinal.

"And it is here thought that the king's grace my brother not only may detain lawfully the said earl, but also should by reason- able occasions and causes do the same, considering it is the desire of his dearest nephew, for the weal and surety of his person, cor- roboration of this his erection and authority, eschewing of many divers apparent inconveniences, and necessary to the combina- tion, unity, and pacifying of these two realms and common weal of the same; which should by all reason be more esteemed than the particular pleasure of the said earl, or whatsoever other pri- vate person.

"And albeit I may not cause nor persuade the king's grace my brother to do herein otherwise than is his grace's pleasure, my lord, you shall hereafter by experience indeed understand and see, that upon the non-detaining of the said earl shall follow great inconveniences, as I have written in the said articles: and for my part I will in no manner way consent to the said earl's coming, for the causes foresaid. And I must in contrary thereof, to the weal and surety of the king my son and me, purchase such friends as I may get, and do the best I may therein. Thinking that if the king's grace my brother, by private solicitation, esteems more the particular pleasure of the said earl than the surety and weal of his nephew the king my son, me and pacifying of these two realms, we must henceforth do for our own weal and sureties, and provide for other support and remedy in such behalf as I doubt shall not be to the pleasure of the king's grace.

"And, my lord, you shall surely believe it is not for no particular displeasure I bear to the said earl that I so expressly write to you, but only to advertise you of the matter as hereafter will ensue and follow, through nondetaining of him. For I know his coming at liberty in this realm shall turn nor rebound to no prosperous success nor good end, but therewith to the displeasure of the said earl and his. Praying you, my lord, to consider this matter, and do your good will and diligence herein, to the weal and surety of the king my son, me, and common weal of these two realms, so that the particular pleasure of any private person be not impediment nor prejudicial thereto. And if there be anything you desire in these parts, I shall to your pleasure and desire reasonably fulfil the same, will God; who have you in his blessed keeping."[53]

This time Margaret's anxieties, her reading of Angus' true nature, her predictions of fatal rivalries came to naught. Henry backed Angus with encouragement, money, and arms, and sent him northward. On November 23 at four o'clock in the morning, he not only entered Edinburgh, he laid siege to the castle. No sooner had ladders and ropes been flung upon the towering walls, than Margaret ordered the guns to fire. In the fearsome darkness of the night, Margaret had again stood against those who sought to take away her authority and to steal away her son. Now, however, it was the man whom she had once raised so high who tried to bring her low. It was a moment of bitter triumph as the guns of Edinburgh Castle echoed across the city, as the curses of wounded men broke the night, as the army withdrew. Margaret listened and briefly considered locking herself and her son behind the massive bastion, but that too was unrealistic. There were few to help her. The force of Angus was too strong, too overwhelming. The castle had not been fortified with either food or munitions. She was forced to capitulate, to give over all that she had struggled for to the man she had come to loathe.[54]

Once again she took up her pen, and anger, frustration, bitterness, and a sense of raw hurt poured forth as she wrote her brother: "Dearest brother, it will please your grace to remember how long I have labored at your hand for to have good peace and love betwixt these two realms; and now, thanked be God, it is likely to come to a good end. For this realm desireth in special to have assured way of England, as at more length your grace will understand by our ambassadors, whom is the first that ever was by me sent; therefore I trust your grace will show you the more loving.

"And because I your sister doth labor in that matter, suppose that any thing that touch me is not well heard with your grace by them that loveth me not, nor credence given to my writing, as well appeareth now by the sending in of the earl of Angus, in contrary my mind and will, and in the contrary of my request and the king my son's; which I think right unkindly, seeing that at my power I did for the pleasure of your grace, as is well understood with all this realm.

"And yet, setting apart my request, I think your grace should not have given me occasion to break this realm, nor to put the king my son in danger of his person, as he hath been now lately through the said earl of Angus coming in the manner as he came within the night, as I wit well your grace will be informed of the truth. But to my part I will say no more of that or little other thing where that I get no credence, but them that loveth me not shall be heard before me and get their desires. Wherefore I will take patience, and do the best I may to keep me from my un-friends; and if I may not keep me here, but that my unfriends shall have help and assistance, against me, then I must provide for myself, beseeching your grace to remember that I have not faulted to your grace, but hath followed your mind in all matters as far as I may.

"And now this realm may understand that your grace hath sent in the earl of Angus to do me displeasure, and to hold me in trouble daily, where I would not have been troubled; but with the grace of God I shall put it off. Not the less it is right unkindly that your grace [hath] done this to me your sister, and to cause this realm to believe the less favor and kindness in your grace, but you may do to me your sister as it pleaseth you."[55]

Whether Margaret liked it or not, she was forced to deal with Angus. Outwardly she summoned control of her face and her voice, in order to look upon her adversary. She would accept Angus, she maintained, on the condition that he drop all claims of matrimony over her, that he deliver her revenues and estates, that she be allowed to bestow all benefices valued less than a thousand pounds. In the meantime, she wrote to Albany and begged that her divorce be quick in coming.[56] But the bitterness between Margaret and Angus merely fomented greater division. As she predicted, faction burst again into pustules and ruptured throughout the body politic. Margaret and Arran against Angus, those were the main choices. The Scots, ever eager to take sides, chose their badges and civil war was once more imminent.[57]

At this uneasy point matters tottered for nearly six months. In July, 1525, parliament again convened—each member increasingly suspicious of the movements and motions of the other. To seek some balance, they arrived eventually at a system of quarterly rotation wherein different factions would have from time to time governance of James V. Angus, as the most powerful member present, became the first keeper of the king. Once he had the boy in his possession, he "would in no wise part with him." When a year later James reached his fourteenth birthday, the Estates declared him free to act on his own royal authority, that the government and governance of the king were to be his own. Again Angus refused, he had the king and the king's power and he refused to give up either.[58]

Margaret throughout this time tried her usual device of one tactic, then another. At times she completely disappeared. At other times she seemed to be at peace with Angus. At still others, she openly brooked his authority. In one thing she was constant— desire for divorce. With Albany's help in Rome, the long-awaited release came on March 11, 1526. She was free at last, but it was too late. Angus' control of the government, his imprisonment or keeping of the king was too strong to challenge.[59] Even Arran found it no longer in his interest to support the dowager queen. Margaret had lost all—authority, government, support from Henry VIII, and her son. When, a short time later, she married without counsel or consultation, the young Henry Stewart, she even lost all persons' respect.

CHAPTER EIGHT

WITH JAMES AND HIS GOVERNMENT NOW FIRMLY IN THE CON-
trol of Angus, Margaret and her new husband withdrew to her
castle at Stirling. There was, for the moment, little else to do. She
was barred from the presence of her son and consulted on neither
the manner of his keeping nor that of his government. All she
could do was watch as Angus replaced, one by one, the offices of
state and church with men of his own faction. With the financial
and political backing of the English and that of his own clan, he
was simply too powerful to oppose openly. But behind the protective walls of Stirling, Margaret studied with the Archbishop of St.
Andrews and the earls of Arran, Argyll, and Murray the potential
for insurrection and the possibilities for overthrow. And as was
her habit, Margaret sought to keep England informed of all that
transpired. Once again she appealed for understanding and relief
as she detailed to Wolsey the awful results of Angus' government:

"Foreasmuch as our dearest son the king's grace has been this
long while by-past after the time of his perfect age, and ordinance
made in parliament by his three estates that his authority should
be used by himself, and yet presently is witholden against his will,
and in thraldom, by the earl of Angus and his partakers; wherethrough his grace, by fear and compulsion of the said earl of
Angus, and against all equity and justice, has granted and sub-
scribed many divers letters inconsonant to reason, as well unto our
holy father the pope as within this his realm, and suchlike unto
the king's grace our dearest brother your master, and yourself;
and in special contrary my lord of Saint Andrews, making mention that he should have usurped our dearest son's authority royal,

and conspired against his grace, which was of no verity, but proceeded all by malice of them that persuaded the same.

"And not the less my said lord of Saint Andrews, because of that wrong relation made on him to his grace, is loath to meddle or concur in the matters wherein his counsel and help are necessary to be had for the weal of our dearest son, while he gets letters of request therefor from the king's grace your master and yourself. Whereupon sundry great enormities and inconveniences has ensued and followed, and not only his grace's authority is all utterly abused in such wise that none manner of justice is executed within this his said realm, by partial ways of the said earl of Angus, which under color of justice causes exercise rigor and cruelty upon his grace's lieges and subjects, whom at the said earl and his partakers has displeasure or indignation by any way; but like wise his grace's most noble person is misguided in all things referring unto the estate royal of his majesty; which were too long and prolix to be written unto you: and therefore this present bearer, master Peter Howston, shall declare you the same; to whom in these behalfs you please give firm credence.

"And all this must our dearest son aforesaid [endure], standing daily under great fear and dread of the said earl of Angus and his partakers, which are continually about his grace, and will suffer none others of his barons nor lieges to resort amongst them; to that end and intent that whatsoever thing he or they will have or devise to be done, his grace for danger of his life, dare not deny the same, howbeit it were never so unreasonable, or might tend to the great hurt of his grace and destruction of the common weal of this his realm; and thereof his grace bears oftentimes great displeasures in his mind, which may not long endure with tenderness of his most noble complexion. And hereupon his grace has moved heavily by his writings unto us his dearest mother, and to my said lord of Saint Andrews, and my lord of Lennox: wherein we and my said lords, with help of God, and others true lieges of this realm, shall do our duty for putting of remedy; as at more large we have written unto our said brother the king's grace your master, presently, by the said bearer.

"And therefore, my lord cardinal, we pray you right affectionately, as in whom we have right singular belief and trust, that you have good and sad consideration hereof with his grace, and aid and assist with the same to the deliverance of our said dearest son his nephew forth from subjection and to kingly freedom: so that the love of his true barons and lieges may safely and surely resort unto his grace, both for obtaining of justice and preserving of his most noble person from such evident dangers and perils as the same stands now daily in. For, if it so happened, as God forbid, that his grace were destroyed or put to confusion by any way, it is not to presume but the king's grace, his dearest uncle your master, should have most high displeasure therefore of any living man, as the case now stands.

"And for putting of hasty and due remedy hereunto, it will please you, my lord cardinal, to cause and solicit his grace [to] write his good affectionate letters unto my said lords of Saint Andrews and Lennox, and to other lords and barons within this realm, as his grace and you think most expedient in that behalf; and that yourself, my lord, write to my said lord of Saint Andrews tenderly in that same effect."[1]

While Margaret's words went unheeded in England, in Scotland the queen and her coalition publicly hurled accusations—not unfounded—upon Angus. He was accused of imprisoning the king, of holding him against his will, of depriving him of the slightest freedom of movement. Privately James fretted at his captivity and in secret messages begged his mother and her friends to set him free. His cries did not go unheard, for his name was a rallying force to noblemen and commons alike. When Angus led a force to subdue raidings and uprisings in Jedburgh, he took James with him. There a smaller force challenged Angus to release the boy. But the differences in armed power made rescue impossible. The challengers fled and James despondently rode home with Angus.[2]

Throughout these months in the custody of Angus, James, ". . . for the tenderness of his years . . . reported to be as fresh wit towardness, and endowed with as many good qualities as may be" —proved himself not lacking in self-reliance.[3] He gradually cultivated the interest and support of the Earl of Lennox. By September 1526, James had so successfully won Lennox's favor that the earl prepared a rescue force. As Lennox's army baited Angus and the entire Douglas clan, James rode in the rear of Angus' host, complaining that he was ill and his horse was lame. He turned aside to rest, and George Douglas realized that the boy was deliberately slowing the march and causing the soldiers to string along the road. In fury Douglas grabbed the king by the arm and snarled: "Sir, rather than our enemies should take you from us, we will lay hold of your body; and, if it be rent in pieces, we will be sure to take one part."[4] James never forgot or forgave those words. When he learned later that the Earl of Lennox had been slain in his cause, the young king wept, swore revenge, and determined to make his own escape.[5]

Lennox's death meant, however, the death of open and concentrated opposition to Angus' rule. The Archbishop of St. Andrews, who had of late made peace with Angus, withdrew from court; Arran shut himself in one of his distant castles and dropped all interest in political affairs. The larger armies broke into petty factions which entertained themselves in raids upon the defenseless. Lawlessness had become the byword of Angus' reign.[6] And in the midst of this total confusion, Margaret was again without friends of influence or allies with power. Silence was all she got from England, and impotence was all she felt in Scotland. She could do nothing of value without the authority of her son. Without him and the military backing of either the lords of Scotland or the King of England, she was totally powerless. Any change must come from Angus or the kings of England or Scotland. It was the boy who took the initiative.

James gained Angus' permission to hunt at the royal manor of Falkland. Although he was under constant guard, he asked that on the morrow all the speediest hounds of his tenants be brought to Falkland "for he was determined that he would slay a fat buck or two for his pleasure." With this order, he dined early and retired early. Once his guards saw him to bed, they too retired, thinking of the morning hunt, the hard ride, the singing hounds. As soon as the watch was set and all things quiet, James dressed himself in the costume of a yeoman. In this disguise, he slipped from his chamber, down the darkened corridors, past the torches at the turnings of the stairs, and into the stable. There he passed for a groom, saddled two horses—one to ride and one for emergency—and called two of his faithful servants to him. With the help of the shadows of night, the small group easily escaped the watch. Once upon the road, spurs dug into horse and by dawn James crossed into Stirling Castle. He ordered the gates slammed behind him and charged that no one else enter. Then he went to sleep.[7]

Before James awoke, Angus and his brother George Douglas

discovered the king's escape and quickly took the road to Stirling. When told of their approach, James sent a herald to the Market Cross and there, "by sound of trumpet commanded Archibald Douglas Earl of Angus, George Douglas, Archibald Douglas the treasurer with all the rest of their kin and friends' allies, that none of them should come near the king's grace within the space of six miles under the pain of treason." The Douglases withdrew while James sent word for the other lords to come to Stirling. Before this assembly James listed his grievances against the Douglases, and the council agreed that the clan be brought to court. By September members of the clan were deprived of all offices and their lands were annexed to the crown; and by November Angus and his brother were driven into exile.[8]

Margaret was again welcomed to court to stand proudly beside the son whose day had finally come. Once again her advice was sought as she became the chief advisor to the seventeen-year-old king. Within a short time James established a five-year treaty with England, led forces out to restore some semblance of order to the long-neglected borders, and gave good heed to the possibility of marrying his English cousin, Princess Mary. Margaret's long-held hopes seemed to be realized at last. The hard years of struggle for the regency were over, her son was securely upon the throne, and peace with England seemed possible. For her long and great labor in the king's cause, James put aside his dislike of Henry Stewart and created him first Lord Methven, "Muffin" as the English nicknamed him. And peace settled in the royal household and began to spread throughout Scotland.[9]

But all was not at peace throughout England. Henry failed to comprehend the danger of the Douglases, welcomed them to court, and gave special heed—against the counsel of Wolsey—to Angus. The king seemed willing to support the outlaw against the government of his nephew. Nevertheless Henry continued to write James flattering letters, to address him as an equal, to send him gifts of hounds and armor, and to encourage the marriage between cousins.

By 1527, however, the King of England was inadvertently cutting the ground beneath the proposed marriage. He was challenging the validity of his own marriage of nearly twenty years to Catherine and, in turn, the legitimacy of Princess Mary. Henry was, no doubt, motivated by the desire to have sons, and Cather-

ine now in her forties seemed incapable of fulfilling his dreams.
He knew he was capable of siring sons—he had the living proof in
his bastard Henry Fitzroy. Upon this boy, Henry showered all the
love he could muster. In 1525, when this "beloved son" was six
years old, he had been created Lord High Admiral of England,
Earl of Nottingham, and Duke of Richmond—hereditary title of
the king's father. As part of the celebrations, so elaborate they
were not unlike those of a legitimate prince, Henry had elevated
two others. The first was the king's cousin Lord Henry Courtenay
Earl of Devonshire, who became Marquis of Exeter. The second
was the king's nephew, the son of Mary and Charles Brandon, the
nine-year-old Lord Henry Brandon, who became the Earl of
Lincoln.[10] By these acts, Henry's bastard took precedence over all
the nobility of England including the Princess Mary herself.[11] It
was a gesture which had thrown the court into confusion and the
gossips into a quiver.

Mary the French Queen and Duchess of Suffolk delighted in
her son's elevation. It was the most certain token of Henry's acceptance of her marriage and the legitimacy of her children. But
his treatment of the bastard troubled her. Catherine had ever
been her friend and champion, and now that Henry was openly
questioning his marriage, Mary suffered for the queen. As the
king talked more and more of the need for divorce, the more Mary
sorrowed. How could the king, as Defender of the Faith, as one
who had so strongly opposed the divorce of his sister Margaret,
seek divorce for himself? Unable to reconcile the questions with
the answers, Mary found herself torn between devotion to her
brother and love for her friend.

As a result Mary came less frequently to court. Throughout
much of the 1520s she spent most of her time in the country
retreats of the county of Suffolk. She came to love the undulating
hills, the rich dark forests which broke to reveal distant horizons,
the spires of churches, abbeys, and holy retreats which stretched
upward against space. This open, quiet countryside brought comfort and release from the suffocating, scandalous intrigues of court.

In the peace of her own home, Mary discovered the pleasure of
building and reshaping the gardens of Westhorpe Hall. In the
neighboring country, she discovered the joys of solitude and silence when visiting the religious houses of Ely and Butley. There
she and Suffolk often visited a month, sometimes two, accepting

the gentle hospitality of the monks. On occasion Mary went alone to these retreats with only her serving women about her. She had discovered the quiet pleasure of lunch in a shady garden, lulled by the chants of the choir. Whenever these retreats ended, her pleasure and gratitude were always marked by rich gifts of money, vestments, or canopies for the altar. It was not that Mary's generosity was generated by the great piety that motivated her brother or her parents. It was not that she opposed or even understood the great theological questions that had been raised by Luther. She had simply discovered the joy of quiet aloneness so different from the life she had always lived.

In such moments Mary no doubt reflected on the great contrasts of her experience: the days of pampered childhood; the days of adoration as queen; the days of festival and game as the king's favorite sister; the days of being in favor and out. She rejoiced that Suffolk remained so constant a friend and welcome companion to her brother, but she lamented that his entire career rested in frequent attendance at court and council. She knew too that to survive he must ever take Henry's part. Now that her brother was determined to have his divorce, she and Suffolk argued. He of necessity stood with the king; she for years of love and devotion would stand with the queen.

When called to court, Mary went. Once there her source of pride, affection, and concern was her niece and namesake, the eleven-year-old Princess Mary. The princess, accomplished beyond her years, was far too intelligent not to grasp the controversy which swept about her. The father, who had loved her, now abhorred her and named her bastard. Pain and confusion haunted her eyes. As she turned to her mother for comfort and reassurance, Catherine gathered the child with love. Mary of Suffolk sought to gather them both in her arms. She could share their grief and understand their humiliation, but she could do nothing to alleviate their pain. When she left court, she sought solace in the solitude and simplicity of her country retreats. There she would try to reason out the painful confusions, these sudden reversals and her relation to them.

Mary saw how easily the seeming stability of a marriage could erupt. It had happened with her sister Margaret. It was happening with her brother Henry. And in both cases, their children's legitimacy became a point of challenge. It made her look to her own marriage. Although neither she nor Suffolk questioned their marriage, there was the problem—or a potential problem—in his previous marriages. Were she not a princess and her son a possible heir to the throne, she would not have bothered to have the matter reviewed. But if Henry could renounce his own daughter, cast the shame of bastardy upon her, might not he or others under some provocation do the same to her own children? Suffolk, as any man of great power and influence, had enemies; and who could tell what the future held.

Consequently both Mary and Suffolk asked Wolsey's help in clearing the matter of their marriage with Rome. In Suffolk's youth he had a verbal contract of marriage with the Lady Anne Browne. He had, however, married the Lady Margaret Mortimer, whom he had later divorced upon the basis of his pre-contract. He then married Anne, and she became the mother of his two daughters. She had died shortly before the marriage of Suffolk and Mary. By slightly bending the facts, the papal bull dated May 12, 1528, allowed for the validity of Brandon's divorce, the legitimacy of his marriage to Mary, and removed all challenge to his heirs. The next year the bull was publicly notarized by the Bishop of Norwich in the presence of witnesses. Any question of the Suffolks' marriage, any slur against the children of his marriages, would result in censure by the pope himself.[12] With these announcements both Suffolk and Mary looked with hope and relief at their handsome young family: Mary and Anne, daughters of Suffolk's second marriage; Henry Earl of Lincoln, Frances, and Eleanor of their own.

The quiet settling of the Suffolks' affairs contrasted sharply with what was fast becoming known as the "King's Great Matter." The contrast was no more sharply marked than in Suffolk's summons to court. He and Mary were visiting Butley Abbey and had ridden out to Slaverton for a day of fox hunting. There they "dined under the oaks . . . with game and sport, merry enough" when the royal messenger appeared. He brought news of the arrival of Cardinal Campeggio, the papal legate, come to judge the proceedings of divorce of Catherine of Aragon and Henry VIII.

The news was filled with awful and multiple meaning. Suffolk as a long-ago attendant upon Catherine's first husband Arthur had been called to testify. There was no doubt that he would do other than support Henry's thesis from Leviticus: "If a man shall take

his brother's wife, it is an impurity . . . they shall be childless."
This adultery Henry believed put him in great peril of his soul
and threatened the throne which had no heirs male. With grave
seriousness, Henry spoke of his marriage of twenty years and
noted with saddened countenance, ". . . although it hath pleased
almighty God to send us a fair daughter of a noble woman and me
begotten . . . yet it hath been told us by divers great clerics that
neither she is our lawful daughter nor her mother our lawful wife.
. . . Think you, my lords, that these words touch not my body and
soul, think you that these doings do not daily and hourly trouble
my conscience and vex my spirits, yes we doubt not but and if it
were your own cause every man would seek remedy when the
peril of your soul and the loss of your inheritance is openly laid to
you. . . ." He then went on to extol the virtues of his wife and
ended with a plea to know the truth.[13]

There were many who knew the truth—that Henry's attentions
were fixed upon a lady of the queen, Anne Boleyn. She, unlike
the legion of royal mistresses, had demanded all or nothing.
Henry was infatuated to the point where he would give her all.
And Catherine knew all. She had watched the mistresses come and
go, she had seen the flirtatious Anne, the "goggled-eyed whore,"
whip Henry's desire to frenzy; and the queen refused to step aside.
She would not consent to annulment; she would not retreat to a
nunnery. She would fight the divorce to the end.

So matters stood through the grim fall of 1529. While the
learned clerics debated before the two cardinals, Wolsey and
Campeggio, the court moved to Greenwich for the annual Christmas festival. Mary came from her country retreat to support her
friend, who presided white-lipped and tense over the banquets,
the masquing, the dancing, and the dicing. But both knew she was
losing. The witnesses against her recalled what they could and
created what they could not remember of the wedding night she
had shared with Arthur twenty-eight years ago. Although Wolsey
and Campeggio might seek to draw out the trial, although her
friends might hope it would all disappear, Catherine and Mary
knew how it would be in the end. But the arguments dragged on
into spring.

Unable to help her friend and unable to encourage her brother,
Mary again retreated from court. Suffolk remained behind as a
peer of the realm, a key witness against Catherine, and a boon

companion to the king. At the hearing in June, Henry again cited his worn and vexed conscience and asked for an answer. When he finished, Catherine left the hall without a word. The arguments continued and dragged their weary weight through the summer, until Campeggio cancelled all hearings by claiming the vacation of the Roman ecclesiastical courts had begun. Henry, disgusted with the delay, turned the matter over to the dukes of Suffolk and Norfolk; he required them to make a judgment "for the quietness of his conscience." When the dukes made their demands before the cardinals, Campeggio refused to listen; furthermore he declared any action null and void and ordered the case closed until October.

Suffolk rose in massive fury before the cardinals, slammed his angry fist on the table, and shouted: "By the Mass! Now I see that the old saw is true—there was never Legate nor Cardinal that did good in England!" With those words, Suffolk drew the line between himself and his old ally Thomas Wolsey the Cardinal of York who answered: "Sir, of all men within this realm, ye have least cause to dispraise or be offended with Cardinals; for if I, simple Cardinal, had not been, ye should have had at his present time no head upon your shoulders, wherein ye should have a tongue to make any such report in despite of us . . . wherefore, my lord, hold your peace, and pacify yourself, and frame your tongue like a man of honor and of wisdom. And not to speak so quickly or so reproachfully by your friends for ye know best what friendship ye have received at my hands, the which yet I never revealed to no person alive before now—neither to my glory nor to your dishonor."[14]

Suffolk was silent as the words poured upon him and a great wave of memory washed over him. It was true, no man had helped him in his hour of need save Wolsey. That both Mary and Suffolk knew. All that was now at an end. For Suffolk was on the other side—the side of the "King's Great Matter." And neither he nor Wolsey could cross over. As they faced each other across the massive table, both knew that their long association was finished.

For Wolsey, it was the beginning of the end. Soon he was denied his old chambers in the king's household. Then Norfolk suggested he attend to his duties in York, and Suffolk demanded from him the Great Seal of England. As cardinal and lord chancellor, Wolsey had failed in the practical business of Henry's demand for a speedy divorce. Henry saw that failure as a personal slight, and he plucked away the honors, dignities, wealth, and power. As they fell to the ground, Suffolk joined his ancient adversary the Duke of Norfolk in picking them up. In short time, there was nothing left to take or give save Wolsey's fool. As a futile attempt at reconciliation, Wolsey gave him to the king, and the fool wept when they took him away.[15]

Later one of Wolsey's wards, the Earl of Northumberland, came with tears in his eyes to arrest his old master. Then the cardinal's grand silver cross, which stood against the wall, suddenly broke from its place and cracked the skull of one of the betrayers. That symbolized the end. Wolsey was arrested, and the broken, sickened man began the journey to London. When he reached Leicester, he could travel no further. In a barren monastic chamber at Leicester Abbey, Wolsey spoke his last discernible words: "Had I served God as diligently as I have done the king, he would not have given me over in my gray hairs; but this is my just reward."[16] Death had saved him from a final public humiliation.

As the great corpulence, once the mightiest prelate and politician in England—sank into the dust of death, political and personal turmoils continued to rise in London. Suffolk's prominence rose with them. Whether he was hearing cases in the Star Chamber, gathering a share of Wolsey's wealth, attending the king's political and personal needs, or scratching out time for his own affairs, it all meant that he spent less and less time with Mary.

The "old pain in her side" was increasingly frequent, and the emotional turmoil brought on by the fall from estate of two of her most valued friends—Wolsey and Catherine—only heightened her distress. When parliament declared "that queen Catherine should thenceforth be no more called queen, but Princess-Dowager of Prince Arthur," Mary grieved from afar.[17] She could only silently agree with her old friend, who refuted all arguments with the simple reply: "Truly I am the king's true wife and to him married; and if all the doctors were dead, or law, or learning so far out of man's mind at the time of our marriage, yet I cannot think that the court of Rome and the whole Church of England would consent to a thing unlawful and detestable (as you call it), but still I say I am his wife, and for him will I pray."[18]

The queen was nonetheless forced from the king's side, and it was apparent that her place had already been seized by Anne

Boleyn. Mary's mind boggled at the presumption of this one-time maid-in-waiting who had gone with her to France, who had since been in the service of Catherine. Her Tudor blood, although encased in a weakened body, rose in absolute disdain for the upstart. Although she could not and would not challenge openly Henry's course, neither would she acknowledge as her queen "the goggle-eyed whore." When, however, Henry demanded loan of Mary's jewels for Anne to wear, Mary had to send them. But she would not come to court. Instead she stayed in Suffolk, most often at Westhorpe Hall. When her health permitted she sought the quiet solitude of nearby abbeys. She sought diversion anywhere but in London.

At Easter, Mary took herself and a large company to the Easter Fair and Market at nearby Bury St. Edmunds. There, under a tent of cloth of gold, Mary held court, receiving friends and acquaintances, speaking with gentry and commons alike, giving gifts and expressing affection. For her sympathy and compassion, she was greatly loved by those who saw and knew her. And in such moments of relaxed affection, the harsher realities of London and the court seemed remote.[19]

Never, whether in favor or out, in good health or bad, in courtly circles or country retreats, did Mary forget those in need. While she could do nothing to help the great ones who fell, she always tried to help the small ones toward greater success. One request, made to Arthur Plantagenet Lieutenant of Calais on behalf of a servant who wanted to be a soldier, was only one of many such petitions: "Right trusty and well-beloved cousin, We greet you well, desiring, at this our intercession, you will be so good lord unto John Williams, this bearer, as to admit him into the room of a soldier in Calais, with the wages of eight pence by the day; assuring you, cousin, in your so doing and acceptable pleasure, which we shall right willingly acquit at your desire in time coming, trusting the conditions, behavior, and personage of the said John be such as you shall be contented with the same."[20]

While Mary found time for these small acts of kindness, there was much that vied for her attention. The pain that wracked her body was intensified by the greater mental conflict—how to justify Suffolk's successes, his heady rise to power at the price of the health, the happiness, the very lives of old friends. The question went unanswered as Mary busied herself in the daily routines of her own household, as she taught her children, as she watched them grow.

As the young wife of Suffolk, Mary had taken great interest in his two daughters, Anne and Mary. When her own family grew to include her son and two daughters more, and Suffolk's wards Henry Grey and Catherine Willoughby, Mary offered affection, interest, and attention that was unusual in many aristocratic homes. Perhaps Suffolk's prolonged absences, coupled with Mary's country retreats, offered more than usual time and preoccupation with the children. Whatever the reason, it was surely with mixed emotion that she watched the little family break apart. In 1531 Lady Anne Brandon married the heir of Baron John Grey of Powis, Wales. Two years later an even more brilliant match was contracted for Mary's elder daughter, the sixteen-year-old Frances, who married Lord Henry Grey Marquis of Dorset.

The wedding ceremony's splendor underscored the important alliance of one of royal blood with one of an ancient and powerful house. To make the wedding more of a public affair, the remote quiet of Westhorpe Hall was deemed inappropriate; instead Suffolk Place near London was sumptuously decorated. To make it more of a family affair, Mary's daughter Eleanor was betrothed to Henry Lord Clifford, heir of the Earl of Cumberland. Unable to consider missing these events, Mary gathered her failing energies for the four-day trip by carriage through the rain and chill of March, 1533. Although she would not go to court, she would not miss the wedding and engagement of her daughters. It was a handsome occasion with hangings and tapestries, feasts, masques, and dancing befitting princesses. Henry came. What he and his favorite sister said to each other is unrecorded. Whether Mary knew that Henry had already, in January, married Anne Boleyn is unknown. That they talked of Mary's loan of jewels to Anne is doubtful. It was something she had had to do, a matter not open to question, but one that had irked her sorely. That they talked of her health is possible, for she was greatly weakened by illness, travel, and the strains of the wedding. Yet in spite of the obvious illness and the conflicting interests of the two, neither suspected it was the last time they would ever meet.

Mary and Eleanor left for Westhorpe Hall as Frances and her husband went to their home at Bradgate in Leicestershire. For the sixteen-year-old bride and her seventeen-year-old groom life was beginning. For the thirty-eight year-old Mary, life was quickly ending. There were days when she could neither stand nor sit for faintness. Physicians from London, from the court itself, came and went from Westhorpe, but none knew of any remedy and none saw any hope. The old sickness seemed to gather intensity, and the sorrow—for Catherine, of Aragon and the confusions at Court— turned to melancholy. Mary's body bordered on death and her spirits on despair. As she had done in times before, she turned in desperation to the distractions of court. With a quivering hand which revealed her great sickness, she wrote to Henry:

My most dearest and best beloved Brother—

I humbly recommend me to your Grace. Sir, so it is that I have been very sick and ill at ease, for which I was fain to send for Master Peter the Physician for to have holpen me of this disease that I have. Howbeit, I am rather worse than better, wherefore I trust surely to come to London with my lord. For if I should tarry here I am sure I should never asperge the sickness that I have. Wherefore, Sir, I would be the gladder a great deal to come thither, because I would be glad to see your grace, the which I do think long for to do. For I have been a great while out of your sight, and now I trust I shall not be so long again. For the sight of your grace is the greatest comfort to me that may be possible. No more to your grace at this time, but I pray God to send you your heart's desire, and surely to the sight of you.

By your loving sister
Mary.[21]

It was Mary's last letter to Henry. While Suffolk was busied at court with preparations for the coronation of Anne Boleyn on June 1, Mary needed no excuse not to give attendance. Whether anyone said so, all who cared knew that she was dying. Suffolk as High Constable for the coronation was, however, too much in- volved in the continuing celebrations at court to make frequent trips to Westhorpe. He, with the agility of a born courtier, had had no outward difficulty in bowing before the upstart maid-in- waiting. What inner turmoil he might have felt, he carefully con- cealed. The same must have been true of his torn allegiances between the king who sought happiness and an heir and the wife who lay dying. Suffolk chose to remain with the king.

On June 26, 1533, the passing bell sounded just before eight in the morning. Mary Tudor Queen Dowager of France and Duchess of Suffolk had died as she had lived her last years—surrounded by her children. Her body was embalmed, wrapped in lead, and placed in its coffin. Over the coffin lay an embroidered pall of blue velvet. The body was moved to the chapel at Westhorpe where it lay for three weeks, surrounded night and day by flaming tapers. The long delay in burial was caused possibly by protocol, which demanded the presence of a French pursuivant.

In London elaborate and costly services were ordered by Henry and Suffolk at Westminster Abbey on July 10 and 11. At these obsequies, punctuated by all the formality and ceremony accorded royalty, were numerous peers of the realm, led by the Earl of Essex as chief mourner. Here knights, the king-of-arms, the herald-of-arms, the king's yeomen and royal pursuivants accompanied the priests and choir in prayer amidst the torch-lit darkness of the ancient abbey.

By July 20 the funeral arrangements for the procession to Bury St. Edmunds and burial in the vast abbey church were complete. Once again the family gathered, although etiquette forbade the presence of Suffolk. The duke retired to Ewelme and Henry stayed at Windsor. Lady Frances Grey led the procession as chief mourner and with her walked her brother the Earl of Lincoln and her husband the Marquis of Dorset. Behind them walked Eleanor Brandon and Catherine Willoughby; behind them came Suffolk's daughters Anne Lady Powis and Mary Lady Monteagle. In the family chapel they gathered for the chanting of the dirge.

The next morning they came again before the coffin for mass, and their offerings that day were given to the poor. Then the funeral procession formed. The coffin was placed on a funeral car, canopied in black velvet, embroidered with Mary's coat of arms, and drawn by six great horses trapped in black. At each corner of the hearse, knelt a gentleman in mourning. Above him fluttered a banner which depicted the lineage and estate of Mary Tudor. Upon the coffin stood a carved likeness of the queen-duchess dressed in robes of estate, a crown upon its head, a sceptre in its wooden hands.

As the procession moved forward, a hundred poor men in black gowns and carrying lighted candles led the way. Then came the priests and attendants of Mary's own chapel, carrying the cross;

after them came members of her household, knights and gentlemen of court; then the funeral car itself surrounded by a hundred yeomen with torches. And the smoke and shadow cast upon the lovely effigy caused it to look as though it lived. Lady Frances reined her horse between her husband and her brother-in-law. Behind them came the rest of the family, the queen-duchess' servants, and "all other that would"—any of the standers-by who wished to show tribute to the royal neighbor who had always been kind.

When the cortège reached Bury, the body was blessed and the mourners were welcomed. The great church itself was already crowded with friends as the coffin was carried to its place. Throughout the ceremonies, the intonement of the priests and the chanting of the choir, the French pursuivant Guisnes, "at the times accustomed," called aloud: "Pray for the soul of the right high excellent princess, and right Christian Queen, Mary, late French queen, and all Christian souls." While a small group of mourners watched before the coffin, the others left the church. And there were many who wept.

The next morning, the family and officials assembled again for their final tribute to the woman who had been the mother to some and a friend to many. After the requiem mass, the four Suffolk daughters presented the four palls of cloth of gold. Then the Abbot of St. Bennett, William Rugg, delivered the sermon and sang a second mass. When it was over, Frances and Eleanor, overcome with exhaustion and grief at this final farewell, withdrew to a private chamber. But they could still hear the song of prayer as the coffin was carried to its grave; afterwards came the great weeping and lamentation as the members of Mary's household broke their staves of office and dropped them into the open grave. The funeral was over; the flags, canopies, banners, the effigy of Mary herself were left behind at the grave or offered at the altar. The final tribute came outside, in the town itself, where "there was also provided for the poor people a great dole in four places in the town of Bury, having meats and drinks, come who would, and every poor body four pence."[22] This last was the most fitting tribute of all, for it was the gesture Mary herself would have made. The poor and the deserving were always her interest and self-imposed responsibility.

The news of Mary's death was not slow in reaching Scotland

although its impact was partially eclipsed by the resolution of the "King's Great Matter," the marriage, pregnancy, and coronation of Anne Boleyn. How Margaret Tudor Queen of Scotland received the news of Mary's death is not known, but there were no public services of mourning in Scotland. There was, however, great interest and concern in the pregnancy of Henry's new wife. Once his daughter, Princess Mary, had been stamped with the stigma of bastardy, James V lost all interest in her. He had greater hopes to look to—the crown of England. As the son of his mother, he was her brother's heir.

During the long years of his miserable minority, James had been alternately flattered and threatened, pampered and coerced. As a result when he grew to manhood, he trusted no one—not even his mother. Instead he seemed rather to take malicious delight in the pain of others. He never forgot a slight, never forgave insubordination. But as ruthless as he was with others, with himself he was self-indulgent. Between his seventeenth and nineteenth years, he had taken five mistresses and fathered five bastards. Little wonder that throughout the late 1520s his mother was anxious to secure the English marriage—she apparently had forgotten her own misery at the infidelities of James IV.

For the time, Margaret and her son, however, were in reasonable harmony as long as they avoided two subjects—marriage with the English Mary and continued peace with the English Harry. Like the Scots kings before him, James saw more hope in continued alliance with France. Unbeknownst to his mother or his uncle, he reopened negotiations with France and renewed the "auld alliance." Margaret continued her flattery of her brother and believed in the reality of the long-cherished dream of continued peace with England.

In this happy frame of mind, Margaret and James entertained the papal nuncio and set off with him on a relaxed progress through the country. The highlight of the tour was a visit in the summer of 1530 with the Earl of Atholl, a mighty Highland chieftain. For the royal entertainment, the earl had built a great rural palace complete with moats, bridges, towers, chambers hung in silk and gold, windows of stained glass, floors of green turf and flowers. About this forest retreat, one chronicler wrote: "In this fairy mansion the king was lodged more sumptuously than in any of his own palaces; he slept on the softest down; listened to the

sweetest music; saw the fountains around him flowing with mus-
cadel and hippocras; angled for the most delicate fish which
gleamed in the little streams and lakes in the meadow, or pursued
the pastime of the chase amid woods and mountains which
abounded with every species of game."[23]

James and Margaret were greatly flattered and the papal nuncio
much impressed, especially since there was neither town nor village within the twenty miles of wilderness. But the charming
rustic palace was filled with every delicacy and every imagined
delight, and it was with regret that the royal party renewed their
journey. As they left the charming spot, they turned for one final
look. Atholl and his men had set the place aflame. While James
and Margaret looked on with delight, the ambassador turned to
Atholl in dismay and said, "I marvel that ye should cause yon fair
palace to be burnt in which your grace hath been so well lodged."
James answered for the earl, "It is the custom of our highland-
men, though they be never so well lodged, to burn their lodging
when they depart."[24] The Scots had proven that they, like the
English, delighted in extravagant waste. And this pleasant interlude was but one of many that the king and his mother shared.

James and Margaret continued to live in general agreement.
But as the king gained confidence in his reign and his abilities, the
queen dowager lost proportionate influence. He consulted her in
the rebuilding and refurbishing of the royal estates of Edinburgh,
Stirling, Dunbarton, Blackness, Linlithgow, and Holyrood; but in
matters of government, he kept his own counsel. Margaret, however, believed—had to believe for her own sense of security and
position—that she was the directress of the policy of Scotland.
James let her think as she would and balked mainly at her constant interest in England.

When an English delegation came into Scotland, they were
warmly welcomed by the king. Margaret greeted them with undi-
luted enthusiasm, talked of their abilities, boasted of their athletic
skills, and issued a challenge that six English archers would gladly
answer six Scots archers at whatever target the Scots might choose.
James laughingly answered his mother's challenge and suggested
that the two pledge a hundred crowns and a tun of wine to the
winning team. When the games were held at St. Andrews, three
landed gentlemen and three yeomen composed each team. Arrow

flew after arrow, some falling wide, some on the mark; but when the tally was taken, the Scots—to James' delight—had won.[25]

The serious part of the English mission was an invitation from Henry for the two monarchs to meet at York. James, at first, seemed inclined to the meeting; but the more his mother urged it forward, the less willing he was to leave. He would go only as far south as Newcastle-upon-Tyne and sent the delegation away with the matter unsettled. Margaret, in a pout, left court and retired to the country, and wrote to her brother with an authority she did not really have: ". . . our dearest son has affectionately desired us to write in his name unto you these words following, that not only will he meet, and commune, and visit you, but also loves your grace better than any man living next himself, and will take your part, his person and his realm, against all living creatures under God. . . ."[26]

James, however, had other matters in mind. He was pleased with his negotiations with England. He had been able to refuse the marriage with Mary while yet renewing the earlier truce. Neither England nor Scotland wanted war. Henry, throughout the 1530s was distracted with the problems of his marriages, the divorce of Catherine, his break with the Roman Church, and the subsequent beheading of Anne. James was simply broke. His treasury was barren, and he saw that the quickest way to replenishment was through marriage and a substantial dowry. He had never interrupted his correspondence with France, and he was prepared now to take a French bride.

To his mother's amazement, James secretly took ship to France. Since he had long been betrothed to the daughter of the Duc de Vendôme, he had long assumed he would marry her. When he met the lady, however, the king changed his mind and took himself to the court of Francis I. There he received the welcome of royalty and fell instantly in love with Francis' daughter, the tubercular Madeleine. Although Francis had hesitations in allowing his frail daughter to leave France for the colder reaches of Scotland, he finally consented. The two lovers were married amidst the majesty of the Cathedral of Nôtre Dame on January 1, 1537.

Upon hearing the news, Margaret, frustrated in her hopes for another Scots-Anglo marital alliance, was angered that her son had acted so independently of her judgment. The deed was done, she could not interfere, she could only agree with Henry's angry protestations. In a carefully worded text, she seconded Henry's anger and shifted all responsibility to James' shoulders. "Dearest brother," she wrote, "as touching the marriage of your nephew the king, my son, insofar as your grace makes rehearsal . . . that your mind and counsel were not had to the same, which would have been both to his honor and profit; as to that, dearest brother, I assure your grace that, when he departed from me, that he said he would have your advice and counsel principally in all his matters that he had to do; and to my part I am very evil content that he did not the same, which of reason and kindness he should have done."[27]

The year 1536 had been a year of revolt for Margaret's children. As James was fast determining his own affairs, so was his half-sister Lady Margaret Douglas. The girl was as much out of her mother's thoughts as out of her life. Her father, Angus, who seemed to have had genuine feeling for the girl, had kept her often with him or under his direction. Consequently she had lived most of her life in England, had enjoyed the favor of her royal uncle, and been placed in the household of her royal cousin Princess Mary. She had had, however, the audacity to violate Henry VIII's trust and fall in love with Lord Thomas Howard. Moreover she had violated her uncle's authority by forming a private contract with Howard. Legally both had broken the law which required Henry's consent to all marriages touching the blood royal. For both offenses Margaret Douglas and Thomas Howard were committed to the Tower of London. Howard died there, and Margaret remained there while her mother begged for her release.[28] After Howard's death, Lady Margaret was released, reprimanded, and kept in England.

With that matter concluded, Margaret Tudor turned attention to matters closer at hand. James and his bride were returning to Scotland. Knowing full well that news of the sumptuousness of the French wedding had been detailed in the English court, Margaret played upon her brother's vanity in order to satisfy her own. She felt she simply had nothing to wear to attend the reception of her daughter-in-law. In order that neither she nor Henry be embarrassed by her tawdry attire she wrote: ". . . you write and maketh mention . . . of the coming of the queen, my son's wife, that I, seeing and considering the great honor that she will be at, that towards myself I would think that I might be in such sort that I might do honor to your grace and myself, I being your only sister, trust your grace will think the more honor I have the more honor is yours. And this cause being considered, I beseech your grace, of your special help and counsel in all sorts, how I shall order me; referring all things to your pleasure, and what you will do to me. . . ."[29]

Henry sent her the money, and Margaret composed herself for the arrival of James and Madeleine. In May they sailed, and true to rumor and Margaret's expectation, the fragile bride brought a healthy dowry, "such substance was never seen in Scotland as this young queen brought."[30] When she came ashore, she knelt upon the ground and took into her hands clods of earth and kissed it. The gesture won the immediate affection of the waiting, watching Scots.[31] While the bride rested, the preparations for the state entry and coronation were underway. But the change in climate tore at the young queen, and her health crumbled. She died on July 7 at Holyrood. Sir David Lindsey, who had planned her ceremonial entry, expressed the sentiments of his countrymen:

> O dreadful dragon with thy mighty dart,
> Which did not spare femininity the flower,
> But cruelly did pierce her through the heart
> And would not give her respite for an hour
> To remain with her prince and paramour
> That she at leisure might have taken license,
> Scotland on thee may cry a loud vengeance.[32]

While Scotland mourned its lovely young queen, James wrote to his father-in-law: "Howbeit there could be nothing in the world more grievous than the occasion which I have for writing you this present letter—that occasion being the passing of your daughter, my most dear companion, which befell this day after long sickness—yet I would in no wise desire to be negligent in apprising you thereof. And were it not for the great comfort and confidence I have in you, that you will forever remain my good father, as I wish never to be anything but your good and humble son, I would be in greater grief than yet I am; and I assure you that you will never find any fault upon my part, who will bear

myself ever towards you as a son bears himself to his father. . . ."[33]
In these words politics and diplomacy contested with those of
grief. It was probably the closest James ever came to expressing
feeling for anyone other than himself.

As the atmosphere following Madeleine's death cleared, James
turned his attention to matters at home, only to find that his
mother—during his absence in France—was fast creating more
scandal. She had arranged for a divorce from her third husband,
Henry Stewart Lord Methven. She had already written Henry,
outlined her complaints, and solicited his aid: "I did take the lord
of Methven, and did him that honor to take him as my husband,
as I understand, at that time, and gave him as much credence as I
could do. He hath spent my lands and profits upon his own kin
and friends, in such sort that he hath made them hope and put me
into great debts, which will be to the sum of 8000 marks Scotch
money; and as yet cannot know how nor in what sort, for he
would never let me understand how my lands was ruled, but said
he would answer for the same.

"Herefore I desire the lords of my son's council to cause him to
make them account, as at more length I have shown my mind in
this matter and in all others. . . . [To which] I trust your grace
will give credence to, and that you will show you a kind prince
and brother toward me, as my special trust and hope is in your
grace, if . . . that the king my son would not do to me in all sorts as
he ought to do, both to the pleasure of God and to his own honor.
. . . And that being known, that he fail to me his mother in
disobeying me of my conjunct feoffment, or in any thing that may
be to my hurt or dishonor, I trust, then, that your grace will look
upon the same for your honor, with your help, and supply a refuge to me, if need asks the same. . . ."[34]

Upon receiving this letter, Henry gently reprimanded his
nephew, who caused the council to look more closely at the matter
of his mother's revenues. But money, of course, was not the only
issue. Methven had taken a mistress, and Margaret was once more
without either money or affection. Moreover she was beginning to
regret her divorce from Angus, and it was rumored that she contemplated remarrying him. From a political view it seemed a
practical thing for Margaret to do. Since her son was so deeply
involved in French interests, she feared for those of England.
Angus, she knew, would be a strong enough presence to counter

the growing French sentiment. With her usual myopia, she counted on her son's cooperation. Indeed she saw divorce as an accomplished fact when she wrote to Henry: "Pleaseth your grace also to know that my divorce and partition is at the giving of the sentence, and proved by many famous folk, to the number of four-and-twenty provers. And with the grace of God I shall not have never such a trouble again, and your grace shall be very sure I shall never do no thing [but] by your counsel and command-ment. . . ."[35]

James, however, refused to cooperate. He saw immediately the ramifications of the divorce and was horrified at the prospects of Angus' returning to haunt the corridors of power. The king wanted no repetition of any part of his miserable history. More-over he had come to accept Methven, honored him with lands and wealth if not with great positions of power. Margaret, however, wanted Methven out of court and out of her life. She remained fervent about the decision for divorce, and James just as fervently refused her. They argued long and passionately. The mother failed to see in the son a king as determined as she, and the son refused the demands of a mother who felt anguished at her situa-tion. The matter of divorce became the occasion for the first break, and it was Margaret who was forced to give in.

Margaret left court and retired to Methven Castle with the full fury of Tudor rage upon her. Her dearest son, like her dearest brother and the series of dearest husbands, had betrayed her. As before she had been forced to give in, but she would not give up. She resorted to her old device of subterfuge and wrote the follow-ing letter to the Duke of Norfolk:

"I must make my complaint to you, how I am heavily done to in this realm; for I have obtained my cause of divorce betwixt me and the lord of Methven, and it is so far past that the judge has concluded and written my sentence, ready to be pronounced these twelve weeks bypast, and the king my son has stopped the same, and will not let it be given, the which is contrary justice and reason; and he promised me, when I gave him my manor of Dun-bar for a certain money, that I should have the same sentence pronounced.

"Thus, my lord, I trust it be the king's grace my brother's will that I have reason done to me, and obeyed of my living, suppose I may not daily write to his grace; and seeing that you are so near to these parts, your good writing and words would do me most good to the king my son, so that he may understand that the king's grace my brother will not suffer me to be wronged, for I am daily holden in great trouble for lack of my sentence [of divorce].

"Herefore I pray you, my lord and cousin, that you will make some errand to the king my son, not letting known that I did advertise you, but that every body speaks of it that I should lack justice, that is mother to him, which is to his dishonor greatly; and that you will pray him to cause my sentence to be pronounced when your said servant is present here with his grace, or else I will not get it. For they cause my son the king to believe that, if the lord of Methven be my husband, that he may give the king my lands and living, as long as he is my husband; and through this way thinks to hold me daily in trouble, and to make him master of my lands.

"Thus, my lord and cousin, you may help me out of my trouble through your good writing; for if they may trust that the king's grace my brother will be displeased at this, they will remedy the same."[36]

This rather pathetic appeal brought none of the hoped-for results. James remained inflexible about his mother's divorce. About her second wish, a meeting with Henry, James was evasive. Margaret insisted that the two kings meet. She believed in the power of her brother's persuasive presence. If only James would talk with Henry, the King of Scots would recognize the advantage of alliance with England and the foolishness in reliance on France. She knew too that Henry was anxious for the meeting. Since his separation from Rome, Scotland had become a refuge for English Catholics. Already they had approached James with an offer of the English crown if only he would undertake the Catholic cause in England.[37] Henry, on the other hand, hoped to win his nephew to the new religion, with its freedom from Roman authority and the tantalizing wealth in the coffers and furnishings of the abbeys, churches, and monasteries. Certainly James was neither ignorant nor impervious to the happenings in the south. But he knew too that the strength of his own throne rested on the strength of the clergy—it had ever been so with Kings of Scotland in a land where the loyalties of the nobility were fickle.

James delayed, hinted agreement, and refrained from a meeting with Henry. The King of Scots was negotiating with the King of

France for another marital alliance. This time the bride was Mary of Lorraine, eldest daughter of the Duke of Guise. Although Mary wanted to marry the King of England—in spite of his record of divorce and beheading—she was under the control of the King of France. Francis directed that she marry James, and so she did. On June 10, 1538, she landed at Crail in Fife. The two were married at St. Andrews, and all the pageantry and festival prepared for the feeble Madeleine was brought out and expanded for this second of Scottish brides in little more than a year.

Mary of Guise was a strong, forceful, capable personality who handled her new mother-in-law with great tact. Consequently Margaret, who still reported all things to her brother, wrote: "Your Grace shall understand that the King my dearest son is in good health and prosperity, and the queen his wife, and great love betwixt them, and great honor done to her, and she is right richly come here in this realm. . . . I trust she shall prove a wise princess. . . . Since her coming in this realm, I have been much in her company, and she bears her[self] very honorably to me. . . ."[38]

Margaret Tudor knew, if she did not admit it, that her star was eclipsed. She had few friends and a husband for whom she cared little. She had no influence at either the Scottish or English court. Her revenues continued to be unreliable and sporadic. She was tolerated by James and, as often as not, ignored by Henry. She continued to write to Henry in a wistful, sometimes pathetic tone: "Henceforth, dearest brother, I beseech you remember that you have no more sister but me, and do in such sort that it may be seen [your] brotherly heart toward me. For I think very [unkindly] that I should be so near you and your realm, I being your only sister, and of long time have no word nor writing from your grace, but like as you set nought by me, nor cared not how I were entreated, which I trust I did never deserve."[39]

Margaret had spent her lifetime serving in her own perverse way the cause of her brother and her son. Now she found comfort in neither. She had been valued all of her life only in respect to the political commodity she represented. When that commodity was spent, she was no longer of value. She was again alone. The sad, lonely wish of the fourteen-year-old bride, expressed to her father so long ago, that "I pray God I may find it well for my welfare hereafter" had never been fulfilled.

Then as now, thirty-seven years later, Margaret's dearest wish was to go home. Time and again she asked of Henry: ". . . if I shall be welcome to come and visit your grace which may be to my great comfort."[40] No invitation ever came. Consequently she spent most of her days in country retirement, most often at Methven Castle while her husband was somewhere, anywhere else. When she could, she came to court. There were still some happy days, days which seemed to offer hope. There was May 22, 1540, for instance, when Mary of Guise produced an heir for the house of Stewart. James Stewart Duke of Ross and Prince of Scotland was born at St. Andrews and brought "such happiness that in every part of the realm fires were kindled, prayers offered, public triumph decreed, which a great happiness of all declared."[41] Margaret, like so many of her subjects, rushed to share the joy, and she joined the Archbishop of St. Andrews and the Earl of Arran as godparents to the young prince.[42]

The following April another prince, Arthur Stewart Duke of Albany and Earl of Fife and Montieth, was born at Stirling. Within the same month, the older brother became dangerously ill. His father heard the news at Linlithgow and made a frantic ride to St. Andrews. By the time he reached the infant's side, the eleven-month-old prince and heir was dead. Word then came that Prince Arthur was also ill at Stirling, and the father again spurred his horse toward his son. The child died before the father could reach him, and the two princes—who died within forty-eight hours of each other—were buried together at Holyrood.[43] Margaret joined the bereaved parents in mourning the two fair princes, and she wrote to Henry: ". . . here hath been great displeasure for the death of the prince and his brother, both with the king, my dearest son, and the queen his wife; wherefore I have done great diligence to put them in comfort, and is never from them, but ever in their company, whereof they are very glad."[44]

While Margaret served as chief comforter to the bewildered parents, she no doubt continued urging her son to visit with her brother. James either capitulated to his mother's demands or was so overwhelmed by his loss, that he suddenly sought—or seemed to seek—a change of policy. Against the advice of his chief counsellors, the bishops of Scotland, he agreed at last to a meeting in September at York. To Margaret's great satisfaction, messengers flew between the two monarchs and the meeting was arranged. Henry, with his accustomed magnificence, set out from London;

James set out from Edinburgh. Henry, the first to reach the destination, immediately ordered elaborate preparations for the reception of his royal nephew.

James had arranged to meet the English ambassador at his castle on the border. With twenty-four companions, he travelled in disguise to the border. When he reached the appointed meeting place, the ambassador was at mass "not knowing the sudden coming of the king. . . . The King of Scotland seeing all quiet and Lord William absent and seeing the breakfast prepared, hastily he and his company eated the same and paid the hosteler of the lodging thereof. And afterwards he lept on horse and when he was on horseback took instruments that he had kept his promise to Lord William and found him absent. . . ." The truth was that the bishops of Scotland feared Henry's seduction of James, that England would turn Scotland to seizure of the wealth of the old church. The bishops, in short, bought the king with a promise of a yearly payment of three thousand pounds.[45]

Henry waited at York, became impatient at the delay, and furious at the insult. He vowed he would never come so far north again. The aborted meeting was the end of Margaret's blighted hopes. Border warfare broke out; Henry once more sent the Duke of Norfolk against Scotland. It had started all over. England against Scotland. Scotland against England. Mistrust and distrust ate at both sides and seemed to turn its devouring teeth toward Margaret. She withdrew from the insinuations and muted abuse at the Scottish court and returned to Methven Castle. Her husband remained at Stirling. No matter to Margaret; she was relieved not to have him near.

Although her spirit never faltered, her body was breaking apart, caught in the shaking grasp of palsy. She retreated to rest, to gather her strength, to try again to bring harmony between her dearest son and her dearest brother. On October 18, 1541, as she sat in the long and darkened gallery of Methven Castle, she was seized by a stroke. Her doctors urged her to pray, to prepare herself for death. She refused and sent instead for her son. They carried her to her bed, and the friars knelt about her. She fretted that James did not come. As the prayers of the friars filled her ears, her thoughts were elsewhere—with Angus. Suddenly she said, "I desire you to beseech the King of England to be gracious to the Earl of Angus." A little later in a voice still firm, she said, "I ask

God for His mercy that I have so offended the Earl." She had written no will but asked that her daughter, the long neglected Margaret Douglas, be given the pathetically few goods the queen had to leave. She asked again for James, asked that he be kind to his sister. After that a coma sealed her senses, and then came death.[46]

When James did arrive, he ordered a grand funeral for his mother. She was taken to the tomb of Scottish kings at the Carthusian Abbey of St. John in Perth. There her grave, noted the chronicler, "was prepared for honorable cause, that who in the affairs of the Realm was noble and seen lusty and clearly shown, as their bodies might be included in the bounds of the same sepulchre righteously." Her son, who gave to his mother in death the attention and splendor he often denied her in life, acted as chief mourner. He was joined by the most influential nobles and members of the clergy, who offered to Margaret Tudor greater honor and dignity in her grave than they had ever given her as queen.[47]

EPILOGUE

FOR THOSE WHO SURVIVED MARGARET AND MARY TUDOR, LIFE, OF course, went on. Within a short space, their husbands remarried and fathered other families. Methven married his mistress Lady Janet Stewart and retreated into a less tempestuous if uneventful retirement. Suffolk, seven weeks after he buried his wife, married his ward—the fourteen-year-old Catherine Willoughby. Through the years he remained the close companion and friend of his king, and Henry's love for Suffolk grew. The old financial debts were replaced by new honors and greater riches. When news came on August 24, 1545, of Suffolk's death, Henry wept. Then he denied his friend's last request—to be buried in a quiet chapel at Lincoln. Instead Henry brought with great ceremony the body of Suffolk to St. George's Chapel at Windsor—the place where the king himself wanted to be buried. The king wished near him in death the friend who had so often been near him in life. That wish was fulfilled two years later when King Henry VIII made his final journey to Windsor.

Before Henry died, however, he made his last will which brought confusion and conflict to those who were to follow. He outlined the succession to his throne. First came his twelve-year-old son Edward by his third wife, Jane Seymour; then, as though anticipating the boy's premature death, Henry designated his daughters—first Princess Mary, born of Catherine of Aragon, and then Princess Elizabeth, born of Anne Boleyn—as rightful claimants. Then, as though anticipating what indeed did happen—that none of his children would have children of their own—Henry directed that the crown pass to the heirs of his favorite sister Mary and his best-beloved friend Charles Brandon Duke of Suffolk. His decision to disregard the rights of priority of the descendants of his older sister was perhaps, as many have claimed, born of general dislike for Margaret and for her son James V.[1] But there is also another suggestion that his reason for doing so was more politic.

Much had happened in Scotland between the death of Margaret in 1541 and that of her brother in 1547. When the Queen of Scots died, the single thread which bound the two nations snapped. Threats of war between the two nations ceased almost immediately, and war became a reality. While Margaret lay dying, the Duke of Norfolk—who years before had served his father the Earl of Surrey at Flodden Field—was gathering an army to lead against the north. James, with the constant encouragement of his clergy, also gathered his forces. The Scots nobility argued against the war, but James held them to their oaths of allegiance and forced them southward. As the two armies moved toward their day of battle, the strain of events brought James to exhaustion, physical and mental, and he retired to Lochmaben Castle. Meanwhile the army moved toward Norfolk; it crossed the border. As the army of Scotland met the advanced force of Sir Thomas Wharton, James' absence was suddenly realized. Word quickly circulated that he had given the command to his minion Oliver Sinclair—a man without experience or authority and whom none respected. Chaos ruptured the ranks of the Scots, who became the easy prey of the English. Although casualties were few, prisoners were many, and the entire army of Scotland was routed. The battle of Solway Moss on November 25, 1542, became for Scotland a total disaster.

As Wharton herded his captives toward London, James learned the awful news. The humiliation of defeat broke him totally. He left Lochmaben for Holyrood. Finding no comfort in either, he rode to Falkland. His humiliation became despair. He turned his face to the wall and refused all food, all counsel. When he was told on December 7 that his wife had given birth to a bonny princess, it was the final blast to whatever hope he might have had. His own minority had been ugly enough, what hope would there be for a girl-queen? He saw none—for his daughter or for himself. A week later he smiled and kissed his hand to those who watched, and then he died.[2] He had lived thirty years. His daughter Mary was only a week old when she was crowned Queen of Scots.

Mary's life is another, more famous story. She, like her aunt, was briefly the Queen of France. Her years as reigning Queen of Scotland were often not unlike the harried reign of her grandmother Margaret. And like her grandmother, Mary Queen of Scots married three times—once for policy and twice for passion. Her second marriage to her cousin Henry Stewart Lord Darnley knit up the strands of Margaret Tudor's heirs. For Darnley was also Margaret's grandson. His mother had been that so-often misplaced and forgotten child of Margaret and Angus—the Lady Margaret Douglas. When the two cousins met and loved, it brought disaster upon them both. Mary's throne was lost and Darnley was murdered. But it was their son who eventually rode southward as King James VI of Scotland to become King James I of England.

When the Tudor line expired with the death of Henry's last child, Elizabeth I, the prophecy of Henry VII came true. "The greater absorbed the lesser"; Scotland came to England. In the long run the purposes for which Margaret Tudor had been sent north had been fulfilled. The wars ceased. England and Scotland, being of one island, had come finally to their one peace. Yet that twisting road to peace and reconciliation had torn viciously at those who carried in their veins Tudor blood. For Mary Stewart Queen of Scots, heritage and blood lines became her curse. And for them she knelt before the block and the executioner who hacked her head from her body.

Nor were the progeny of Mary Tudor Dowager Queen of France and Duchess of Suffolk left unscourged. Of all her children, the luckiest perhaps was her only son, Henry Brandon Earl of Lincoln. He died young—two years after his mother. His sisters lived to have children of their own. For their nearness to the throne, they found themselves in prison as often as out, depending on the politics and fortunes of their cousins who were also queens. The saddest of them all was the seventeen-year-old Lady Jane Grey, who was forced by ambitious men to seize the throne upon the death of her cousin Edward VI. Jane Grey is known to history as the Nine Days' Queen. And for whatever part she played in the revolt, she was forced to watch the execution of her own young husband before she too followed him to the block on the Tower green. If the spirits of the dead care for the living, surely the shades of Margaret and Mary Tudor mingled their tears at the horror wrought upon their unhappy grandchildren.

By all rights this story should end here. Except for the very famous who even in death influence the living, most biographies, as do lives, end with the grave. That is not so in the case of either Margaret or Mary Tudor. They shared in death the ironies of fate they had often shared in life.

When the tomb of Margaret Tudor was closed in 1541, no one knew or imagined that it would not rest in the peace in which it had been left. She lay among the noblest of the land. But in 1559 amidst the fervor of Reformation fanaticism, a band of marauding Calvinists violated the sacred grounds of the Carthusian Abbey. There they broke open the tombs of the kings and queens of Scotland. Corpses were stripped, rings were plucked from fingers turned to bone, and the bodies—or what was left of them—were burned. The ashes of Margaret Tudor were kicked and scuffed about the abbey grounds. Today a simple blue slab marks the spot where once she lay.

Mary Tudor lay in her grave only three years before Reformation zeal destroyed the abbey in which she lay, crushed the alabaster monument to her memory, and broke open her tomb. Her coffin, however, was left intact and was moved without ceremony to St. Mary's Church on the grounds of the abbey. In later years the church underwent remodelling, and Mary's body was exhumed three times—in 1731, 1758, and 1784. The coffin on the last two occasions was opened, and her body, said to be in a remarkable state of preservation, was placed on view. The last time that Mary's coffin was opened, the thousands—who came to gawk at one who had been a queen and a sister of England's most famous king—were so fascinated by Mary's golden hair that they snipped away locks for souvenirs.

Today Mary's grave is marked by a plain marble slab. Above it stands a commemorative tablet bearing her coat of arms. It faces a handsome stained glass window, a gift of Queen Victoria, whose scenes depict the chief events of one whose life so captured the imagination of those in whose time she lived. There are no such monuments to Margaret Tudor in either England or Scotland— although she gave her life and all her efforts to bring the harmony so essential to the land she loved and the country in which she lived. She could have done better. She could have done more. But it was her dream of unity that came to fruition—through her England and Scotland married. Yet she remains in death, as she was so often in life, ignored and forgotten because even her memory is no longer a valuable commodity. It is the final, ironic consistency of her life.

NOTES

Chapter One

1. Henry Ellis, ed., *Original Letters Illustrative of English History* (London, 1824), series 1, vol. I:41–42. The letter is in the hand of an unknown scribe except for the last two paragraphs, which are in Margaret's hand.

2. Ibid., series 2, I:171.

3. Francis Bacon, *Historie of the Raigne of King Henrie the Seventh*, ed. James Spedding (New York, 1869), p. 361.

4. John Leland, *De Rebus Britannicis Collectanea*, ed. Thomas Hearne (London, 1774), 4:253–255.

5. Ibid., pp. 254–257.

6. Although the date of Mary's birth has been open to controversy, I agree with Walter C. Richardson's statement: "I have accepted the date, March 18, as given in the calendar to the psalter belonging to Mary's mother, now in Exeter College Library, Oxford, which also verifies the year as 1495." *Mary Tudor: The White Queen* (Seattle, 1970), p. 273.

7. Charles L. Kingsford, ed., *Chronicles of London* (Oxford, 1905), pp. 202–203; James Gairdner, ed., *Letters and Papers Illustrative of the Reigns of Richard III and Henry VII* (London, 1861), I:388–404; Robert Fabyan, *New Chronicles of England and France*, ed. Henry Ellis (London, 1811), p. 485.

8. C. H. Williams, ed., *Great Chronicle of London, English Historical Documents 1485–1558* (London, 1967), 5:121; Kingsford, *Chronicles of London*, p. 222. Another more colorful, explanation for the renaming of Sheen states that after Henry VII "had finished a great part of the building of his manor of Sheen, which as before is said was consumed by fire, for consideration that in the time of the said burning great substance of Riches, as well in Jewels and other things of Riches,

was perished and lost; And also that the Reedifying of the said Manor had cost, and after should cost or it were pursued, great and notable sums of money, where before that season it was once called or named Sheen, from this time forward it was commanded by the king that it should be called or named Rich mount." *Chronicles of London*, p. 233.

9. Polydore Vergil, *Anglicae Historiae Libri*, trans. Denys Hay (London, 1950), pp. 109–115; Edward Hall, *Chronicle (The Union of the Two Noble Families of Lancaster and York)*, ed. Henry Ellis (London, 1809), pp. 480–488; Raphael Holinshed, *Chronicle of England, Scotland, and Ireland* (London, 1577), 3:511–519.

10. Vergil, *Historiae*, p. 121; Holinshed, *Chronicle*, 3:521.

11. Erasmus describes his visit to the royal children by saying, ". . . I was staying at lord Mountjoy's country house when Thomas More came to see me, and took me out with him for a walk as far as the next village, where all the King's children, except prince Arthur, who was then the eldest son, were being educated. When we came into the hall, the attendants not only of the palace but also of Mountjoy's household were all assembled. In the midst stood prince Henry, then nine years old, and having already something of royalty in his demeanor, in which there was a certain dignity combined with singular courtesy. On his right was Margaret, about eleven years of age, afterwards married to James, King of Scots; and on his left played Mary, a child of four. Edmund was an infant in arms. More, with his companion Arnold, after paying his respects to the boy Henry, the same that is now [1523] king of England, presented him with some writing. For my part, not having expected anything of the sort, I had nothing to offer, but promised that on another occasion I would in some way declare my duty towards him. Meantime I was angry with More for not having warned me, especially as the boy sent me a little note, while we were at dinner, to challenge something from my pen. I went home, and in the Muses' spite, from whom I had been so long divorced, finished the poem within three days." Desiderius Erasmus, *Epistles*, trans., F. M. Nichols (London, 1901), I:201.

12. Richard Davey, *The Pageant of London* (New York, 1906), p. 266; Agnes Strickland, *Lives of the Queens of Scotland* (New York, 1859), 1:6–7.

13. Charles Wriothesley, *A Chronicle of England during the Reign of the Tudors: 1485 to 1559*, ed. William Douglas Hamilton (London, 1875), p. 405; Holinshed, *Chronicle*, 3:526–527; Hall, *Chronicle*, pp. 493–494.

14. John Leslie Bishop of Ross, *The History of Scotland from the Death of King James I to the Year 1561*, ed. E. G. Cody (Edinburgh, 1888), 2:117–118.

15. James Gairdner, *Henry the Seventh* (London, 1889), p. 169: "This was the first 'peace' as opposed to a 'truce' between England and Scotland since the treaty of Northampton in 1328. . . . Each king . . . was to abstain from a direct attack upon the terrorists of the other king to whom he was now contract in the bonds of perpetual peace." J. Mackie, "Henry VIII and Scotland" in *Transactions of the Royal Historical Society*, series 4, 29 (1947):97.

16. Mackie, "Henry VIII and Scotland" in *Royal Historical Society*, pp. 97–98.

17. Peter Hume Brown, *History of Scotland* (Cambridge, 1929), pp. 313–314.

18. John Pinkerton, *History of Scotland from the Accession of the House of Stewart to that of Mary* (London, 1797), 2:40–42; Bacon, *Historie of Henry the Seventh*, p. 323.

19. Leland, *Collectanea*, 4:258–262.

20. Strickland, *Queens*, 1:8.

21. Bacon, *Historie of Henry the Seventh*, p. 322.

22. Leland, *Collectanea*, 4:263–264; Fabyan, *Chronicles*, p. 687; Raphael Holinshed, *Chronicle of Scotland* (London, 1585), p. 412. Cited hereafter as *Scotland*.

23. Leland, *Collectanea*, 4:262–381; Holinshed, *Chronicle*, 3:599.

24. Strickland, *Queens*, 1:7.

25. Nancy Lenz Harvey, *Elizabeth of York* (New York, 1973), pp. 189–193.

26. Hall, *Chronicle*, p. 497.

27. Leslie, *History of Scotland*, 1:120.

28. Strickland, *Queens*, 1:24.

29. Mackie, "Henry VIII and Scotland" in *Royal Historical Society*, p. 95.

30. Leslie, *History of Scotland*, 1:121.

31. Lady Margaret Drummond. Her sisters were also poisoned at the same time.

32. Leland, *Collectanea*, 4:265–283. All students of the Tudors are indebted to John Yonge, Somerset herald, who accompanied Margaret to Scotland and carefully recorded the details of the journey, the wedding, and the coronation. Fortunately these descriptions were then preserved by John Leland.

Chapter Two

1. Don Pedro de Ayala, cited in Peter Hume Brown, ed., *Early Travelers in Scotland* (New York, 1970), pp. 39–40.

2. Robert Kerr Hannary, ed., *The Letters of James IV: 1505–1513* (Edinburgh, 1953), p. xxxiv; Holinshed, *Scotland*, p. 409; Leslie, *His-*

tory of Scotland, 2:122; Patrick Fraser Tytler, *History of Scotland* (Edinburgh, 1864), 2:267.

3. Leslie, *History of Scotland*, 2:110–111.

4. Robert Lindsay of Pitscottie, *The Historie and Chronicles of Scotland*, ed. J. G. Mackay (London, 1899), p. 231.

5. Tytler, *History of Scotland*, 2:266.

6. J. W. Baxter, *William Dunbar* (Edinburgh, 1952), p. 96.

7. Lindsay, *Chronicles*, p. 218; Brown, *History of Scotland*, 1:306; Holinshed, *Scotland*, p. 408; Tytler, *History of Scotland*, 2:280.

8. De Ayala in Brown, *Early Travelers*, p. 40.

9. Hannary, *Letters of James IV*, p. lxix; Mackie, "Henry VIII and Scotland," p. 101.

10. Baxter, *William Dunbar*, p. 99.

11. William Dunbar, "The Thistle and the Rose" in *Works*, ed. James Paterson (Edinburgh, 1863).

12. Leland, *Collectanea*, 4:265–300.

13. Holinshed, *Scotland*, pp. 412–413; Hall, *Chronicle*, p. 498.

14. De Ayala in Brown, *Early Travelers*, p. 40.

15. Holinshed, *Scotland*, p. 413.

16. Tytler, *History of Scotland*, 2:246.

17. Neville Williams, *The Royal Residences of Great Britain* (London, 1960), pp. 183–184.

18. Baxter, *William Dunbar*, p. 120.

19. Dunbar, "Of a Dance in the Queen's Chamber," in *Works*, pp. 164–166.

20. Hannary, *Letters of James IV*, p. 13, no. 16.

21. Holinshed, *Scotland*, p. 413.

22. Baxter, *William Dunbar*, p. 139.

23. Leslie, *History of Scotland*, 2:123–124; Holinshed, *Scotland*, pp. 413–414.

24. Holinshed, *Scotland*, p. 414.

25. Ibid., p. 415.

26. Ibid., p. 414; Leslie, *History of Scotland*, 2:123.

27. Leslie, *History of Scotland*, 2:128.

28. Ibid., pp. 124–125.

29. Strickland, *Queens*, 1:63.

30. Leslie, *History of Scotland*, 2:129.

31. Vespasian C XII, 239b.

32. Bacon, *Historie of Henrie the Seventh*, p. 353.

33. Mary Anne Everett Green, *The Lives of the Princesses of England* (London, 1854), 5:12. Cited hereafter as *Princesses*.

34. Galba B III, 109; *see also* Mary Croom Brown, *Mary Tudor, Queen of France* (London, 1911), pp. 19–22.

35. Green, *Princesses,* 5:14–15.

36. Ibid., 5:7–8.

37. Ibid., p. 16.

38. John Gouge Nichols, ed., *The Chronicle of Calais in the Reigns of Henry VII and Henry VIII to the Year 1540* (London, 1846), pp. 54–63.

39. Henry Ellis notes: "In the Copy of King Henry the Seventh's will published by Mr. Astle, no such legacy certainly occurs; but it is noticed in different papers and public documents, and there can be no doubt that such a bequest was made; though whether as supplementary to the Will, or by any verbal allotment does not appear." *Letters,* series 1, 1:64.

40. M. A. S. Hume, ed., *Calendar of State Papers Spanish* (London, 1892), I:603; Brown, *Mary Tudor,* p. 23.

41. Leland, *Collectanea,* 4:303–309; Hall, *Chronicle,* pp. 506–507.

42. Holinshed, *Chronicle,* 3:547.

Chapter Three

1. Hannary, *Letters of James IV,* p. 148, no. 251.

2. Vespasian F III, 36; Ellis, *Letters,* series 1, 1:63. Although the year of this particular letter by James IV is not given, it is typical of his early correspondence with Henry VIII.

3. Hall, *Chronicle,* pp. 516–517.

4. Ibid., p. 517.

5. Ibid., p. 519.

6. Green, *Princesses,* 5:1.

7. J. S. Brewer, *Letters and Papers, Foreign and Domestic of the Reign of Henry VIII,* revised by R. H. Brodie (London, 1920), I:1777.

8. J. S. Brewer and James Gairdner, *The Reign of Henry VIII from his Accession to the Death of Wolsey, Reviewed and Illustrated from the Original Documents* (London, 1884), 1:46.

9. Williams, *Royal Residences,* pp. 18–20.

10. Holinshed, *Scotland,* p. 415; Leslie, *History of Scotland,* 2:133; Hannary, *Letters of James IV,* p. xxxvi.

11. Leslie, *History of Scotland,* 2:134.

12. Lindsay, *Chronicles,* pp. 250–251.

13. Hannary, *Letters of James IV,* p. 166, no. 294.

14. William Croft Dickinson, *Scotland from the Earliest Times to 1603* (London, 1961), p. 242.

15. Dunbar, "Blythe Aberdeen," *Works,* pp. 288–291.

16. Mackie, "Henry VIII and Scotland," p. 105.

17. Ellis, *Letters,* series 1, 1:64.

18. Ibid., pp. 64–65.

19. Tytler, *History of Scotland*, 2:280.

20. Brown, *History of Scotland*, 1:328–329; Leslie, *History of Scotland*, 2:135–136.

21. Hall, *Chronicle*, p. 525; Marguerite Wood, ed., *Flodden Papers* (Edinburgh, 1933), pp. xxiii–xxiv.

22. Holinshed, *Scotland*, p. 414; Leslie, *History of Scotland*, 2:129.

23. Leslie, *History of Scotland*, 2:122; Strickland, *Queens*, 1.68.

24. Holinshed, *Scotland*, p. 416; Leslie, *History of Scotland*, 2:137.

25. Brown, *Mary Tudor*, pp. 83–84; Brewer, *Letters and Papers Henry VIII*, 1:4844; Holinshed, *Scotland*, pp. 416–417.

26. Brewer, *Letters and Papers Henry VIII*, I:791–792.

27. Ellis, *Letters*, series 1, 1:70.

28. Ibid., p. 74.

29. Ibid., p. 75.

30. Ibid., p. 77.

31. Lindsay, *Chronicles*, p. 253.

32. Hall, *Chronicle*, p. 555.

33. Ellis, *Letters*, series 1, 1:78–79.

34. Hall, *Chronicle*, pp. 545–548; Brewer, *Letters and Papers Henry VIII*, 1:973.

35. Brewer, *Reign of Henry VIII*, 1:26–27.

36. Lindsay, *Chronicles*, p. 258; Brown, *History of Scotland*, 1:332.

37. William Drummond of Hawthorndon, *History of Scotland* (London, 1655), pp. 144–145.

38. Brewer, *Letters and Papers of Henry VIII*, 1:2192.

39. Pinkerton, *History of Scotland*, 2:96.

40. Lindsay, *Chronicles*, pp. 258–259.

41. Tytler, *History of Scotland*, 2:288–289.

42. Lindsay, *Chronicle*, p. 260.

43. Ibid., p. 261.

44. Tytler, *History of Scotland*, 2:289.

45. Ellis, *Letters*, series 1, 1:83.

46. Tytler, *History of Scotland*, 2:288–289.

47. Leslie, *History of Scotland*, 1:144–145.

48. Ellis, *Letters*, series 1, 1:86–87.

49. Lindsay, *Chronicles*, 1:270.

50. Holinshed, *Scotland*, p. 421.

51. Lindsay, *Chronicles*, pp. 368–369.

52. "An Exclamatioun of James the Fourt / And Quat He Was In his Lyf / Tyme, How He was / Exteimit," in Lindsay, *Chronicles*, 1:277–278.

53. Holinshed, *Scotland*, p. 421; Brown, *History of Scotland*, 1:335–

339; Hall, *Chronicle*, pp. 561–563; Dickinson, *Scotland Earliest Times*, p. 260; Brewer, *Letters and Papers Henry VIII*, I:2283, 2246.

54. Brewer, *Letters and Papers Henry VIII*, 1:2283.

55. Ibid., 2325.

56. Hall, *Chronicle*, p. 564.

57. Lindsay, *Chronicles*, p. 272.

58. Leslie, *History of Scotland*, 1:146.

59. Hall, *Chronicle*, p. 564.

60. Ellis, *Letters*, series 1, 1:88.

61. Dickinson, *Scotland Earliest Times*, p. 244.

62. Holinshed, *Scotland*, p. 423.

63. Drummond, *History of Scotland*, p. 156.

64. Wood, *Flodden Papers*, p. lxx; Leslie, *History of Scotland*, 2:148; Eva Scott, *Six Stuart Sovereigns, 1512–1701* (Port Washington, N.Y., 1971), p. 18; Dickinson, *Scotland Earliest Times*, p. 302.

65. *The Scottish Antiquary*, 12 (1898):115–122.

66. Mackie, "Henry VIII and Scotland," in *Royal Historical Society*, p. 104–105.

67. Ibid., p. 109.

68. Stow notes that after the dissolution of the monasteries, Sheen Priory became a private residence and that James' body was "thrown into a waste room amongst the old timber, lead, and other rubble. Since the which time, Workmen there for their foolish pleasure hewed off his head; and Lancelot Young, Master Glaser to her Majesty, feeling a sweet savor to come from thence, and seeing the same dyed from all moisture, and yet the form remaining, with the hair of the head, and beard red, brought it to London to his house in Woodstreet, where for a time he kept it for sweetness, but in the end caused the Sexton of that Church to bury it amongst other bones, taken out of their Charnel [of St. Michael's Parish]. John Stow, *A Survey of London* (London, 1603), p. 300.

Chapter Four

1. Hall, *Chronicle*, p. 543.

2. Nichols, *The Chronicle of Calais*, pp. 70–76.

3. Brewer, *Letters and Papers Henry VIII*, 1:2391.

4. Brown, *Mary Tudor*, p. 72; Hall, *Chronicle*, p. 566.

5. At the same time Lord Howard the High Admiral was created Earl of Surrey; and Sir Charles Somerset Lord Herbert, the Earl of Worcester. Hall, *Chronicle*, p. 567.

6. Lindsay, *Chronicles*, p. 280.

7. Wood, *Flodden Papers*, pp. lxxv–lxxvi.

8. Ellis, *Letters*, series 1, 1:93–99.

9. Drummond, *History of Scotland*, p. 157.

10. Richardson, *Mary Tudor*, p. 77.

11. Tytler, *History of Scotland*, 2:301.

12. Wood, *Flodden Papers*, p. lxxxvii.

13. Drummond, *History of Scotland*, p. 158.

14. Richardson, *Mary Tudor*, p. 78.

15. Brewer, *Reign of Henry VIII*, 1:36–37.

16. Hall, *Chronicle*, p. 567.

17. Karl Brandi, *The Emperor Charles V*, trans. C. V. Wedgwood (London, 1939), p. 53.

18. Richardson, *Mary Tudor*, p. 47.

19. R. Brown and G. C. Bentinck, eds. *Calendar of State Papers, Venetian* (London, 1890), 3:1485.

20. Lord Edward Herbert, *The Life and Raigne of King Henry the Eighth* (London, 1649), p. 48; Richardson notes: "The jointure lands were numerous but scattered, lying chiefly in the west-central and south-eastern part of France: the counties of Saintonge and Pezenas; the towns of Rochelle, Loudun, Roquemare, and Chenon with its adjacent castle; the lordships of Montigny, Cessenon, and Cabrières; the profits or privy seal of Montpellier; the revenues from Saintonge, St. Jean d'Angély, Rochford, Bourg, St. Andrém, Villeneuve, and Beaucaire near Avignon; and salt profits derived from Pezenas, Montpellier, Fronlingnan, and Narbonne, valued at 10,400 *livres tournois* annually. These revenues represented a sizable income yearly, though it varied appreciably from year to year. Polydore Vergil's estimate, probably too high, was some 302,000 crowns annually. In later years, when as Duchess of Suffolk she lived in England, Mary seldom realized more than 6,150 pounds per year from her French possessions." *Mary Tudor*, p. 83.

21. Mary Anne Everett Green, ed., *Letters of Royal and Illustrious Ladies from the Commencement of the Twelfth Century to the Close of the Reign of Queen Mary* (London, 1846), 1:172–173.

22. Brown and Bentinck, eds., *Calendar of State Papers, Venetian*, 2:505; *see also* Brown, *Mary Tudor*, pp. 90–91.

23. Brown, *Mary Tudor*, p. 105.

24. Wood, *Flodden Papers*, p. lxxxv.

25. Lindsay, *Chronicles*, pp. 280–281; Dickinson, *Scotland Earliest Times*, p. 302.

26. Wood, *Flodden Papers*, p. lxxxvii.

27. Brown, *History of Scotland*, p. 354.

28. Leslie, *History of Scotland*, 2:155.

29. Dickinson, *Scotland Earliest Times*, p. 6.

30. Green, *Letters*, 1:166–169.

31. Caligula D VI, 198.

32. Green, *Princesses*, 5:35–37.

33. One person dismissed on moral grounds by Louis XII was Jane Popincourt, a childhood companion of Mary Tudor. While the Duke of Longueville was a prisoner in the court of Henry VIII, he and Jane Popincourt became involved in an amorous affair. "After hearing of the scandal Louis would have no part of her; rather she were burnt alive than serve his Queen, he told the English ambassador . . . Jane remained behind." Richardson, *Mary Tudor*, p. 88.

34. Brown and Bentinck, eds., *Calendar of State Papers, Venetian*, 2:500.

35. John Stow, *The Annals of England* (London, 1580), p. 828.

36. J. Speed, *Chronicle* (London, 1846), pp. 75–76.

37. Brown, *Mary Tudor*, pp. 114–116; Green, *Princesses*, 5:41–43; Hall, *Chronicle*, p. 570.

38. Brown, *Mary Tudor*, pp. 117–118.

39. Green, *Princesses*, 5:43.

40. Richardson, *Mary Tudor*, p. 91.

41. Worcester to Henry VIII, Ellis, *Letters*, series 2, 1:240.

42. Hall, *Chronicle*, p. 570.

43. Ellis, *Letters*, series 1, 1:115–117.

44. Ibid., pp. 118–119.

45. Green, *Princesses*, 5:48.

46. Ibid., p. 49; Ellis, *Letters*, series 2, 1:244–247.

47. Green, *Princesses*, 5:52–53.

48. Ibid., p. 53.

49. Worcester to Henry VIII, Ellis, *Letters*, series 2, 1:241.

50. Green, *Letters*, 1:178–179.

51. Ibid., p. 180.

52. Ibid., pp. 182–183.

53. Richardson, *Mary Tudor*, p. 111.

54. Ellis, *Letters*, series 2, 1:250–251.

Chapter Five

1. Green, *Princesses*, 5:55–59; Suffolk to Henry VIII in Ellis, *Letters*, series 2, 1:253–254; Brown, *Mary Tudor*, pp. 135–137; Charles Read Baskerville, ed., *Pierre Gringore's Pageants for the Entry of Mary Tudor into Paris* (Chicago, 1934); Hall, *Chronicle*, p. 571.

2. Suffolk to Wolsey, Caligula D VI, 156; Ellis, *Letters*, series 2, 1:257–258.

3. Richardson, *Mary Tudor*, p. 118.

4. Hall, *Chronicle*, pp. 570–572.

5. Suffolk to Wolsey in Ellis, *Letters*, series 2, 1:258.

6. Louis XII to Henry VIII in Ellis, *Letters*, series 2, 1:261.

7. Ibid., pp. 255–256.

8. Brewer, *Letters and Papers Henry VIII*, 2:1025.

9. Richardson, *Mary Tudor*, p. 121.

10. Brown, *Mary Tudor*, p. 148; Green, *Princesses*, 5:69.

11. Hall, *Chronicle*, p. 581.

12. Alexander Charles Ewald, *Stories from the State Papers* (London, 1882), 1:114.

13. Green, *Princesses*, 5:76–77.

14. Ellis, *Letters*, series 1, 1:120–121.

15. Green, *Letters*, 1:185–186.

16. Ibid., pp. 187–189.

17. Brown, *Mary Tudor*, p. 173.

18. The old-style calendar was still in use when Mary issued this proclamation. Hence the actual year was 1515, new style. *See also* Brown, *Mary Tudor*, pp. 162–163; Brewer, *Letters and Papers Henry VIII*, 2:237.

19. Green, *Letters*, 1:190–192.

20. Brown, *Mary Tudor*, pp. 161–162.

21. Green, *Letters*, 1:195–196.

22. Ibid., p. 196.

23. Hall, *Chronicle*, p. 581.

24. Ewald, *Stories from the State Papers*, 1:118–119.

25. Green, *Letters*, 1:197; Brown, *Mary Tudor*, pp. 191–194; Brewer, *Letters and Papers Henry VIII*, 2:224.

26. Ewald, *Stories from the State Papers*, 1:122.

27. Caligula, D VI, 176.

28. Brewer, *Letters and Papers Henry VIII*, 2:223.

29. Green, *Letters*, 1:199–200.

30. Ibid., p. 201.

31. Brown, *Mary Tudor*, p. 181.

32. Caligula D VI, 247.

33. Brown, *Mary Tudor*, pp. 210–211.

34. Green, *Letters*, 1:204–206.

35. Ewald, *Stories from the State Papers*, 1:130.

Chapter Six

1. Green, *Letters*, 1:202.

2. Ibid., pp. 193–195.

3. "Three years later, when the city was returned to France, Wolsey received a pension of twelve thousand livres per year for the surrender of his diocesan rights." Richardson, *Mary Tudor*, p. 170.

4. Ibid., p. 183.

5. Brewer, *Letters and Papers Henry VIII*, 2:468.

6. Green, *Princesses*, 5:110.

7. Green, *Letters*, 1:209–210.

8. Holinshed, *Scotland*, p. 425.

9. Tytler, *History of Scotland*, 2:301–302.

10. Holinshed, *Scotland*, p. 425; Lindsay, *Chronicles*, 1:288–289.

11. Tytler, *History of Scotland*, 2:302.

12. Ibid., p. 303.

13. Brewer, *Reign of Henry VIII*, 1:214; Brown, *History of Scotland*, p. 357.

14. Green, *Letters*, 1:212–213.

15. Ellis, *Letters*, series 2, 1:265–267.

16. According to Dacre, Margaret's disease, which was in her hip joint, was sciatica.

17. Brewer, *Reign of Henry VIII*, 1:218–219.

18. Hall, *Chronicle*, p. 584.

19. Brewer, *Reign of Henry VIII*, 1:219.

20. Ibid., 1:217–218.

21. Brewer, *Letters and Papers of Henry VIII*, 2:1024, 1030.

22. Tytler, *History of Scotland*, 2:304.

23. Kingsford, *Chronicles of London*, p. 263.

24. Caligula, B VI, 99.

25. Brewer, *Letters and Papers Henry VIII*, 2:1387.

26. Ellis, *Letters*, series 1, 1:129.

27. Harvey, *Elizabeth of York*, p. 159.

28. Green, *Princesses*, 5:112–113.

29. Richardson, *Mary Tudor*, p. 196.

30. Hall, *Chronicle*, pp. 584–585.

31. Wolsey was raised to the cardinalate on September 10, 1515; he was created Lord Chancellor on December 24, 1515.

32. Leslie, *History of Scotland*, 2:165.

33. Ellis, *Letters*, series 1, 1:132–133.

34. Green, *Letters*, 1:220–221.

35. Ellis, *Letters*, series 1, 1:130.

36. Hall, *Chronicle*, pp. 585–586.

37. Caligula B VI, 106; Ellis, *Letters*, series 1, 1:123–125.

38. Titus B I, 69.

39. Brown, *Mary Tudor*, p. 222.

40. Brewer, *Reign of Henry VIII*, 1:237–241.

41. Brown, *Mary Tudor*, p. 229.

42. Ibid., p. 231; Green, *Princesses*, 5:118–119; Richardson, *Mary Tudor*, p. 211.

43. Hall, *Chronicle*, p. 591.

44. Green, *Letters*, 1:223–225.

45. Brewer, *Reign of Henry VIII*, 1:221.
46. Ibid., 223–225.

Chapter Seven

1. Green, *Letters*, 1:228–230.
2. Cited by Hester Chapman, *The Thistle and the Rose* (New York, 1972), p. 141.
3. Ida Woodward, *Five English Consorts of Foreign Princes* (London, 1911), 1:36.
4. Leslie, *History of Scotland*, 2:173–174.
5. Dacre's charges to Margaret:

"Item, ye shall show unto her Grace that it is thought marvellous that she should bear so great favor unto the Duke of Albany seeing her Grace [has] request made unto the king my Sovereign lord, and labor made to my lord Cardinal's Grace to most his Highness, that the said Duke should not come into Scotland, as well for the surety of the king her son as of herself; seeing the sudden departure of the prince her son, and that incontinently after the said Duke proclaimed himself Prince of Scotland; and that also the said Duke's father took upon him and usurped to be king against his elder brother, being King, and in the time of his usurping made diverse knights.

Item, ye shall show unto her Grace, that I doubt not but it is in her remembrance that the King her husband (whose soul god pardon) in his time would never take the said Duke as Duke of Albany, for because of the pretense that his father made to the crown of Scotland.

Item, ye shall show unto her Grace that it is common to the knowledge of the King my said Sovereign, that her Grace is departed from my Lord of Angus her husband, contrary to all good order and the agreement made betwixt her and my said lord by the good and virtuous father friar Henry Chadworth; and also the common *brute* [rumor] runneth that her Grace departed Edinburgh by night, and there was met without the Town by Sir James Hamilton being deadly enemy to my said lord of Angus and by him conveyed to Linlithgow.

Item, ye shall show unto her Grace, that it standeth not with her honor to leave her husband by counsel of any man, and so it is thought be counsel of the said Duke of Albany, giving her fair words and promises, under color whereof her Grace will be deceived at length, which peradventure will shortly appear, and then it will be hard to be amended.

Item, ye shall say unto her Grace to call unto her remembrance how the King my late Sovereign Lord her father of noble memory (whose soul god pardon), married her Grace into Scotland for that purpose to have a perpetual Peace, and that the issue of her body should be King of that realm, whereby and by reason of the nearness and proximity of blood betwixt my said Sovereign that now is, and her said issue, a perpetual peace should grow: and now to lean to that counsel that by all likelihood is not good and profitable for the continuance of the same, what hurt and reproach shall come of thereof I refer to the wisdom and discretion of her Grace.

Item, ye shall show unto her Grace, the keeping that the King her son is in is right suspicious, seeing that her Grace cannot come at him but with a few persons with her: and that his person is in the keeping of the said Duke, except that every quarter once there cometh a Lord to have the name thereof: and as well his Schoolmaster, as all other persons that are officers about him, are of the said duke's appointing, and not of the Lord's that is above [over] him which attendeth his quarter.

Item, ye shall say unto her Grace, to call unto her remembrance of whereof she is come, and of what House, and that there is few Scots men that will give unto her fruitful counsel, but only for their singular weal and profit; wherefore, good it were to take some regard to such as be naturally born to give her Grace good counsel, and to lay all dissimulation apart, and to remember what dishonorable *brutes* are spoken of her Grace in Scotland, in the leaving of her said husband and following the advice of such as finally may, and of likelihood shall be her destruction, *both in fame and otherwise*, which cannot stand with the pleasure of God nor with the King my said Sovereign's honor.

Item, finally ye shall show unto her Grace that in thus ordering herself in the premises, neither regarding her own honor, the surety of the King her son, nor yet of her said husband or of herself, her Grace may not look for any favor at the King my said Sovereign's hand; for it is thought she is sore abused under color of fair promises which be but illusions; and finally shall bring her Grace in the displeasure of God to her dishonor and undoing at length." Ellis, *Letters*, series 2, 1:282–285.

6. Ibid., 276–278.

7. Green, *Letters*, 1:250–252.

8. Leslie, *History of Scotland*; 2:168; Drummond, *History of Scotland*, pp. 170–171; Holinshed, *Scotland*, 428.

9. Leslie, *History of Scotland*, 2:174.

10. Hall, *Chronicle*, p. 595.

11. Ibid., p. 596.

12. Ibid., pp. 597–598; Brewer, *Reign of Henry VIII*, 1:198–200.

13. Green, *Princesses*, 5:121.

14. Harleian MS 6986, 6.

15. Hall, *Chronicle*, pp. 603–605.

16. Nichols, ed., *Chronicle of Calais*, p. 18.

17. Hall, *Chronicle*, p. 613.

18. Ibid., p. 619.

19. Ibid., pp. 605–620; Brewer, *Reign of Henry VIII*, 1:348–356; Brewer, *Letters and Papers Henry VIII*, 3:303–313.

20. Nichols, ed., *Chronicle of Calais*, pp. 29–30.

21. Hall, *Chronicle*, pp. 620–621.

22. Brewer, *Reign of Henry VIII*, 1:519–520.

23. Leslie, *History of Scotland*, 2:180–181.

24. Ibid.

25. Drummond, *History of Scotland*, p. 187; Leslie, *History of Scotland*, 2:173–174; Herbert, *Henry VIII*, p. 133.

26. Brewer, *Reign of Henry VIII*, 1:530.

27. Ibid., pp. 523–538.

28. Hall, *Chronicle*, p. 650; Leslie, *History of Scotland*, 2:190.

29. Green, *Letters*, 1:254–256.

30. Wolsey to Charles V in Brewer, *Reign of Henry VIII*, 1:543.

31. Brewer, *Letters and Papers Henry VIII*, 3:3268, 3327.

32. Ellis, *Letters*, series 1, 1:226–227.

33. Brewer, *Reign of Henry VIII*, 1:554.

34. Hall, *Chronicle*, p. 665.

35. Green, *Letters*, 1:283–287.

36. Brewer, *Reign of Henry VIII*, 1:554–564.

37. Green, *Letters*, 1:288–290.

38. Ibid., p. 291.

39. Ibid., pp. 292–293.

40. Ibid., pp. 297–298.

41. Mackie, "Henry VIII and Scotland" in *Royal Historical Society*, p. 101.

42. Green, *Letters*, 1:298–305.

43. Ellis, *Letters*, series 1, 1:249–250.

44. Green, *Letters*, 1:324–328.

45. Leslie, *History of Scotland*, 2:198.

46. Brown, *History of Scotland*, 1:369.

47. Margaret to Surrey in Green, *Letters*, 1:267.

48. Ellis, *Letters*, series 1, 1:251.

49. Brewer, *Letters and Papers Henry VIII*, 4:551.

50. Margaret to Norfolk in Green, *Letters*, 1:342–345.

51. Brewer, *Letters and Papers Henry VIII*, 4:55.

52. Green, *Letters*, 1:347.

53. Ibid., 349–352.

54. Tytler, *History of Scotland*; 2:332; Brown, *History of Scotland*, 1:370.

55. Green, *Letters*, 1:354–355.

56. Tytler, *History of Scotland*, 2:334.

57. Leslie, *History of Scotland*, 2:199–200.

58. Dickinson, *Scotland Earliest Times*, p. 306.

59. Brown, *History of Scotland*, p. 372.

Chapter Eight

1. Green, *Letters*, 2:6–9.

2. Holinshed, *Scotland*, p. 436.

3. Johannis de Whethamstede, *Chronicon, e Registro Ejus In Bibliotheca Collegii Armorum Londini* (London, 1732), 2:628.

4. Caroline Bingham, *James V King of Scots 1512–1542* (London, 1971), pp. 64–65.

5. Leslie, *History of Scotland*, 2:201–209; Brown, *History of Scotland*, 1:370–375.

6. Tytler, *History of Scotland*, 2:340.

7. Lindsay, *Chronicles*, 1:324–325.

8. Ibid., 326–328, 330–334; Brown, *History of Scotland*, 1:374–375; Leslie, *History of Scotland*, 2:216.

9. Leslie, *History of Scotland*, 2:217.

10. Hall, *Chronicle*, p. 703.

11. Brewer, *Letters and Papers Henry VIII*, 1:cxlii–cxliii.

12. Green, *Princesses*, 5:246; Richardson, *Mary Tudor*, p. 163.

13. Hall, *Chronicle*, pp. 753–754.

14. George Cavendish, *Life and Death of Cardinal Wolsey*, ed. Richard S. Sylvester (London, 1959), pp. 90–91.

15. Ibid., p. 106.

16. Herbert, *Henry VIII*, p. 313.

17. Hall, *Chronicle*, p. 795.

18. Ibid., p. 782.

19. Richardson, *Mary Tudor*, p. 214.

20. Green, *Letters*, 2:87.

21. Ellis, *Letters*, series 1, 1:304–305.

22. Green, *Princesses*, 5:138–141; Richardson, *Mary Tudor*, pp. 260–263.

23. Tytler, *History of Scotland*, 2:353.

24. Lindsay, *Chronicles*, 1:336–338.

25. Ibid., 340–341.

26. Green, *Letters*, 2:130–131.

27. Ibid., p. 324.

28. Herbert, *Henry VIII*, p. 400; Hall, *Chronicle*, p. 819.

29. Green, *Letters*, 2:324.
30. Lindsay, *Chronicles*, 1:355–368.
31. Ibid., p. 369.
32. Ibid., p. 370.
33. Bingham, *James V*, p. 133.
34. Green, *Letters*, 2:325–326.
35. Ibid., p. 332.
36. Ibid., pp. 334–335.
37. Bingham, *James V*, p. 136.
38. Green, *Letters*, 3:19.
39. Ibid.
40. Ibid., 2:277.
41. Leslie, *History of Scotland*, 2:243.
42. Holinshed, *Scotland*, p. 445.
43. Bingham, *James V*, p. 177.
44. Green, *Letters*, 3:167.
45. Lindsay, *Chronicles*, 1:339–344.
46. Brewer, *Letters and Papers Henry VIII*, 16:601.
47. Leslie, *History of Scotland*, 2:243–244.

Epilogue

1. Woodward, *Five English Consorts*, p. 1.
2. Lindsay, *Chronicles*, pp. 404–408.

BIBLIOGRAPHY

Original Manuscripts

Cotton Manuscripts: Caligula B I, 28, 164, 246, 251; Caligula B II, 211, 262, 278, 292, 364, 367; Caligula B VI, 68, 74, 76, 80, 99, 105, 106, 119, 121, 123, 124; Caligula D VI, 145, 147, 156, 176, 220, 247, 249, 268; Vespasian B II; Vespasian F III, 21, 36, 37, 38, 39; Vespasian F XIII, 74, 134; Vitellius C XI, 156b; Titus B I, 69.

British Museum Additional Manuscripts: 3246; 34208, 27, 28; 45132, 1b–9; 4797, 142.

Harleian Manuscripts: 3462, 142; 6986, 6.

Royal Manuscripts: 13 B II, 54b, 55b, 62, 76b, 83b, 87b.

Other Works Consulted

Adamson, J. W. "The Extent of Literacy in England in the Fifteenth and Sixteenth Centuries: Notes and Conjectures." *The Library*, 4th series. 10 (1929–30):163–193.

Agrippa, Henry Cornelius. *The Glory of a Woman: or a Looking-Glasse for Ladies.* Translated by Edward Fleetwood. London, 1652.

———. *A Treatise of the Nobilitie and Excellencye of Woman Kynde.* Translated by David Clapham. London, 1542.

Allen, P. S. *The Age of Erasmus.* Oxford, 1914.

Anglo, Sydney. "The Court Festivals of Henry VIII: A Study Based upon the Account Books of John Heron, Treasurer of the Chamber." *Bulletin of the John Rylands Library* 43 (1960):12–45.

Auton, Jean de. *Chroniques de Louis XII.* Edited by R. de Maulde La Claviere. 4 vols. Paris, 1889–95.

Bacon, Francis. *Historie of the Raigne of King Henrie the Seventh.* Edited by James Spedding. New York, 1869.

Bailly, S. *Francois I.* Paris, 1954.

Baskerville, Charles Read, ed. *Pierre Gringore's Pageants for the Entry of Mary Tudor into Paris.* Chicago, 1934.

Baxter, J. W. *William Dunbar.* Edinburgh, 1952.

Bellenden, John. *The History and Chronicles of Scotland.* n.d.

Belloc, Hilaire. "Casual Papers: Charles Brandon, Duke of Suffolk." *New Statesman* 35 (1930):443–444.

Bennett, H. S. *English Books and Readers: 1475–1557.* Cambridge, 1952.

———. *The Pastons and Their England: Studies in an Age of Transition.* 2d ed. Cambridge, 1932.

Bergenroth, G. A. *Calendar of Letters, Dispatches and State Papers relating to the Negotiations between England and Spain.* Vol. I. London, 1862.

Besant, Sir Walter. *London in the Time of the Tudors.* London, 1904.

Bingham, Caroline. *James V King of Scots 1512–1542.* London, 1971.

Bowle, J. *Henry VIII.* London, 1959.

Brandi, Karl. *The Emperor Charles V.* Translated by C. V. Wedgwood. London, 1939.

Brayley, Edward Wedlake, and John Britton. *The Ancient Palace of Westminster.* London, 1836.

Brewer, J. S. *Letters and Papers, Foreign and Domestic of the Reign of Henry VIII.* Revised by R. H. Brodie, London, 1920.

——— and James Gairdner. *The Reign of Henry VIII from his Accession to the Death of Wolsey, Reviewed and Illustrated from the Original Documents.* 2 vols. London, 1884.

Bridge, John S. C. *A History of France from the Death of Louis XI.* Vols. IV and V. Oxford, 1921–1936.

Brodie, R. H. *Letters and Papers, Foreign and Domestic of the Reign of Henry VIII.* Vol. I. London, 1920.

Brook, Roy. *The Story of Eltham Palace.* London, 1960.

Brown, Mary Croom. *Mary Tudor, Queen of France.* London, 1911.

Brown, Peter Hume. *History of Scotland.* Vol. I. Cambridge, 1929.

———, ed. *Early Travelers in Scotland.* First pub. 1891. New York, 1970.

Bruto, Giovanni Michele. *The Necessarie, Fit, and Convenient Education of a Yong Gentlewoman.* Translated by W. P. London, 1598.

Buchanan, George. *Rerum Scoticarum Historia.* Translated by James Aikman. London, 1827.

Buchon, Jean-Alexander C. *Choix de chroniques et mémoires relatifs à l'Histoire de France.* Orléans, 1861.

Burke, Maurice. "Charles Brandon, Gentleman Adventurer." *Contemporary Review* 179 (1951):111–116.

Burton, Robert. *The Anatomy of Melancholy.* New York, 1932.

Bury St. Edmunds. Bury St. Edmunds, 1973.

Busch, Wilhelm. *England Under the Tudors.* Translated by Alice M. Todd. New York, 1965.

Bush, Douglas. "Tudor Humanism and Henry VIII." *University of Toronto Quarterly* 7 (1938):162–177.

Calendar of State Papers relating to Scottish Affairs. Edited by J. Bain. Vols. I and II. London, 1898.

Calendar of State Papers, Spanish. Edited by M. A. S. Hume. London, 1892.

Calendar of State Papers, Venetian. Edited by R. Brown and G. C. Bentinck. Vol. 2. London, 1890.

Camden, Carroll. *The Elizabethan Woman.* Houston, 1952.

Campbell, William. "Erasmus in England." *Dublin Review* 211 (1942): 36–49.

———, ed. *Materials for a History of the Reign of Henry VII.* London, 1877.

Carmelianus, Petrus. *Solennes ceremoniae et triumphi or the solempnities & triumphs doon & made at the spouselles and mariage of the kynges daughter, the ladye Marye to the Prynce of Castile, archduke of Austrige.* Edited by Henry Ellis. London: Camden Society, new series, 9 (1893).

Cavendish, George. *Life and Death of Cardinal Wolsey.* Edited by Richard S. Sylvester. London, 1959.

Caxton, William, ed. *Le Grande's Boke of Good Maners.* Westminster, 1487.

Chapman, Hester W. *The Thistle and the Rose: The Sisters of Henry VIII.* First pub. 1969. New York, 1972.

———. *Two Tudor Portraits.* London, 1960.

Chronicles of London. Edited by Charles L. Kingsford. Oxford, 1905.

Cocheris, Hippolyte. *Entrée de Marie d'Angleterre, Femme de Louis XII, à Abbeville et à Paris.* Paris, 1859.

Commines, M. Phillipe de. *Mémoires.* Paris. 1903.

Conway, Agnes Ethel. *Henry VII's Relations with Scotland and Ireland: 1485–1498.* Cambridge, 1932.

Cooper, C. H. *Memoir of Margaret Beaufort, Countess of Richmond and Derby.* Edited by J. E. B. Mayor. Cambridge, 1874.

Crawford, George. *The Lives and Characters of the Officers of the Crown and of the State in Scotland from the Beginning of the Reign of King David I to the Union of the Two Kingdoms.* 1726.

Cruden, Stewart. *The Scottish Castle.* New York, 1961.

Davey, Richard. *The Pageant of London.* New York, 1906.

Dickinson, William Croft. *Scotland from the Earliest Times to 1603.* London, 1961.

Donaldson, Gordon. *Scottish Kings.* London, 1967.

Douglas, Gavin. *Poetical Works.* Vol. I. Edited by John Small. Edinburgh, 1874.

Drummond, William, of Hawthorndon. *History of Scotland*. London, 1655.

Dunbar, William. *Works*. Edited by James Paterson. Edinburgh, 1863.

Einstein, Lewis. *Tudor Ideals*. London, 1921.

Ellis, Henry, ed. *Original Letters Illustrative of English History*. Ser. 1, vol. I. London, 1824. Ser. 2, vol. I. London, 1877.

Emmison, F. G. *Tudor Food and Pastimes*. London, 1964.

Erasmus, Desiderius. *Epistles*. Translated by Francis Morgan Nichols. Vol. I. London, 1901.

Ewald, Alexander Charles. *Stories from the State Papers*. Vol. I. London, 1882.

———. "An Historical Love Match." *Living Age* 147 (1880):290–301.

Fabyan, Robert. *New Chronicles of England and France*. Edited by Henry Ellis. London, 1811.

Fisher, H. A. L. *The History of England From the Accession of Henry VII to the Death of Henry VIII, 1485–1547*. London, 1928.

Fleuranges, Robert de la Marck, Seigneur de. *Histoire des choses mémorables advenues aux règnes de Louis XII et de Francois I*. Edited by l'Abbé Lambert. Paris, 1753.

Ford, Francis. *Mary Tudor, A Retrospective Sketch*. Bury St. Edmunds, 1882.

Gage, John. *History and Antiquities of Suffolk*. London, 1838.

Gairdner, James. *Henry the Seventh*. London, 1889.

———, ed. *Letters and Papers Illustrative of the Reigns of Richard III and Henry VII*. London, 1861.

———, ed. *Memorials of King Henry the Seventh*. London, 1858.

———, ed. *The Paston Letters, 1422–1509*. London, 1904.

———, ed. *Three Fifteenth Century Chronicles*. London, 1880.

Glenne, Michael. *King Henry's Sister: Queen of Scotland*. New York, 1953.

Godwin, Francis. *Rerum Anglicarum Annales: 1509–1558,* Broun, 1653.

Grafton, Richard. *Chronicle*. Edited by Henry Ellis. London, 1809.

Great Chronicle of London. Edited by A. H. Thomas and I. D. Thornley. London, 1938.

Green, Mary Anne Everett. *The Lives of the Princesses of England*. London, 1854.

———, ed. *Letters of Royal and Illustrious Ladies from the Commencement of the Twelfth Century to the Close of the Reign of Queen Mary*. London, 1846.

Grose, F. *Antiquities of Scotland*. Vol. III. Edinburgh, 1800.

Hall, Edward. *Chronicle (The Union of the Two Noble Families of Lancaster and York)*. Edited by Henry Ellis. London, 1809.

Hannary, Robert Kerr, ed. *The Letters of James IV: 1505–1513*. Edinburgh, 1953.

Harvey, Nancy Lenz. *Elizabeth of York*. New York, 1973.

Herbert, Lord Edward. *The Life and Raigne of King Henry the Eighth*. London, 1649.

Holinshed, Raphael. *Chronicle of England, Scotland, and Ireland*. London, 1577.

————. *Chronicle of Scotland*. London, 1585.

Jerdan, William, ed. *Rutland Papers*. Camden Society, 21. London, 1842.

Kendall, Paul Murray. *The Yorkist Age*. London, 1962.

Leland, John. *De Rebus Britannicis Collectanea*. Edited by Thomas Hearne. Vols. IV and VI. London, 1774.

————. *Itinerary*. Edited by Lucy T. Smith. London, 1906–1908.

Leslie, John Bishop of Ross. *The History of Scotland from the Death of King James I to the year 1561*. Edited by E. G. Cody. Vol. II. Edinburgh, 1888.

Letters and Papers of Henry VII and Henry VIII. London, 1881.

Levine, Mortimer. *Tudor England 1485–1603*. New York, 1968.

Lindsay, Robert of Pitscottie. *The Historie and Chronicles of Scotland*. Edited by J. G. Mackay. London, 1899.

Mackie, J. *The Earlier Tudors, 1485–1558*. Oxford, 1952.

————. *James IV*. London, 1950.

————. "Henry VIII and Scotland." *Transactions of the Royal Historical Society*. Series 4, 29 (1947):93–114.

Mackie, R. L. *King James IV of Scotland: A Brief Survey of His Life and Times*. London, 1958.

Major, John. *A History of Greater Britain*. Edinburgh, 1892.

"Mary Tudor and Brandon, Duke of Suffolk." *The Edinburgh Review* 123 (1866):248–263.

Mattingley, Garrett. *Catherine of Aragon*. Boston, 1941.

Maulde La Claviere, Marie Alphonse Rene de. *Histoire de Louis XII*. Paris, 1889–1893.

————. *Les Femmes de la Renaissance*. Translated by George Herbert Ely. London, 1900.

————. *Louise de Savoie et Francois Ier*. Paris, 1895.

Mitchison, Rosalind. *A History of Scotland*. New York, 1970.

Morpurgo, J. E., ed. *Life Under the Tudors*. London, 1950.

Murison, W. *Sir David Lindsey*. Cambridge, 1938.

Nichols, John Gouge, ed. *The Chronicle of Calais in the Reigns of Henry VII and Henry VIII to the Year 1540*. Camden Society, 35. London, 1846.

Nicolas, Sir Nicholas Harris, ed. *The Privy Purse Expenses of Henry VIII from November 1529 to December 1532.* London, 1827.

Noble, Mark. "An History of the Illustrious House of Brandon." Bodleian Library.

Page, William, ed. *The Victoria History of the County of Suffolk.* Vol. II. London, 1907.

Pardoe, Julia. *The Court and Reign of Francis the First.* London, 1849.

Paul, John E. *Catherine of Aragon and Her Friends.* New York, 1966.

Pinkerton, John. *History of Scotland from the Accession of the House of Stewart to that of Mary.* Vol. II. London, 1797.

Plumpton Correspondence. Edited by Thomas Stapleton. London, 1839.

Pollard, A. F. *Henry VIII.* London, 1902.

———. *Wolsey.* London, 1929.

Richardson, Walter C. *Mary Tudor: The White Queen.* Seattle, 1970.

Robson-Scott, William Douglas. *German Travellers in England, 1400–1800.* Oxford, 1953.

Roper, William. *The Life, Arraignement and Death of Syr Thomas More.* EETS, 197. London, 1935.

Routh, E. M. G. *Lady Margaret. A Memoir of Lady Margaret Beauford.* London, 1924.

Rye, William Brenchley. *England as Seen by Foreigners.* London, 1865.

St. Mary's Church, Bury St. Edmunds: An Illustrated Description. Gloucester, n.d.

Salter, Emma Gurney, *Tudor England through Venetian Eyes.* London, 1930.

Salzman, L. F. *England in Tudor Times.* London, 1926.

Scarisbrich, J. J. *Henry VIII.* London, 1968.

Scott, Eva. *Six Stuart Sovereigns, 1512–1701.* Port Washington, 1971.

The Scottish Antiquary 12 (1898):115–122.

Simons, Eric N. *Henry VII: The First Tudor King.* New York, 1968.

Sneyd, Charlotte Augusta, ed. *A Relation of the Island of England about the Year 1500, with Particulars of the Customs of these People and of the Royal Revenues.* London, 1847.

Spanish Chronica del rey Engrico Ottavo de Inglaterra. Translated by M. A. S. Hume. London, 1889.

Speed, J. *Chronicle.* London, 1846.

Stow, John. *The Annals of England.* London, 1580.

———. *A Survey of London.* London, 1603.

Strickland, Agnes. *Lives of the Queens of Scotland.* Vol. I. New York, 1859.

———. *Lives of the Tudor Princesses, Including Lady Jane Grey and Sisters.* London, 1868.

The Suffolk Garland: or a Collection of Poems, Songs, Tales, Ballads, Sonnets, and Elegies, Legendary and Romantic, Historical and Descriptive, Relative to that Country. Ipswich, 1818.

Sylvester, Richard, and Davis P. Harding, eds. *Two Early Tudor Lives: The Life and Death of Cardinal Wolsey,* by George Cavendish, and *The Life of Sir Thomas More,* by William Roper. New Haven, 1962.

Thorton-Cook, Elsie. *Royal Marys: Princess Mary and her Predecessors.* London, 1930.

Tyler, Royall. *The Emperor Charles the Fifth.* London, 1956.

Tytler, Patrick Fraser. *History of Scotland.* Vol. II. Edinburgh, 1864.

Vergil, Polydore. *Anglicae Historiae Libri.* Translated and edited by Denys Hay. London, 1950.

Vives, Juan Luis. *A Very Frutefull and Pleasant Boke called the Instruction of a Christen Woman.* Translated by Rycharde Hyrd. London, 1540.

Warner, Philip. *The Medieval Castle: Life in a Fortress in Peace and War.* New York, 1971.

Watson, Foster, ed. *Lives and Renaissance Education of Women.* New York, 1912.

Whethamstede, Johannis de. *Chronicon, e Registro Ejus In Bibliotheca Collegii Armorum Londini.* Vol. II. London, 1732.

White, Beatrice. *Royal Nonesuch: A Tudor Tapestry.* New York, 1936.

Williams, C. H., ed. *English Historical Documents 1485–1558.* Vol. V. London, 1967.

Williams, Neville. *The Royal Residences of Great Britain.* London, 1960.

Williams, Penry. *Life in Tudor England.* London, 1964.

Wood, Marguerite, ed. *Flodden Papers.* Edinburgh, 1933.

Woodward, Ida. *Five English Consorts of Foreign Princes.* Part I. London, 1911.

Wormald, Francis. "The Solemn Entry of Mary Tudor to Montreuil-sur-Mer in 1514." *Studies Presented to Sir Hilary Jenkinson.* Edited by J. Conway Davies. London, 1957.

Wright, Louis B. "The Reading of Renaissance English Women." *Studies in Philology* 28 (1931):671–688.

Wriothesley, Charles. *A Chronicle of England during the Reign of the Tudors: 1485 to 1559.* Edited by William Douglas Hamilton, London, 1875.

Yonge, John. "The Fyancells of Margaret, Eldest Daughter of Henry VII." John Leland, *Collectanae.* Vol. IV. Edited by Thomas Hearne. Oxford, 1710–1712.

INDEX

Albany, Duke of. *See* Stewart, John
André, Bernard, 19
Angus, Earl of. *See* Douglas, Archibald, I
Anne of Brittany, Queen of France, 61, 62, 64, 79, 83, 112
Argyll, Earl of. *See* Campbell, Colin
Arran, Earl of. *See* Stewart, James
Arthur, King of England, 18, 27
Arthur, Prince of Wales, 5, 6, 15, 18, 212–213, 240*n*.; marriage 9–10; death 16–17
Atholl, Earl of. *See* Stewart, John

Barton, Andrew, 56–57, 60, 65
Barton, Robert, 170
Baynard's Castle, 151, 153, 159
Beaton, James, Archbishop of Glasgow, 71; as Archbishop of St. Andrews, 196, 199, 205–208, 230
Beaufort, Margaret, Countess of Richmond, 4, 5, 9, 20, 46, 47
Bergues, Lord Jean de, 41, 42
Berwick Castle, 23, 69, 89
Boleyn, Anne, 103, 159, 213, 215–218, 221, 223, 233
Bonnivet, Guillaume de, Lord High Admiral of France, 174
Bothwell, Earl of. *See* Hepburn, Patrick
Brandon, Lady Anne, 137, 217, 219
Brandon, Charles, Duke of Suffolk, 39, 42, 46; as Viscount Lisle, 60, 75–76; as Duke of Suffolk, 77, 82–83, 100–103, 105–106, 107–111, 116–133, 135–138, 148, 152–153,